HUMAN INFANCY:
AN EVOLUTIONARY
PERSPECTIVE

CHILD PSYCHOLOGY

A series of volumes edited by **David S. Palermo**

HUMAN INFANCY: AN EVOLUTIONARY PERSPECTIVE

BY DANIEL G. FREEDMAN
UNIVERSITY OF CHICAGO

LEA **LAWRENCE ERLBAUM ASSOCIATES, PUBLISHERS**
1974 **HILLSDALE, NEW JERSEY**

DISTRIBUTED BY THE HALSTED PRESS DIVISION OF

JOHN WILEY & SONS
New York   Toronto   London   Sydney

Lawrence Erlbaum Associates, Publishers
62 Maria Drive
Hillsdale, New Jersey 07642

Distributed solely by Halsted Press Division
John Wiley & Sons, Inc., New York

Library of Congress Cataloging in Publication Data

Freedman, Daniel G.
   Human Infancy.

   (Child psychology)
   Bibliography: p.
   1. Developmental psychobiology. I. Title.
II. Series. [DNLM: 1. Child development.
2. Child psychology. 3. Infant. WS105 F853h]
RJ131.F74   155.7   74-13497
ISBN 0-470-27726-2

Printed in the United States of America

CONTENTS

ACKNOWLEDGEMENTS

Since this book covers some 17 years of work, ranging from my studies of puppies at the Jackson Laboratories in Bar Harbor, Maine, through recent studies of newborns of different ethnic groups, there are many people to thank. Although the book is dedicated to my most influential teachers, Kurt Goldstein and Abe Maslow, I owe J. Paul Scott a great deal. His help and encouragement over my two years at the Jackson Laboratories have remained a source of strength and comfort ever since. Jack King, too, whom I was supposed to be assisting there, was exceedingly generous in allowing me the freedom to go my own way.

After a postdoctoral stint at Langley Porter Neuropsychiatric Clinic, where I learned a great deal about children, especially from Frank Gorman, Dr. Enoch Callaway, Director for Research there, and George Ellman made room for me in George's lab so that I might carry out the studies of infant twins reported in Chapter 4. My association with Langley Porter has continued over the years, and Paul Ekman and Wallace Friesen were directly helpful in filming follow-up visits of the twins. My heartfelt thanks to Barbara Keller for assisting in these studies, and I am forever grateful to Marjory Honzik and Nancy Bayley, both for recommending Barbara to me and for their general encouragement. Thanks also to the California State Department of Mental Health for generous support of these twin-studies.

I should like to thank the people at the National Institute for Mental Health, whoever they were, for awarding me a Special Fellowship to study human genetics in Uppsala, Sweden, and similarly, the National Institute of Education for support over the last seven years via our Early Education Research Center.

There are many people who helped with the most recent research on newborns. First and foremost, Dr. T. Berry Brazelton, with whom the Cambridge Neonatal Scales were developed, and who thereby helped initiate these studies. Thanks also to Dr. Jock Roby, Nina Freedman, Joan Kuchner, and Joan Durfee who also helped to develop these scales, and again to my wife, Nina, who collaborated in the initial studies. Dr. Saul Cohen, a pediatrician and an old friend from my postdoctoral days in San Francisco, helped arrange for the first study which compared Chinese and Caucasian newborns. For similar help, my thanks go to the following: Drs. Allen Ross, Kaiser Hospital, Hawaii, and David Crowell of the University of Hawaii; Dr. Howell Wright and Mary Wilhelm, R.N., University of Chicago; Dr. Rosita Pildes, Cook County Hospital, Department of Pediatrics; Norbett Mintz, an old friend, and Dr. Robert Bergman, a new friend, who made arrangements on the Navajo reservation; Prof. Shoshiro Kuromaru and Dr. Sadaaki Shirataki, Kobe University School of Medicine; Dr. W. H. Lo, University of Hong Kong; Mr. H. L. Giese, Assistant Administrator for Aboriginal Affairs, Northern Territory, Australia, and Dr. Alan Walker, Darwin Hospital; and last but not least, Prof. Robert LeVine, my colleague at the University of Chicago, who made possible my trip to Northern Nigeria. I should like to thank him as well for consistent intellectual stimulation and guidance on cross-cultural matters.

My thanks also to the administrative and secretarial staff of the Committee on Human Development, University of Chicago, especially the two mainstays, Alice Chandler and Bernice Spivek, for their ever-present willingness to help. Finally, thanks to the readers of the manuscript, including several anonymous referees. Known readers who provided me with useful feedback were Marc Seifer and Drs. Wilbur Haas, Susan Stodolsky, Ruth Kraines, William Henry, Bernice Neugarten, and Robert LeVine. And for their painstaking care with the final stages of the manuscript, my thanks to Janet Bare and Dodie Hillger.

DEDICATED TO

Kurt Goldstein
Abe Maslow
and
Bella Freedman

INTRODUCTION

My interest in the biological approach to behavior started in 1955 when I studied groups of inbred dogs for my thesis work at the Jackson Memorial Laboratories in Bar Harbor, Maine. Previously, I had been, like most other clinical and personality psychologists of the time, a rather complete environmentalist, but in my work at Bar Harbor, I came face to face with the great importance of genotype in the actualization of behavior. Briefly, I found that while some breeds of dogs were indeed malleable and changed, depending on how they were reared, in other breeds constitutional factors over-rode essentially the same modes of rearing (Freedman, 1957, 1958).

This study with puppies started me on the path detailed in this book, for once I had been caught up by the concept of genotype, it was a small step to evolutionary theory and ethology. Prior to my thesis work, my primary theoretical affiliation was to psychoanalysis, and the neo-Freudianism of the forties and fifties was part of my daily sustenance. Also, to this day, Kurt Goldstein's Holism (Goldstein, 1963a) is an essential part of my thinking. But in becoming a participant in the ethological movement, with its thorough zoological and evolutionary grounding, I felt myself within the swell of an important new force in social science. Indeed, there was a period in the early sixties when, by asking of any and every human structure or behavior the evolutionary questions, How is it adaptive?—What is its evolutionary function?—I seemed to experience one insight after another. I recall with some nostalgia the sense of elation that came through realizing the potential of these questions to account for many aspects of human behavior, and a number of empirical studies were subsequently developed. First came a series on the possible adaptive function of beardedness in males

1

(Freedman, 1971a); then a master's thesis dealing with the differential responsivity of adults to baby cries and other noises (Omark, 1967); and now a number of students, working within an evolutionary model, are studying human sex differences and a related topic, the development of human peer groups. These studies will eventually be detailed in a separate volume, so it will suffice to say here that the joining of biological theory with the concerns of the behavioral sciences appeared to me as an important step, albeit a small one, toward the unification of science.

I should like to focus the reader's attention on a single example of behavior, the baby's smile, and note the various interpretations of this simple, profound event. For me, it provides a paradigmatic example of the power in an evolutionary explanation and the problem surrounding most other interpretations. (Please see Appendix 1 for a documentation of the research on infant smiling.)

As a student of Katherine Wolf's at City College of New York in the early fifties, I became familiar with the literature on socialization in early infancy, particularly of studies with psychoanalytic significance. Wolf, along with René Spitz (Spitz & Wolf, 1946) had performed the most detailed study to date on the baby's smile. They were able to demonstrate that 3-month-old babies responded with smiles to a model of a nodding face as well as to an actual face, but never to the profile of either model or actual face. These were fascinating findings, but aside from a bow to Gestalt psychology, the authors had little to say about the theoretical importance of the findings. This was especially curious since both authors, most particularly Spitz, were major psychoanalytic theorists. It appeared that psychoanalysis, as a theoretical structure, could not "handle" the baby's smile. Later Spitz, in a deviation from psychoanalytic theory (Spitz, 1959), compared the smile with embryological organizing centers, calling it the major "organizer" of the first trimester of life. However, his continued concern with orality and libido theory seemed to prevent a clearcut statement of what he meant by the smile as "organizer".

T. C. Schneirla (1959), the influential leader of the American Museum of New York's animal research section, also wrote about the baby's smile. Schneirla, who found the term "innate" distasteful and politically reactionary, insisted that the smile develops gradually, through social reinforcement by the parents, from a generalized grimace. This fit with his view that it is the immediate environment and not the historical, phylogenetically adaptive environment that shapes behavior. The fact is that the early smiles of newborns ("reflexive" smiles) are not grimaces, but fully recognizable smiles (see Chapter 2 and Appendix 1), and a theory proposing the gradual acquisition of smiling is simply wrong.

Piaget, too, great observer that he was, failed to see that most infants smile more readily, if not exclusively, at people rather than things (cf. Piaget, 1952, pp. 72–74). Perhaps because of his over-riding interest in intellectual development, he could not conceive of behavior which had primary adaptive value in the realm of social interaction.

At the very same time that Wolf gave her course on the psychoanalytic approach to infancy, the father of the holistic approach, Kurt Goldstein, who was also teaching at C.C.N.Y. in the 1950's, gave his interpretation of the baby's smile (Goldstein, 1957). To this day I consider his article the best discussion on the adaptive function of human smiling. He wrote sensitively and appreciatively of the ties between mother and infant which the smile helps facilitate, and of the experience of being *one* that is felt by two people united in a smile. What was lacking in Goldstein's explanation was the further insight that smiling is a phylogenetically adaptive mechanism, achieved by evolving hominids through the evolutionary processes of genetic variation and natural selection. The added dimension of *phylogeny,* we will see, can generate exciting hypotheses and open new avenues to research, and it is, in fact, the explication of such hypotheses and research that is the purpose of this book.

It is interesting that both Goldstein and Konrad Lorenz were students of Jacob von Uexküll, the great biologist, and each has said that von Uexküll was his most influential teacher. Clearly, Lorenz never took seriously von Uexküll's rabid anti-Darwinism, whereas Goldstein did, and like von Uexküll, could never quite believe that the awesome organization of living systems could have come about through the so-called random events of natural selection. It will perhaps become apparent, especially in the first chapter, that I am somewhere in between on this issue.

Finally, a few words about behavior genetics as it relates to ethology. For a number of reasons, these fields have remained separate. Genetics, of course, necessarily studies within-species variation exclusively, since the very definition of two "good" species is that mating does not ordinarily occur between them, and thus a geneticist usually works exclusively within one species or another. The great message of ethology, on the other hand, is that of phylogenetically adaptive species-specific mechanisms, and this can only be illuminated by comparisons between species. As a consequence, within-species variation has been somewhat slighted in ethological literature.

Considered separately, each field is somewhat weakened. A typical study in the behavior genetics area, for example, usually demonstrates that yet another aspect of behavior has a genetic component, but in itself this is of little interest. The field is by now rife with such findings, and a demand for an understanding of such data is beginning to be heard. As I wrote elsewhere about the twin method (Freedman, 1968), "It strikes me as a safe prediction that most correlations obtained with twin studies will dry and blow away with time, and only those that attain comprehensibility in the light of our evolved nature will remain."

On the other hand, one of the notable weaknesses of ethologists is their tendency to speak of species-specific behavior as if the entire species were represented by a single ideal type. But as they well know, within any species there are distinguishable individual differences on almost any behavioral trait, for it is upon such differences that evolutionary change depends.

In this book, therefore, it may be difficult at times to delineate one field from another, but that is an exact reflection of the author's intention. For ethology and behavior genetics are but two facets of a single biological approach to behavior, and each is strengthened by reference to the other.

ORGANIZATION OF THE BOOK

Chapter 1 deals with a wide range of theoretical issues, ranging from the mind-body problem to Lamarckism vs. Mendelism. This chapter serves to introduce the issues, but they are referred to time and again throughout the text.

Chapter 2 then deals with the behavior of human infants, which one presumably sees in all members of the species, and which is therefore termed *species-specific behavior*. There the unity of *Homo sapiens* will be emphasized—the fact that the entire species shares certain behavioral capacities.

In Chapter 3 the behavioral concomitants of the male–female sexual division are discussed from the bioevolutionary point of view. This is essentially a continuation of Chapter 2 because the sex differences discussed appear to be characteristic of the entire species.

Chapter 4 goes on to deal with individual variations on these species-wide themes, especially variations which can be correlated with genetic variations. This topic is better known in the psychological literature as the study of individual differences.

Finally, in Chapter 5, behavioral differences between groups are discussed within the bioevolutionary framework. Since this is perhaps the most controversial chapter, it is important to indicate that in the evolutionists' view, group differences are as important as are individual differences for the survival of life. The process of speciation, while starting with individual variation, then depends upon reproductive isolation of groups from one another. In fact, any time groups of plants, animals, or men are even partially isolated, each isolate takes on a unique cast. In other words, nature seems eager to form new species, and raciation or subspeciation is a step along this path. In our view, then, genetically based behavioral differences between human races or between isolated breeding populations are not something to shun or explain away, but are rather highly probable expectations. As we shall discuss in Chapter 5, the trouble in raising the issue of human group differences is the universal tendency among humans to rank such differences in a value-laden hierarchy of better or worse. The arguments then become red-hot and reasoning disappears or becomes incidental. But more on this later.

1

THE EVOLUTIONARY
PERSPECTIVE

HOLISM

A book on infancy cannot exclude reference to parents, to siblings, to culture, to nutrition, to phylogeny, and ultimately, to the entire context into which the infant is born. Thus any modern approach is necessarily a *holistic* one. That is, it is assumed at the outset that no simple "cause and effect" logic can adequately deal with the phenomena of infancy, and that biological reality always involves the whole organism-in-environment complex.

Since, however, we must necessarily focus on one or another phenomenon, we frequently will have to relinquish our interest in context, however temporarily. To use the figure-ground analogy, a phenomenon that is central to one discussion may be relegated to part of the background as another item becomes central. That is, there are no "primary" phenomena in biology, only temporarily salient ones. While not as neat as a linear cause and effect model, this ebb and flow is, for better or worse, a reasonable approximation of the way biological phenomena work. To quote a pioneer of the holistic approach, Kurt Goldstein (1963b):

> . . . With our holistic approach, we are faced with a very difficult epistemological problem. For us there is no doubt that the atomistic method is the only legitimate scientific procedure for gaining facts. Knowledge of human nature has to be based on phenomena disclosed in this way. But is it possible to proceed from material gained by the use of this method to a science of the *organism as a whole,* to a science of the nature of man?
>
> If the organism were a sum of parts which one could study separately, there would be no difficulty in combining the parts to form a science of the whole. But all attempts to understand the organism as a whole directly from these phenomena have met with

5

very little success. They have not been successful, we may conclude, because the organism is not such a sum of parts.

Holism does not try to construct the architecture of the organism by a mere addition of brick to brick; rather it tries to discover the actual *Gestalt* of the intrinsic structure of this building, a *Gestalt* through which some phenomena may be intelligible as belonging to a unitary, ordered, relatively constant formation of a specific structure, and other phenomena may become intelligible as *not* belonging to it.

We can arrive at this only by using a special procedure of cognition—a form of creative activity by which we build a picture of the organism on the basis of the facts gained through the analytic method, in a form of ideation similar to the procedure of an artist. It is a sort of ideation, however, which springs ever again from the empirical facts, and never fails to be grounded in and substantiated by them [p. 9].

It follows from the holistic position that one eschews explanatory systems based on a division of life processes into parts, such as heredity vs. environment, or culture vs. biology. Our major theoretical point throughout is that phylogeny, our evolutionary history if one will, has fashioned a balance between organism and environment so that all the human animal does is based on a marriage of cultural practice and biological predisposition.

Even where it may appear that culture is the sole architect as in differences in the mode of transport of newborn infants, it will be shown (Chapter 5) that biological traits also play a substantial role. In other words, our position is that neither "biology" nor "environment" means anything without the other.

It should be noted that this is not an interactionist position, since interaction implies that biology and environment are separable entities which come together at an interface and affect one another. As we shall see in Chapter 4, only when used as a statistical description of *populations* can one speak of interaction between environment and heredity; and it is used there as a formal property of a mathematical formula and not as a description of life processes within individuals. Instead, we have here taken a monistic position (which follows directly from holism), in which biology and environment are participating in a single life-process. While it is not at once clear what advantage such a position has over interaction, it at least appears to be more logically defensible, as the next section should illustrate.

THE ISSUE OF INNATE VS. ACQUIRED

It has been said by the Zen scholar, Suzuki, that "innate vs. acquired" is a man-made problem and that man, having divided life into two parts, is now harassed with the problem of fitting them together again.

If one examines carefully the use of the innate-acquired dichotomy, it would appear that Suzuki is right. The famous phenomenon known as "imprinting" (cf. Lorenz, 1935) will provide a good illustration. Briefly, imprinting involves the tendency of newly hatched precocial birds, such as ducklings, to follow closely and to become intensely attached to the parent, or to the human caretaker in the case of experimental imprinting. While all would agree that this phenomenon is extremely important for the survival of ducklings, for in this way they achieve the constant care and guidance of the parent, is such imprinting innate (unlearned) or acquired (learned)?

If this question is pursued we soon get into a logical problem, since it appears that imprinting is an "unlearned capacity to learn." That is, the ability to learn *quickly* whom to follow is considered an innate structure, whereas the learning per se is presumably without structure. Needless to say, there is no actual or logical boundary separating structure and learning in the imprinting process, for learning itself must have a material or structural basis. The dichotomy, then, is less than helpful for it is misleading.

Instead of posing a dichotomized process, it makes considerable sense, when dealing with complex behavior like imprinting, to speak of an "evolved" capacity to imprint. Evolved refers only to the fact that imprinting has a clearly perceived adaptive function, but does not suggest opposition to "acquired" as does "innate." It simply designates probable phylogenetic origin of the entire process.

Thus, when we hereafter refer to evolved or phylogenetically adaptive behavior, we will be designating a behavioral unit that has probably been produced by the evolutionary process in much the same way that physical or biochemical characteristics of the species have been produced. We will *not* offer an analysis of the complex interaction of gene and environment that went into the development of the behavior in question even as we do not make such analyses in speaking of a physical characteristic, such as the pink color of the flamingo. This color is properly discussed as an adaptive characteristic of the species even though experiment has shown it is only expressed under particular nutritive conditions. In the same way, a particular behavior is properly examined from the evolutionary or ecological viewpoint as an evolved unit whether or not the particular genetic and environmental interaction necessary for its expression has been analyzed, or whether or not learning plays a role in its expression.

Learning and phylogeny must, of course, be completely interrelated in that each species learns to do a different set of tasks easily and well: Human children all can learn to speak, all chimps can learn to build tree shelters, all cats can learn to stalk, and such talents are rarely interchangeable between species. One can therefore speak of inherited thresholds or pathways of learning which were developed over the history of the species.

In very broad phyletic perspective, it may be looked at this way: As we go from simple to more complex organisms on the phylogenetic scale there is greater and greater independence from the environment and more complex homeostatic mechanisms with which to maintain this independence. From the pre-cellular co-ascervates of three billion years ago, which were completely immersed in their surroundings, to the cell with its selective membrane, through passive ocean feeders, through active ocean hunters with their bony jaws, amphibians, homeotherms, mammals, through man, there has been a steady progression in self-sufficiency. The increasing role of learning has certainly been a concomitant trend, and man's ability to plan for the future and to take cognizance of the past in such planning, may well be viewed as the current culmination of this phyletic progression. Thus, learning itself must be considered an important product of natural selection—as a sort of mechanism of homeostasis which has served to increase fitness (Lewontin, 1951), and as having species-specific characteristics.

In general, the dichotomization of life processes into acquired and innate, environmental and biological, learned and unlearned, is misleading and produces more problems than it solves.

The Issue of Causal Mechanism in Biology

Much has been written about science as a false god, and these attacks have been largely directed at unfounded claims for causal mechanisms in biology. The fact is that only when things go wrong in biological systems can we find the cause, as, for example, in successful medical research. But attempts at causal explanation for normally organized biological systems usually end in circularity.

For example, the substance deoxyribonucleic acid (DNA) is said to contain the *Bauplan,* or genetic code, of the organism-to-be, and some have implied that when we fully understand coded DNA we will simultaneously understand the cause of life. But where does DNA itself come from? We know that for its production an enzyme, DNA polymerase, is required. But the production of this enzyme is perforce dependent on DNA, and the only way out of this circle is to hold that "natural selection" has somehow accomplished this.

Mutation of genes is similarly problematic as a causal mechanism. Mutation is frequently pointed to as the ultimate cause of biological variation, and many biologists consider mutations as random events out of which organization of genetical material has emerged. Unfortunately for this theory, random mutation is nowhere to be observed. It appears instead that genetic systems *permit* mutations where it may do good, and do not permit it where it may do harm. That is, there are "hot" spots and "cold" spots on chromosomes, so that genes mutate at different rates and some not at all (cf. Stern, 1960). It appears that some traits are "safely" varied and others not, and that mutation rates themselves have been subject to natural selection (Crow, 1961). Thus we have a situation in which a mechanism of natural selection was brought about *by* natural selection.

Yet a third example involves embryological development. C. H. Waddington, having begun his work in Spemann's laboratories in the 1920's, was fascinated by Spemann's discovery of an "organizing center" into which streamed random cells and out of which emerged organized cellular patterns. But as he continued his search for a single organizing substance, Waddington found instead that even inert chemicals, such as methylene blue, could evoke a certain degree of organization. He came to the reluctant conclusion that there is a "readiness" in cells to become organized, and that activation and readiness were, so to speak, two sides of the same coin (Waddington, 1962). Again, what started as a search for a causal agency, ended in a series of circular concepts.

The behavioral sciences are not immune to this problem, and the weakest aspect of psychoanalytic theory, for example, is that it is constructed in the form of a linear model in which early events determine later character and personality (Bowlby, 1969).

The disappointment in causal, linear thinking has thus been profound, and cybernetic or feedback models may be seen as attempts to grapple with this issue. In the next section, we discuss one such model.

SYSTEMS-THEORY AND EVOLVED BEHAVIOR

One of the consequences of present-day sophistication in the behavioral sciences is that we realize that there are no independent behavioral systems, and that everything is to some extent related to everything else. The very act of verbalizing this situation with regard to any bit of behavior has therefore become a serious problem. One recent attempt at its solution is systems-theory, especially as presented by Bowlby (1969).

Systems-theory is actually modified cybernetics (Wiener, 1948) and is based on the feedback model. As applied to human social behavior, the elements of the feedback schema are individuals within a relationship, as in a courting pair, a mother and baby, a nuclear family, or, for that matter, a village hierarchy. The advantage of this approach is that it calls for the simultaneous consideration of all actors. For example, in the mother–infant pair, the dyad is the unit of interest. Each is seen as a participant in a complex system of growth, with sufficient "phyletic preprogramming" to enable each to adapt to the other.

Thus while the infant is helpless, the parent is most helping, and as the infant's capacity enlarges, the normal parent adjusts so that its growth is constantly facilitated. During the reckless courage of toddlerhood, for example, parental authority and anger act as a protective brake. Then, as the child matures, the net species-wide pattern is of a youngster who gradually achieves greater autonomy and of caretakers who reciprocally relinquish their hold. We can therefore speak of the parent–child system, and thus the term systems-theory.

The systems-theory scheme for dealing with "instinctive" behavior can be most helpful since it appears to provide a language congenial to mechanistic or inductive scientists while acknowledging the holistic nature of biological processes. In this scheme behavior in its most primitive form is based on reflexive reaction, such as the eyeblink to dust, or the hungry infant's rooting to pressure on the cheek. In order to accomplish more complex necessities, however, such as courtship, mating, and nest-building, *chains* of reflexes have evolved. Building a nest for a canary, for example, has been analyzed by Hinde (1965) into distinct units of behavior, each depending on the successful expression of the foregoing unit for its own proper expression. Any break in the reflex-chain as necessitated by the absence of appropriate nest-building materials, may cause the whole chain to collapse.

However, in the nest-building of other birds a more advanced modality is exhibited, and in the raven (Thorpe, 1963) we may speak of nest-building as a *set-goal*. It differs from the reflex-chain in that only the goal is constant. In the absence of the preferred nesting materials, for example, nest-building is not halted, but a make-do nest is executed out of those materials that are available. As may be surmised, *set-goals* and not chained reflexes typify mammalian behavior. Courtship among mammals, for example, is not conducted via a series of chained innate responses in the male and a coordinated series in the female, as in stickleback fish (Baerends & Baerends, 1950). Rather, the precise interactions in courtship are not preordained and only the set-goal of attachment and mating remains invariable.

In man, variability in attainment of set-goals is furthered by his ability to engage in abstract thought. This involves the ability to *plan* for the future, take account of the past, and act "as if" something were true (Goldstein & Sheerer, 1941). As Cassirer (1944) has pointed out, language usage is completely intertwined with this ability. In man, then, the term *plan* is introduced to represent a development beyond the set-goal.

Bowlby (1969) has also introduced the phrase "environment of evolutionary adaptedness." By this is meant the environment to which a species has become adapted over its phylogenetic history. In this way he emphasizes that evolutionary developments lie as much in the environment as they do in the organism. To use an ecological example, the grass of the African plains is as much a product of ungulate hooves, eating, and defecation as the hooves and alimentary activities are due to the available grassy plains. Each evolved in terms of the other (Bateson, 1972). And so it must be with hominid adaptations. In Chapter 2, for example, we will see that the human infant's behavioral repertoire is as much a product of the capabilities of human parents as parental behaving is a response to human infancy.

The environment of evolutionary adaptedness, then, is the environment to which living things are especially attuned since survival in the past has required this. The usual innate-acquired dualism is avoided since in this approach "instinct" means readiness of response to the particular set of circumstances that make up the environment of "evolutionary adaptedness": and organism and environment are here two aspects of a single schema.

While systems-theory terminology will be used only occasionally, its congeniality with our preceding discussion should be apparent; additionally, the treatment of the adult–infant dyad as a system should be noticeable throughout the book.

THE EVOLUTIONARY PERSPECTIVE
TYPOLOGICAL VS. POPULATION APPROACH

When we speak of an evolutionary perspective in child development, what precisely do we mean, and in what way is this an improvement over more traditional psychological approaches? The contrast in approaches has been called by Mayr (1963) the typological vs. population approach; that is, the approach that has as a basic unit the *individual* (typological) vs. the approach that considers the basic unit as the *deme*, or breeding population. The consequences of taking one position or the other are considerable, as we shall see, although one does not exclude the other. Let us first consider how the population approach and evolutionary theory go hand in glove.

Modern evolutionary theory is quite straightforward regarding its major principles. As in Darwin's initial formulation, the major principles today are still: (1) Species are *not* immutable and species' members, to the contrary, vary continuously about almost any trait; (2) there is a tendency for only the favorable variations to survive, i.e., natural selection.

Today, the principle of continuous variation coincides largely with the science of genetics, especially population genetics. In this field, variation of traits *within* a population is seen as primarily due to the reshuffling of genes in sexually reproducing species. Such continuous variation in combination with natural selection provides the material for new subspecies, species, and, ultimately, for all animal and plant diversity.

The next question is, How does one account for the fact that despite "continuous" variation within species, members of different species are readily distinguished one from another? A general answer is that two forces are always simultaneously operating on the gene-pool of a population (gene-pool refers to the total genetic material, or alleles, available within a breeding population), one pushing toward genetic diversity (heterozygosity) and the other pushing toward genetic unity (homozygosity). Each has its own advantages and disadvantages, and a compromise is always achieved.

Genetic diversity yields unending variation and possibility to a group, and therefore enables adaptation to the unpredictable events of changing circumstances. But if diversity becomes too great, communication and mating itself can become crippled; for a fruitful courtship entails two sexes in a commonly "understood" ritual. Thus there is at the same time a conservative pull toward conformity in any mating population. Further, as Darlington (1958) has stressed, these rules must hold for all breeding groups at any phyletic level.

Let us consider some behavioral phenomena at the human level which operate in the interests of heterozygosity on the one hand, and homozygosity on the other. Certainly, heterozygosity is served by the incest taboo, the rule, apparently universal in mankind, that forbids coitus between close relatives and thereby prevents "excessive" inbreeding. On the other hand, no people engage in purely random mating, and in-group affiliation, tribalism, and ethnocentrism are probably universally human (cf. Sumner, 1906). That is, few matings take place across such designated lines, and the genetic character of a group therefore changes very slowly. As a result of these apparently opposed behavioral institutions, dynamic compromise is invariably achieved between homozygosity and heterozygosity, unity and diversity, within any human population.

We can now start to answer the question, "What advantage does the evolutionary perspective or population approach have over the typological approach in which the individual is the basic unit of interest?"

It would appear that as long as the individual is our main unit of interest, as in traditional psychology, we will always be impressed by variation from one individual to another, but remain unable to say much about why such variation exists. The reason for this is that it is logically not possible to explain something by itself. Put another way, understanding comes as context is clarified, and this requires going outside of the phenomenon itself. For example, in the past the behavioral sciences have tended to explain individual variation by postulating causal variations in either environment or genotype. In both types of typological explanation, environmental and hereditarian, the nature of individual variation has been the issue, not its context, and as we have seen, some insoluble and diversionary arguments have resulted.

Only when one views individuals in the context of their *deme*, or breeding population, do individual differences and similarities become understandable. For it is within the dynamic balance of forces at the population level that evolutionary viability lies. Also, as will be seen in subsequent chapters, differences between male and female and between breeding populations also become intelligible within the population context, whereas the typological approach again leads to thankless arguments about where such differences might have originated. This is to say that the perspective offered by looking at the entire population allows us to make greater sense of diversity and similarity at the level of individuals, and it is therefore a necessary complement to the direct study of individuals themselves.

It would seem a certainty, then, that the future growth of a typological science such as psychology would necessitate an appreciation of these forces in life which are now within the exclusive aegis of evolutionary biologists, and it is the avowed purpose of this book to assist in this task.

HEREDITY AND ENVIRONMENT IN EVOLUTION

How does one conceive of the evolutionary process, i.e. the origin of new forms? As we have just inferred, it is to be thought of in population terms, that is, as the change in the gene-pool of a population. It is true that individuals make up the population, but unless population means change we cannot speak of evolutionary change.

Unfortunately this sort of thinking was not available to Darwin, and he found himself resorting to Lamarckian explanation, that is, an organism's hereditary material is affected by what it does within its lifetime.

To illustrate, we will present an example from Chapter 8 of the *Origin of the Species* (1859). In this selection Darwin documented transitional behavior between European cuckoos which lay their eggs in other birds' nests, and a member of the same zoological family which does so only occasionally, the American cuckoo. Since both species lay eggs at 2- or 3-day intervals, Darwin speculated as follows:

> Now let us suppose that the ancient progenitor of our European cuckoo had the habits of the American cuckoo, and that she occasionally laid an egg in another bird's nest. If the old bird profited by this occasional habit through being enabled to migrate earlier or through any other cause; or if the young were made more vigorous by advantage being taken of the mistaken instinct of another species than when reared by their own mother, encumbered as she could hardly fail to be by having eggs and young of different ages at the same time; then the old birds or the fostered young gain an advantage. And analogy would lead us to believe, that the young thus reared would be apt to follow by inheritance the occasional and aberrant habit of their mother, and in their turn would be apt to lay their eggs in other birds' nests, and thus be more successful in rearing their young. By a continued process of this nature, I believe that the strange instinct of our cuckoo has been generated [p. 251].

We see in this passage Darwin's attempt to explain change at the level of the individual organism rather than at the population level as we now do. The result is a Lamarckian-sounding exposition in which the habits developed by one generation affect the inheritance of their offspring.

Today, the principle of natural selection as utilized by Darwin in this passage would stand more or less unchanged. However, in explaining the "change in inheritance" over succeeding generations we would now start with the complementary concepts of *phenotype* and *genotype*. In the present example, the parasitization of song birds by cuckoos is the phenotype, or overt trait, while the genes that support such behavior form the genotype.

We now know from innumerable experiments that similar phenotypes may eventuate from many different genotypes. Thus, the early appearance of parasitization in the cuckoo population may well have involved a number of different genotypes. Assuming, then, that the tendency toward parasitizing was supported by different genes in different individuals and that natural selection favored all such individuals, these genes would in time become available to the entire breeding population. That is, they would become part of the gene-pool. Then, given a variety of genes supporting parasitizing behavior, the trait could be passed on at higher dosage and with greater consistency in succeeding generations. It is likely, then, that such a process accounts for the transition from the American cuckoo, who only occasionally parasitizes, to the European cuckoo, who does so consistently.

Waddington (1954) has called a process such as this the "genetic assimilation of an acquired trait," assuming that in the initial instance the trait, being barely supported by the genotype, may come about largely through current circumstances and appearing to be no firmer than a habit. Then, as supporting genes accumulate over subsequent generations, what initially appeared as an adjustment to new circumstances might become a universal trait. Waddington (1954) has achieved such results experimentally with fruit flies, and there can be no doubt that such selective and accumulative processes exist. Insofar as selection pressures were similar on all members of the group in these experiments, we can speak of the gene-pool of the breeding population as the main medium of adaptation rather than individuals.

This, then, is the resolution that has been reached from over a century of debate between Lamarckian and anti-Lamarckian forces. The typological approach itself was the major problem, and reconsideration of the issues at the population level, made possible by present-day genetics, appears to have effected a solution.

However, it must be acknowledged that some evolutionary biologists will cavil at these remarks on the score that all selection and therefore all evolutionary change must logically occur through the reproductive success of *individuals*, and not groups. The only point of evolution, so to speak, is to maximize one's genetic contribution to the next generation. Accordingly, an opposition has developed between Wynne-Edwards (1962), who claims evidence for selection at the group level, and Williams (1966), who presents a forceful argument that such a view is patently illogical, and that evolutionary explanation must rely only upon individual reproductive success. Williams' argument, however, does allow for selection at the level of relatives in addition to one's offspring, and once one accepts the legitimacy of such "kin selection," selection at the level of breeding groups is but one logical step away. The point is that all members of most breeding groups are highly related (cf. Harrison, 1964) so that mechanisms which enable the survival of kin could logically include everyone in the breeding group. Additionally, insofar as selection pressures are similar in all members of a group, as in the Waddington (1954) experiments, those traits which enable the survival of offspring will become universal.

Thus, my own view is that natural selection does indeed operate at the level of individual reproductive success, but that through a complex feedback system the breeding group develops a dynamic balance of forces best described and understood at the group level. In effect, group selection does occur, but it operates via the reproductive success of individuals. More remarks about the related issues of reproductive success, parental investment, and kinship genetics will be made in Chapter 3.

BASIC CONCEPTS IN EVOLUTIONARY THEORY

In addition to the basic principles of continuous variation and natural selection, it is important to mention a few derivative principles of modern evolutionary theory, which have proved useful in behavioral work. Closely related to natural selection is the notion of *adaptive function*. That is, the evolutionist asks of all traits and behavior, "What phylogenetically adaptive function has this or that structure, trait, or behavior served?" And experiments may be performed to find the answer.

In one such study, Tinbergen (1965) wondered about the adaptive function of the herring gull's removal of eggshells following the hatching of the young. Why would they "bother" to transport the broken shells to sites remote from the nesting area, and thus leave their young temporarily unprotected? Tinbergen hypothesized that the shells glistening in the sun served to attract flying predators, and he consequently laid out an experimental area with shells scattered about, to see if indeed more predators investigated there than in a control area without shells. His hypothesis proved correct, and it appears that natural selection via predation had fixed this behavioral pattern into the species.

In general, there appear to be few epiphenomena in evolution, and the evolutionist usually starts with the assumption that all species' characteristics have some adaptive function, even before such a function appears plausible. Something of the flavor of the intellectual problem can be gleaned from David Lack's (1947) decision, in the first edition of *Darwin's Finches*, that not all differences among the Galapagos finches need be considered as adaptive; and his subsequent decision that he had initially been too hasty. Upon reconsideration, most traits indeed gave evidence of either being or having been adaptive (1961).

Another concept, that of *ecological niche,* states that there is the tendency for life in any geographic area to fan out and fill all noncompeting slots. Thus the marsupials of Australia and the mammals of North America, although essentially unrelated, spread into all available niches in their respective continents, and have duplicated one another in what is termed *convergent evolution* (cf. Mayr, 1963).

The principle of *correlation* will be quite useful to our discussion in Chapter 2 and it is best explained by example. If we compare mammalian predators and mammalian prey with this principle in mind, we will see patterns emerge in which the structures of various zoologically unrelated predators (or prey) resemble one another because of similar selective pressures. Large predators, such as lions, may sleep for hours at a time; their prey, the impala, rarely sleep for over a minute at a time. Large predators are often alone in open sight; prey, from rabbits to wildebeests, are never alone in open sight. Predators invariably have eyes in front of the head, which helps in the kill; prey invariably have eyes to the side, which helps to escape.

Predators may take hours to mate; prey, such as impala, achieve intromission in seconds. Prey eat small morsels and digest as they eat or else eat now and digest later, as in ruminants; predators usually relax and digest for hours after a meal (cf. Etkin, 1967; Hediger, 1965).

As for *speciation*, the current view is that a new species arises when relatively small numbers of an extant species become isolated from others of their kind; and when, through the action of *natural selection* and *random genetic drift*, or both, the *gene-pools* of both populations become sufficiently dissimilar so that viable mating between the two populations is no longer possible (cf. Mayr, 1963).

Random genetic drift means that, through chance, genes without demonstrative selective value may either be lost or else take over in a small breeding group. For example, in a breeding group of about 500 individuals, a single gene for green eye color might easily be lost or else take over as normal (assuming neutral selective value for this trait). In large randomly mating populations, on the other hand, it can be shown that it is much more difficult for either event to occur [see especially Hardin (1961) for an excellent discussion of these processes]. That is, large populations are stable populations, so that evolutionary change probably depends on many small subpopulations more or less isolated from one another.

Lastly, evolution *above* the species level need involve no further principles than those already discussed, save that progressively longer time spans would be needed for progressively greater departures (cf. Rensch, 1960).

2
A SPECIES APPROACH TO
HUMAN INFANCY

Our intention in the present chapter is to look at human infancy as a zoologist or ethologist might look upon some animal species. We will be primarily interested in adaptive behavior in infants, that is, in how their own nature helps them to survive and flourish. A baby bird, for example, demands to be fed by fiercely gaping and cheeping; or a young duckling will not allow its parent out of its sight and thereby assures itself of care and guidance. We will seek answers to the following three questions. Can we learn principles from studies of lower species that will aid in our understanding of human babies? Are specific behavioral potentials "built-into" the human infant? And, finally, to what extent can environmental deprivation alter the course of such species-specific patterns?

Before getting to the answers, however, it will be appropriate to consider further the characteristics of modern evolutionary thinking. For one thing, evolutionary thought is often seen as circular. Something is said to have adaptive value for a species, and the proof offered for this contention is that the species has survived. For example, imprinting, or the rapid formation of primary attachments, is seen as an adaptation of ground-nesting precocial birds to intense predator pressure, and the proof is said to be that these birds have survived predator pressure.

The point is, however, that evolutionary thinking depends on a nexus of relationships in which each datum, although weak by itself, grows in strength when considered in the context of other evidence. Evolutionary theory is thus holistic and is primarily oriented toward understanding the adaptive function of an event rather than, say, the biochemical process underlying it. The latter form of research is sometimes called the "atomistic approach'' (Waddington, 1966), and ideally the two approaches are coupled in mutually supporting theory and discovery.

In this regard, it is assumed that all the genes within an organism act in concert and that, for example, the XX chromosomally constituted female and the XY male are not dimorphic as *direct* action of the different chromosomes and genes involved; rather the XX or XY takes the entire genome in the direction of maleness or femaleness via complex interactions, which have in turn come about phylogenetically, presumably by a series of discrete molecular processes. In other words, evolution has yielded organization, and it is up to the scientist to discover the mechanisms involved, always having in mind total functioning.

The same holistic logic holds for the analysis of behavior, i.e., any item of behavior takes on meaning only when examined in light of the total species' adaptation (Von Uexküll, 1938). *Thus, an item of infant behavior, e.g., the smile or cry, must be considered in terms of total hominid adaptation, including the total life span.*

From this point of view, the equation of development with ontogeny alone is erroneous and can lead to false conclusions; it is no more logical to start with the baby in a description of human behavior than with any other stage of life, for species survival and the evolution of adaptations involve all phases of the life span.

THE COMPARATIVE APPROACH

Part of an evolutionary approach involves comparisons of different phylogenetic levels, usually with two purposes in mind. The first involves the search for general principles of behavior which seem to hold at widely diverse levels, as in comparisons of lower animals and humans. The second is the search for homologous structure and behavior. This usually involves comparisons of closely related species, since similarities in widely separated species may be due to convergent evolution and may not be homologous at all (Mayr, 1963).

Man is the only species in his taxonomic family (Hominidae), and although comparisons with other primates sometimes strongly suggest homology, we can never be sure. Consequently, the major part of the evolutionary argument as it regards man involves within-species analyses of adaptive behavior, while nevertheless borrowing insights from studies and observations of lower animals. To start with, then, we will look to animal behavior to see if this might help us better understand human infancy.

Precocial vs. Altricial Development

The evolutionary principle of correlation states that certain traits group together because of consistencies in natural selection. For example, brightly colored male birds rarely sit on eggs or even associate with the female once the nesting site is established, for his presence would be an invitation to predators. Where predation is a possibility, birds that sit on the nest, whether male or female, are dully or cryptically colored (cf. Etkin, 1967).

Similar groupings of traits exist around the two major forms of infancy—*altricial* and *precocial* development. In precocial development, the newborn are on their feet in a matter of hours or fractions of an hour, whereas in altricial development there is a substantial period—weeks to months—during which the young are relatively immobile and dependent on the parents. In birds the situation is fairly well known and provides us with one of the beautiful examples of phylogenetic adaptation. As one might perhaps predict on the basis of a hypothetical "predator pressure," it is ground-dwelling birds, such as the Anatidae (ducks, geese, and swans), which are precocial. That is, the young are able to follow the parents within hours of hatching. Not only are these youngsters precocial, but as Lorenz (1935) so vividly described, they have a built-in drive or need to follow the adult as soon as they can move about. This tendency to closely follow the moving, and particularly an excited, fleeing adult, is known as *imprinting*, for indeed, a specific imprint or attachment tends to occur to the individual being followed. As proof, Lorenz himself replaced the parent soon after hatching and the birds thereafter followed Lorenz as if he were the parent. This has proved true over a wide variety of precocial birds, but as Hess (1959) has pointed out, such experiments are easier to accomplish in some species than in others.

Long-nesting (altricial) birds show nothing so dramatic. In an elegant experiment with doves, Klinghammer (1967) found that there is considerable variation in their attachment patterns. In some species, the attachments developed during nesting led to later sexual selection, whereas in other species there was no necessary relationship of this sort. Also, the development of fear responses to strangers was highly varied. In other words, the so-called critical periods for attachment are not quite so critical for birds raised in trees and away from predators, and there is consequently much more variation in patterns of attachment and fear. By contrast, if a newly hatched ground-dwelling bird did not soon follow the escaping parent into the pond or bushes, the last duck or the last game bird would have been eaten long ago. The altricial system is a much looser one, "because" it has developed under relatively relaxed predator pressure.

Mammals exhibit a similar distinction, although here we have to speak of altricial predators and precocial prey. The most commonly preyed-upon animals in Africa are the flocking ungulates, and for them, like precocial ducks, it is important that the young be on their feet and ready to run with the flock shortly after birth. This is also true of goats, sheep, horses, cows—all of them flocking, potentially preyed-upon mammals.[1] The baby lamb, for

[1]Note that relatives of precocial prey (all flocking or herd animals) are our major domesticated sources of meat, whereas we keep relatives of predators as our major pets (Canidae, Felidae).

example, is on his feet about 20 minutes after birth, ready to follow his mother. He quickly learns her characteristics as she does his, and a mutual imprinting results, largely based on smell (cf. Hafez & Scott, 1962). In a short time visual and auditory recognition occur also, although the lamb's visual recognition is not so good as that of the ewe; she will recognize the strayed lamb's bleating from quite a distance and answer in kind, and on his way back he may try several females (who will reject him) before he finds her.

There are other correlates of being a potentially preyed-upon mammal aside from motoric and sensory precocity. Eyes at the side of the head enlarge the area of peripheral vision, which permits simultaneous grazing and watching for potential danger. The frontally located eyes of predators, on the other hand, enable zeroing-in on prey. Among prey, erect and mobile outer ears enable detection of unusual sounds, and rapid mating (some 30 seconds among impala) avoids the immobility associated with extended copulation. Compare this with bears that have been observed to mate over an entire morning at the Zurich zoo (Hediger, 1965).

An interesting further consequence of precocial birth is that the newborn must be fairly mature and therefore rather large. Consequently single or at the most double births are the rule, compared with the slower growing *litters* of canid and felid predators. Slower growth among predators, in turn, has made possible a number of further correlated traits which have had great consequences for man. These will be discussed next.

Play in Mammalian Predators and Prey

A further correlate of differential time spans in infantile dependency involves play. In ungulates, a male-male play group starts within a matter of weeks after birth, with head butting as the favorite game, as if in preparation for adult battles over dominance or territory. However, compared to the offspring of prey animals, the ungulates play little, and their allotted play age is soon over (cf. Ewer, 1968).

Predator mammals can afford to support a lengthened infancy and therefore a prolonged period of play. As in ungulates, sib play prepares for later behavioral patterns, but the longer period, coupled with the physical prowess of Felidae and Canidae, allows for more subtle learning, most particularly in the areas of hunting and fighting. Kittens start stalking one another soon after they are on their feet, while puppies engage in play fighting at a comparably young age, and both species continue playful interactions through sexual maturity, many months later. Another aspect of these constant peer (litter) interactions is a growing attachment to and knowledge about one's kin, and the stage is thereby set for cooperation in the hunt. As we shall see later, social cooperation and dominance-submission hierarchies are not at all antithetical, and in both the Canidae and the Felidae, in a matter of months, play has given way to true hunting and serious fights for social dominance.

Another important and related aspect of play is curiosity. Both puppies and kittens, for example, examine everything in and around the nest as soon as they can move about. Although his insatiable curiosity is said to have killed the cat, it has in fact served to make it aware of every nook and cranny in its gradually expanding territory. As we shall see, curious little human investigators are impelled by much the same forces. For all these predator species, the fact that something different is out there is sufficient reason for investigation.

Growth and Development among the Primates

When we get to our primate relatives, we see an interesting mix of predator and prey traits. Since none are more than occasional predators and most are exclusively vegetarians, preparation for hunting has probably not played a role in selection. Nevertheless, prolongation of the infancy and juvenile play periods here exceed all other phyletic groups. How can we understand this within the concepts developed so far?

For one thing, just as in birds, predator pressure is reduced by tree dwelling or, in ground-foraging species, the ability to escape into trees and onto cliffs. Second, unlike ungulate young who must escape predation by either hiding or running along with the herd, the primate infant can remain helpless since he can be transported in haste by clinging to the parent, as in the monkeys, or in the great apes through his being carried and/or clinging. As in herd animals, there is mutal protection in group living, but among primates manual manipulation, inventiveness, cooperation, subtle social interaction, and complex bonds are present as parts of the prehominid adaptation.

Learning has a greater role than ever within the primates, and a definite concomitant trend can be seen. While relative gestation time and age to menarchy does not vary greatly among the great apes and man, the time taken to complete physical growth is doubled in man (Table 2-1). When we

TABLE 2-1

Prenatal and Postnatal Growth Periods[a]

Primate	Gestation (in weeks)	Menarche (age)	Completion of growth (age)	Life span (years)
Macaque	24	2	7	24
Gibbon	30	8.5	9	30
Orangutan	39	?	11	30
Chimpanzee	33	8.8	11	35
Gorilla	36	9	11	40
Man	38	13.7	20	75

[a] From Campbell (1966).

add the fact that the brain of the chimpanzee is already one half its full size at birth, whereas the human newborn's brain is only about one fourth of its final size (Schultz, 1968), we see that man spends more time maturing experientially in the world (see also Fig. 2-1).

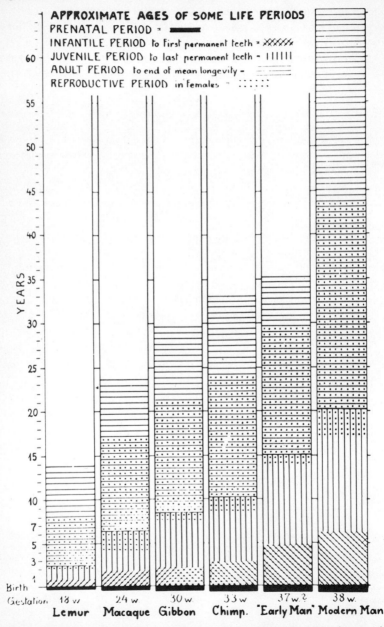

FIG. 2-1 Diagrammatic representation of the approximate average durations of same periods of life among recent primates (Schultz, 1968).

This relatively prolonged state of immaturity in the human young is made possible, in turn, by strongly developed "parenting" behavior in the adults, and the human *male's* prolonged interest in the young is unmatched by any other primate. In Table 2-2 we see that, despite the trend toward theoretically lower reproductive capability, hominization has been highly successful with regard to reproductive success, mainly, one would surmise, because of the high interest human mothers and fathers maintain in their offspring.

In the next sections we will see what the newborn and young infant are capable of, and how the relationship with the caretaking adult develops.

THE HUMAN INFANT

What Is He Capable of at Birth?

Newborns are frequently alert, selective in what they turn to, and, in general, capable of coming to terms with a variety of environmental challenges. Speaking first of optimal cases (or newborn "geniuses"), my co-workers and I have seen several 2-day-old infants correctly localize sounds by repeatedly turning toward the varied source of a sound, which they could not see. Other exceptional neonates have proven capable of accurately following visually presented objects in the horizontal, vertical, and in a complete circle. If we turn to Fig. 2-2 and Fig. 2-3, we see that *most* newborns are capable of some visual following and of visual discrimination as well (discussed further below). Motoric "geniuses" were seen, too, and one African baby, 45 minutes old, was pulled to a sitting position with back straight, head up, and looking from one side to the other.

With regard to social responsivity, which will also be discussed below, very few crying newborns cannot be consoled by picking-up, soft words, and rhythmic rocking (Fig. 5-7; see also Korner and Grobstein, 1967). Since this can be demonstrated in the first trial and before the first feeding, this is not a conditioned response. There are, of course, the obvious adaptive responses of sucking, crying when hungry or in pain, and withdrawing the limbs from painful stimuli. However, there are other less obviously adaptive

TABLE 2-2

The Reproductive Potential of Higher Primates[a]

Primates	Period of fertility of female (in years)	Fertility commences (years from birth)	Theoretical maximum number of offspring after 45 years
Marmoset	7	3	20 million
Chimpanzee	16	9	408
Man	28	17	64

[a]From Campbell (1966).

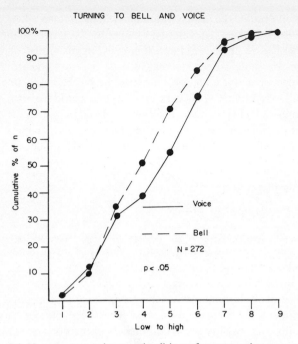

FIG. 2-2 Neonates turn to human stimuli in preference to other types of stimuli.

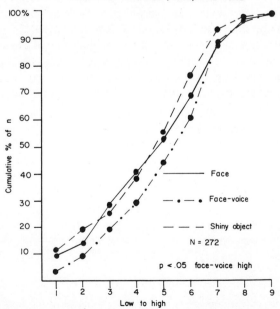

FIG. 2-3 Neonates follow human stimuli in preference to other types of stimuli.

responses already present at birth: the palmar grasp, the ability to bring the hand to the mouth, the ability to remove a smothering object from the face, and the ability to shut out excessive stimulation (the infant simply drifts into a sleep state).

Additionally, a number of reflexive behaviors can be elicited in newborns, which, at their initial appearance, have no apparent function, although they clearly do later in the first year. Peiper (1963) has reasoned that these behaviors appear because the motor circuits have been completed before the appropriate inhibiting mechanisms have developed. While there is no direct evidence for this, these reflexes do normally drop out after the first months. Examples of this class of behavior are the automatic walk (Fig. 5-11), crawling movements, the support reaction of the legs (Fig. 5-10), and eyes-closed smiling (Fig. 3-5). The automatic walk and leg-support reactions appear when the newborn is supported under the arms and the dangling feet are placed on a flat surface. Successful leg support occurs when the legs stiffen on contact and support the body in a stand. Apparently the same response may be elicited by placing pressure on the soles of the feet, so that this may as well be called a pushing-off response. The "automatic" walk may also occur in both positions, but it is usually elicited by holding the baby over a flat surface and guiding his feet forward, and the walk may then take over. This involves very much the same movement as does our own walking, although babies range from those who trip on their own feet to those who do a splendid series of high steps. Recent work by Zelazo (1974) indicates that with forced practice this "reflex" need not drop out, but can be maintained until normal walking starts later in the first year.

Crawling appears in the prone, looks like later crawling, and may achieve forward locomotion, although it usually does not. Peiper (1963) has suggested that crawling, leg stiffening (pushing-off), and the tendency for babies to push forward when pressure is placed on their heads, all help in the birth process. While there is no proof of this, it is easy to imagine that they do, and these reflex behaviors may well facilitate viable birth.

Nonsocial eyes-closed smiling usually occurs after a feed as the infant dozes off. This phenomenon is discussed below, but let us note now that it is not to be confused with grimacing or contortions due to gas; it is instead quite distinguishable as the same phenomenon we later call "smiling," even as reflexive walking and crawling are also fairly clear replicas of the later phenomena. Wolff (1963) and Korner (1969) have reported that spontaneous erections in newborns also occur in their dozing state, and to judge by EEG records both smiling and erections occur in the state which in later life typifies the time of maximal dreaming (Petre-Quadens, 1967).

Perceptual Capacities of Young Infants

The hypothetical perceptual capacities of infants were frequently at issue in the 300-year-old nativist-empiricist controversy [see Hochberg (1966) for a review]. The nativist position, as exemplified by Descartes, maintained that the mind is provided with innate capacities to understand the world. He claimed that we are born with innately valid ideas of size, form, position, and motion. Berkeley, Hume, and Locke, on the other hand, maintained that all ideas derive from something previously experienced. In the last century Kant revitalized the Cartesian view, while James Mill and the associationists championed the empiricist position.

At the century's turn, the sensory physiologists brought the controversy into experimental science, as Helmholtz took over the empiricist's mantle and Hering that of the nativists. They carried on a long debate concerning phenomena of space perception, including the questions of how we perceive patterned vision and achieve depth perception; but, since the evidence on either side was weak, little was actually resolved. In our century, experimental psychology inherited the controversy, and the new empiricists became known as behaviorists and the new nativists were called Gestaltist. Out of Gestalt psychology came the holistic movement and promise of a resolution to the debate (see especially Goldstein, 1963), but it was not until the recent experimental work on perception in infancy that sufficiently convincing evidence was accrued.

This very recent development can be traced to the influence of ethology. Robert Fantz, a student of Eckhard Hess, an avowed and active nativist-ethologist, worked with innate perceptual preferences in newborn chicks. In his doctoral thesis, Fantz clearly demonstrated that the barnyard chick will peck *preferentially* from the first, although modification with experience invariably occurs. The notion of a built-in guidance system to initial pecking led quite directly to his questioning whether or not similar systems might be present in higher animals, including the human infant.

Fantz (1961) thereupon developed a simple, unique, and easily quantifiable measure for judging visual preferences in babies. He presented two visual stimuli to the reclining infant, and measured the amount of time the reflection of each target appeared in the infant's pupils. Significantly more time spent attending one or the other target was quite properly accepted as evidence of a preference. While there is some controversy about the validity of using as a measure the reflection in but one eye, an enormous literature has accrued since this method was first published [see Vine (1971) for a review]. While it is still too early to properly assess this large literature, one result is clear. Newborns are capable of distinguishing one pattern from another, and we now know they can attain a visual acuity of at least 20/150 (Dayton et al., 1964). Many adults can do no better. In general, given the progressively increasing powers of resolution in the first year, targets of moderate complexity are usually preferred. (A further trend, an apparent preference by infants for facelike patterns, will be discussed in the next subsection, ''The Social Capacities of Young Infants.'')

Thus, while visual resolution in neonates is much better than once suspected, and while we know that visual accommodation becomes an active and accurate function by 2 months (Haynes et al., 1965), these facts do not in themselves resolve the nativist-empiricist controversy. The work of Bower (1966a, 1966b, 1967a, 1967b, 1968, 1972), however, *is* crucial. Perhaps because they are so critical, his findings are also controversial, with many claims afoot that some of his results are not reproducible. At any rate, Bower, addressing himself to classic problems of perception such as phenomenal identity, size constancy, shape constancy and slant perception, visual apperception of texture, and object permanence, has shown, in a brilliant series of experiments, that infants exhibit these capacities in early infancy. As a result of these studies there now seems little doubt that whatever learning is involved in the achievement of the perceptual constancies, it accrues around built-in abilities. In one experiment, for example, a projected *virtual* image of a soft, puffy ball was presented to 1- to 2-week-olds who had never seen such an object before. (A virtual image is an optical illusion created by mirrors; an object appears three-dimensionally in space, but it is actually not there.) Infants were then observed to reach for the image with the fingers of both hands set appropriately to touch a soft round object of the projected size. A projected metal ball, by contrast, drew quite another set to the hands, clearly appropriate for the surface of a hard sphere. Also, when the projected ball was small, only one hand was reached out. In each case, the absence of the object (since it was a virtual image) elicited unmistakable surprise (Bower, 1968, 1972).

In the same series of studies of 1- to 2-week-olds, infants could distinguish a small near object from a large far object, although both should have produced identical images on the retina. By reaching more often for the small near object they demonstrated the immediate ability to determine relative distance (Bower, 1972). Young infants can thus be said to perceive the distal properties of objects rather than their retinal correlates, and this seems to hold for solidity, size, and distance.

In another experiment, which can be called a demonstration of movement constancy, unpracticed 6-week-old infants visually followed a target moving in a constant arc, and continued following the target after its disappearance behind a screen—so that the eyes met the target as it emerged on the other side of the screen (Bower & Patterson, 1973).

Very young infants (6 weeks old) are also capable of recognizing an object in its various aspects (shape constancy). For example, a rectangle when placed at an angle, impinges on the eyes as a trapezoid, but it is nevertheless distinguished from a true trapezoid and recognized as a rectangle. This was determined by conditioning head-turning responses to the rectangle, and then noting when this conditioned behavior again occurred (Bower, 1966a).

Bower (1966a) concludes, as follows:

> The most notable set of false premises stems from the belief that perception is caused by the momentary retinal image. What the experiments seem to show is that evolution has turned the human perceptual system to register not the low-grade information in momentary retinal images but rather the high-fidelity information in sequences of images or in simultaneous complexes of images—the kind of information given by motion parallax and binocular parallax. Rather than being the most primitive kind of perceptual ability, it would seem, the ability to register the information in a retinal image may be a highly sophisticated attainment and may indeed have to be learned [p. 92].

After noting that young infants do not have the capacity to deal with several perceptual dimensions at once, Bower continues:

> If capacity is limited, it also seems plausible that the infant perceptual system should give priority to information that has definite survival value. On this reasoning one would expect the shape of an object to have greater priority than its orientation and the orientation of a surface to have greater priority than its shape. Objects must be responded to, and their shape will often indicate the proper response, whereas surfaces are things to be landed on or used as supports, and their orientation is surely their most important attribute. One would also predict low priority for retinal shape and size, variables that are of no survival value except to a representational artist [p. 92].

While these experiments and conclusions are exciting, the evolutionist is not surprised at their results. Given the basic adaptive value of the perceptual constancies, is it possible that they have to be relearned in each lifetime? Evolutionary logic yields a negative answer, and the behavioral sciences are fast learning a rule that seems universal: Learning proceeds easiest in directions determined by phylogenetic evolution; i.e., evolution has dug the major channels through which the river of experience runs. Said another way, natural selection frequently yields differential *thresholds* for learning rather than full-blown species-specific behavior.

The Social Capacities of Young Infants

As we have seen, the infant has come into the world with a substantial array of talents. Not the least of these are his socializing abilities, which, like the perceptual constancies, appear without reinforcement and as an immediate accommodation to the environment.

In systems-theory terms, the species' goal is for infant and caretaker to become socially attached, for this assures survival of the young. Each member of this partnership is equipped to contribute to this goal, and although cultural rules to some extent determine adult participation, the infant nevertheless appears to develop in all cultures according to a regular pattern.

Crying, holding, and caretaking. The very first behavior exhibited by the newborn is the cry, a nearly universal mammalian occurrence. Detailed analyses of the behavior around human crying are only now being made (e.g., Wolff, 1969), but crying seems to share the common mammalian function of exciting the parent to caretaking activities. In dogs, for example, a puppy removed from the nest immediately starts to cry and continues until exhausted. The bitch will usually become extremely excited, seek the source of the cry until the puppy is found, and then fetch him back. What we have here are two complementary evolved mechanisms, and neither has to be learned.

It should be added that while crying and whining exposes the young to predation, they would die in any event without parental aid; so that, like many evolutionary mechanisms, a compromise is reached between two opposing possibilities. Few mechanisms do not to some extent compromise the chances of survival, and this fact occurs with such frequency that compromise can be termed a general rule of evolution.

In the human, we have demonstrated (Fig. 5-7) that within hours after birth most crying infants will quiet when held and carried, and of 252 crying newborns in our study only three could not be quieted in this way. Consider how this cessation of crying coordinates beautifully with the intense anxiety felt by the parent or caretaker until the infant is quieted, for there are few sounds which humans find as unnerving as the infant's cry. Aside from caretaking and feeding, body contact is the usual outcome of crying, and the human baby does as well as the macaque in getting next to the parent without the ability to cling. There seems little doubt that such contact is a mutually edifying experience, and in the human, as in most social mammals, physical contact of one form or another remains an important means of relating throughout life.

It should be noted, however, this does not imply, as does psychoanalytic logic, that behavior occuring earlier in time is necessarily causal to related behavior appearing later in time. Within evolutionary logic, attachments between adults of a social species are as "primary" as are attachments between infant and adult.

Seeking out the face. As has already been mentioned, Fantz's method of measuring what an infant is looking at brought on an avalanche of similar studies (cf. Vine, 1971). Of interest to us, in the present context, is that the overall trend in these studies indicates that young infants show a general preference for looking at cards, or models, in the likeness of the human face.

A crucial question has been whether this is the result of conditioning or whether it is an unconditioned preference. The answer would seem to lie in testing very young inexperienced infants. However, newborns rarely fixate for long on a static object—and the Fantz methodology necessitates a stationary stimulus. On the other hand, newborns will readily follow a *moving* object and, in our studies, 75% of all the babies tested ($n = 272$, average age 42 hours) followed a moving object, 68% turned to a voice, 72%

followed a silent moving face, while 80% followed a moving and speaking human face. [Hutt et al. (1966), Wolff, (1963), L'Allier (1961), and Eisenberg et al. (1964) have all contributed evidence that the human voice, especially the higher-pitched female voice, is the most preferred auditory stimulus in young infants.] Figures 2-2 and 2-3 present the results of our rating scales, but for details on their administration, please see Brazelton and Freedman (1971).

As a result of these observations, Jirari (1970) decided to use head-following rather than eye-fixation as the basis for a quantitative study and was consequently able to use infants of 24 hours of age and less. Four stimuli were used: a schematic face, a scrambled symmetrical face, an unsymmetrical face, and a blank card equated to the others for reflectance (Figs. 2-4a and b). Using a large protractor behind the baby's head, Jirari measured how far 36 newborn infants followed each card from midline to either side, up to 90 degrees. The stimuli were randomly varied and unseen by the experimenter. A quite distinct ordering emerged, face > moderately scrambled > scrambled > blank, with all points significantly different from each other. She subsequently repeated this experiment with 40 infants whose average age was *10 minutes* (range 2–17 minutes)! Once again the face was followed significantly more; while there was no differentiation of moderately scrambled and scrambled, the blank again ranked significantly last.

EXPERIMENT I STIMULI

FACE   MODERATELY SCRAMBLED FACE

SCRAMBLED FACE   BLANK

FIG. 2-4a Figures used in test.

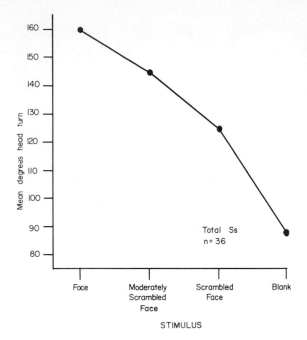

FIG. 2-4b Averaged head turning in newborns to stimuli varying in degree of "faceness" (maximal score is 90° to each side or 180°). On the Wilcoxin matched-pair assigned-ranks test, all the comparisons were significant ($p < .005$). (From Jirari, 1970.)

In a second experiment, an attempt was made to ascertain which aspect of the face was salient for infants. Thus a schematic face, two normal-sized eyes, six normal-sized eyes, two large eyes, and a mouth were used as stimuli, with the same methodology as above (Fig. 2-5a and b). Once again the full schematic was preferentially followed, with six eyes and two large eyes tied for second. We may then assume that, given a face, it is the eyes which are salient for the infant, a conclusion also reached by Ahrens (1954).

In yet a third experiment, however, in which a series of three checker-boards of increasing complexity were used, the checkerboard of inter-mediate complexity was followed about as well as the schematic face. It would appear, then, that two different continua may be operating in newborn preferences—"faceness" and complexity.

Finally, Jirari found that *all* stimuli were followed better when babies were propped in the lap than when propped at the same angle on an apparently comfortable little bed.

All told, then, the best following thus far obtained is to the human face-voice combination while being held in the lap, and, unsurprisingly for an evolutionist, it would appear that there is a lowered threshold for follow-ing a real-live human.

EXPERIMENT 4 STIMULI

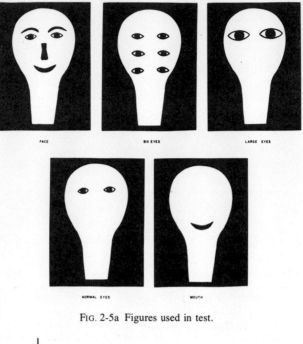

FIG. 2-5a Figures used in test.

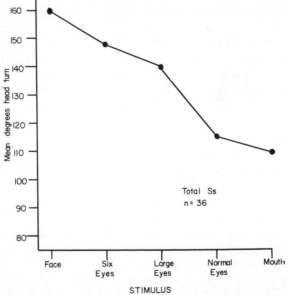

FIG. 2-5b Averaged head turning in newborns to schematic drawing of a face and face-parts. On the Wilcoxin test: Face > Six Eyes, $p < .01$; Six Eyes > Normal Eyes (as in schematic face), $p < .005$; Face > Large Eyes, $p < .03$; Large Eyes > Normal Eyes, $p < .01$; Six Eyes = Large Eyes and Normal Eyes = Mouth. (From Jirari, 1970.)

Figures 2-6 through 2-11 are a series of stills from a motion picture record of a crying 24-hour-old infant as it is picked up and cuddled for the very first time. She quiets in a matter of seconds and turns almost immediately to the caretaker's face.

Smiling. The experimental work on infant smiling appears to sustain the above data in that the most efficient visual elicitor of social smiles yet found is a full-face view of a nodding human face or model of a face. The essential points of Ahrens' (1954) relatively crude study seem to be surviving the test of time. Using staring and/or smiling as his measure of interest, Ahrens had found a general preference for "eye"-spots in the first month, followed by a progressive preference for targets which more realistically resemble a face, until only a real face could elicit smiling. Ahrens reported, as did Kaila (1932) and Spitz and Lolf (1946) before him, that the most efficient visual elicitor of a smile, after social smiling starts, is a full-face view of a nodding model. L'Allier (1961) and Wolff (1963) found, additionally, that the human voice alone can elicit smiling, but that the best elicitor of infant smiles is a live, vocalizing human adult. That is, if the experimenter is seeking to build, element by element, an ideal model for the elicitation of smiles, the model would, according to the trends in the literature, end up a human. Again, for an evolutionist this is not terribly surprising. But for a

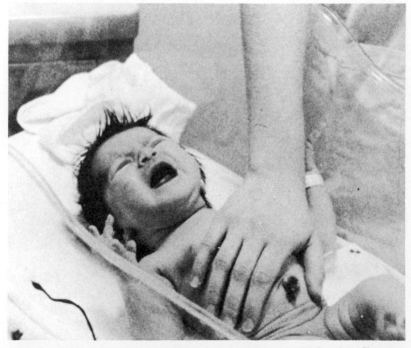

Figs. 2-6 through 2-11 One-day-old girl is consoled in arms for the first time. She ceases crying almost immediately and looks to *E*'s face. From a motion-picture film covering approximately 12 seconds of action.

field steeped in the tradition that behavior, such as the smile, accrues through subtle reinforcement from the environment, such a conclusion finds many detractors. However, Freedman (1964; see also Appendix) in a review of the literature on smiling, has shown that reinforcement cannot be the causal mechanism in smiling, so that we will confine ourselves here to a brief summary.

Smiling is first seen in reflexive form in newborns, including prematures, when they are dozing with eyes closed, usually after a feeding. These smiles are frequently ascribed to intestinal gas. Accordingly, we have carefully recorded facial expressions and body activities which precede gas burps and eyes-closed smiling. The former event is preceded by facial reddening, general writhing, and shifting contortions of facial muscles. The smile is invariably preceded by a distinctly different state characterized by complete relaxation of the face and body. Clearly, these are two distinctly different events, and we hope that these observations will help lay to rest the theory of gaseous smiling. Even at these early ages, smiles can also be elicited by a voice or by rocking the infant and, since it occurs in infants whose gestational age is as low as 7 months, there seems little doubt that smiling can also occur *in utero*. Visually elicited smiles usually occur considerably later than sound elicited ones, by 2 to 2½ months, though they are occasionally seen within the first week of life. These occur most readily when the eyes of infant and adult meet, and so they are called social smiles. In the auditory

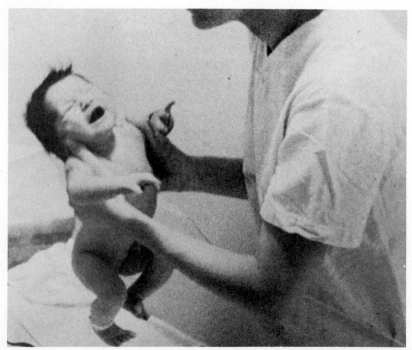

Fig. 2-7

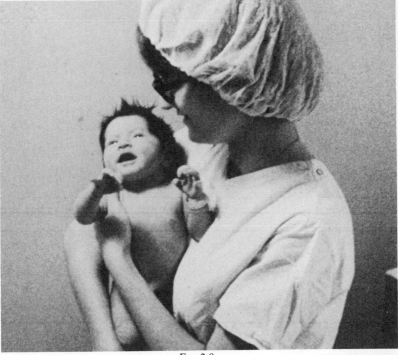

FIG. 2-8

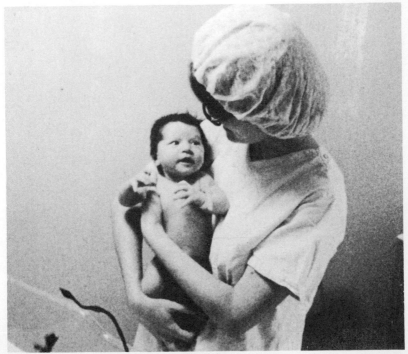

FIG. 2-9

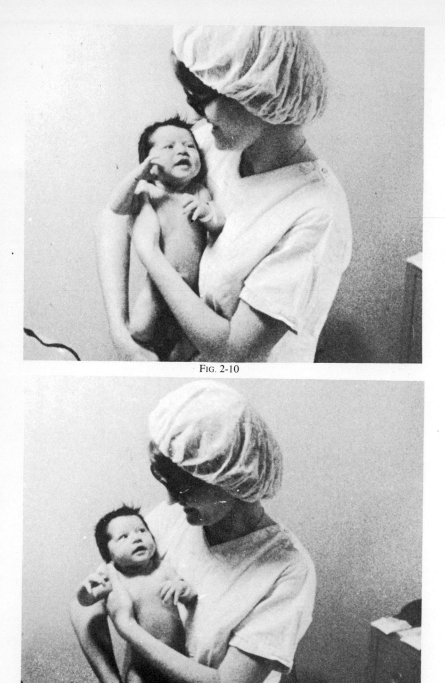

Fig. 2-10

Fig. 2-11

mode, increased smiling to a voice over other sounds also marks such smiles as "social" (Wolff, 1963).

Regarding individual differences in smiling, some newborns never, or rarely, exhibit so-called reflexive smiling while others may become the pets of the nursery because of their constant display. From a 5-year longitudinal study, we have found consistency in the use of smiling as a social technique dating back to the reflexive eyes-closed smiles; e.g., a frequent eyes-closed smiler in the first months tends to be a frequent social smiler at 5 years (see case of Arturo and Felix, Chapter 4).

As for the origins of smiling, the endogenous nature of the phenomena is perhaps best illustrated in the spontaneous smiling of blind infants. The following is a report on a blind infant closely observed over the first half-year of life (from Freedman, 1964):

> Yvonne was an infant with Rubella induced cataracts in whom there were no other significant sequelae. According to the ophthalmologist's report (Akademiska Hospital, Uppsala), Yvonne had less than 20/200 vision in both eyes, and on our tests there was no following of the test objects, including a bright pen light. She did, however, attend to a very bright light, and although no pupillary response was noted, she furrowed her brow to light shone directly on her eyes.
>
> As in seeing babies, Yvonne smiled frequently as she was going off to sleep but never to social contact in the first month (information from mother). Then came a period of reduced nonelicited smiling (also a normal development), followed by social smiling to voice and touch early in the second month (the time of onset for visual social smiling in precocious normals). When observed at 2 months 13 days her smiles, while beautiful, were not normal. They seemed to be a series of reflexes firing in rapid succession, so that they appeared and then faded rapidly. Of great interest was the fact that at this visit Yvonne's otherwise constant nystagmus became arrested during a smile. At this time she smiled most often to voices, but also briefly to our test bell and a familiar squeaking toy.
>
> By 3 months 8 days her smiles were rather prolonged, especially to the human voice (Fig. 2-12). However, if one observed closely, the prolonged smile still consisted of a discrete series, i.e., regular twitching at the corners of her mouth. Again, nystagmus halted during the social smile. At this age it was noted that nystagmus was also arrested when she turned toward a sound or, in one series of observations, the source of a breeze caused by fanning. It was also noted that her eyes characteristically turned toward the source before her head turned, and that the eyes were always bilaterally coordinated.
>
> We have tentatively concluded that the arrest of nystagmus and the directing of eyes towards voice and sound were manifestations of highly motivated states which enabled processes, isolated by disease, to become temporarily integrated.
>
> In the third month, Yvonne was observed "peering" at her hands, a maturational event that occurs regularly in seeing children, i.e., the hands are brought before the eyes and wiggled there for long periods of time. When she did this, Yvonne's eyes converged to the center and down, as if she were trying hard to see her hands. It seemed unlikely that shadows had been cast on the retina since these observations were made under dim lighting conditions. Also, she did not touch her face, so that tactile sensations were not a factor. It appears, therefore, that the motor pattern of wiggling the hands before the eyes may operate independently of peripheral stimulation. Even if one argues that forms must have been cast on the retina, it is still of singular interest that this phenomenon developed; for it is now clear that very little

visual stimulation is necessary for its performance. Evolutionally this may have come about as a "guarantee" that eye-hand coordination would occur. The hands-before-the-eyes behavior dropped out a few weeks after it appeared, and at the sixth-month visit Yvonne was still not reaching for objects introduced by sound or touch [pp. 177–178].

Since blind infants, deaf infants, deaf-blind infants, even retarded infants eventually smile fully and normally (Appendix), there is no doubt as to the built-in nature of this phenomenon. The evolutionary questions then loom in importance: Are there homologs to be found in lower apes? What is the phylogenetically adaptive value of human smiling?

It is pure surmise, of course, as to whether the smiling response appeared phylogenetically as an adult-adult mechanism or as an adult-infant mechanism. It is most akin to the "frightened grin" in other primates, a gesture that occurs quite frequently by a subordinate animal when passing close to a dominant one (Hall and DeVore, 1965). Human smiling may well have originated with such a gesture in the evolutionary "turning to the opposite," but more than this we cannot say.

With regard to adaptive value, the most obvious hypothesis is that smiling facilitates attachments between baby and caretaker, and evidence for this is readily attainable. Consider the following observation:

> Jock is 7 weeks old. The Experimenter and two strangers enter his room and Jock looks past them at the window. *E* speaks and Jock looks at *E*, but only briefly. *E* walks back and forth before Jock's crib, but Jock does not follow with his eyes.

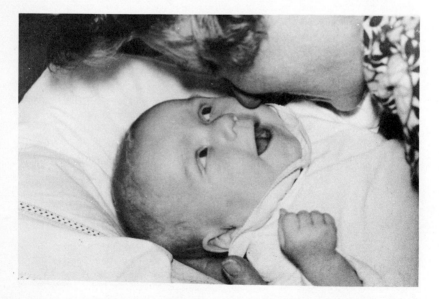

Fig. 2-12 Yvonne, 2-month, 20-day-old blind infant, is spoken to by her mother. Her nystagmus is momentarily arrested, she "faces" the source of the sound and smiles.

E then bends over Jock and starts baby talk. Jock soon fixes on *E*'s face, staring intently for a full 20 seconds, and then smiles. Several more smiles are similarly elicited.

E again walks back and forth before Jock's crib, but now Jock follows him visually everywhere he goes, even craning his neck when *E* wanders out of sight. Jock picks *E* from among the strangers in the room, even when *E* walks back of them. This continues over the remainder of the 10-minute observation period.

For his part, *E* reports feeling much closer to Jock now that Jock has returned his cooing and smiling and is following him with his eyes.

If one then multiplies this event many hundredfold between the same twosome, as in a common caretaker-baby relationship over, say, the first 6 months of life, it is not difficult to imagine how this interaction contributes to the development of strong, lasting attachments.

In later life, of course, smiling lends ease and promotes positive feelings in a wide variety of social encounters, and it plays a particularly important role in courtship behavior. It is also widely displayed between adults as a means of either overcoming or precluding dissension and angry feeling, so that one might speak of smiling as an important lubricant in one's daily encounters. It appears to have these same functions in *all* cultures in which studies have been made (Eibl-Eibesfeldt and Hass, 1967), so that it must be considered a product of hominid evolution.

Perhaps the most interesting discussion of the adaptive function of smiling is that in Goldstein (1957). Briefly, he considers man's highly developed social nature as the basis for any consideration of this phenomenon:

> Ultimately the concern for the other's existence is an intrinsic property of man's nature, and man is not to be understood without a consideration of his belonging together with the "other." This is the foundation of understanding language. It is the basis of all friendship, of all love, where with surprise and astonishment we recognize that what is taking place in the "other" is identical with what is taking place in us. This belonging of individuals to each other . . . reveals itself as a characteristic experience for human existence in the smiling of the infant in primitive form, and later conspicuously in the "encounter" of the adult with another person [p. 91].

For Goldstein, then, the smile is a means by which the biological unity of mother and child, once broken, may be reestablished, however briefly, as social unity. Thereafter smiling remains a major means of establishing and reestablishing the oneness of people who feel close to one another, while expressively, it reflects feelings of personal adequacy throughout life.

Many new mothers have reported to me that their infants did not become "real persons" until after social smiling started (although this is by no means a rule). The question then arises: What possible adaptive advantage is served by a non-smiling period from birth to 2 or 3 months of age? Visual incapacity could not be the reason since blind and seeing infants follow the same basic developmental course of smiling. Instead, the answer would appear to lie in the potential advantage of a relatively loose mother-infant attachment in the first months, when a large percentage of infants die, particularly in subsistence cultures; presumably, the depression and pain caused by infant death after attachment could impair future child-bearing. The postponement of deep attachments also enables infanticide with nonviable infants, a common eugenic practice in many cultures (cf. Carr-Saunders, 1922), as well as easing adoption when the mother cannot care for the baby. Possibly, the fact that neonates are frequently seen as "ugly" also serves the same functions.

Cooing, babbling, and language. Soon after *en face* smiling starts, the infant begins to coo at the beholding adult who in turn feels the irresistible urge to respond, and as a result much time may be spent in such happy "conversation." Feedings and sleeping have then decreased and normally more and more time is spent in direct social interactions.

Although Lenneberg (1967) reports that the frequency of cooing in infants of deaf, silent parents is about the same as in infants of normal parents, several studies (Wolff, 1963; Rheingold et al., 1959) have found that infants of 4–8 weeks are stimulated to cooing by parental cooing (and vice versa), and that phrasing and "waiting one's turn" are present at the very inception of this behavior. Thus, there seems to be a "preprogrammed" aspect not only to the appearance and frequency of cooing, but to vocal interchange as well. That is, the infant seeks out and appears to enjoy vocal give and take. As the study by Rheingold et al. (1959) demonstrates, such behavior may be either encouraged or discouraged by parental behavior and, one consequently assumes, by cultural expectations.

At about the time of the social smile, cooing begins to give way to more complex vocalizations, usually of the consonant–vowel–consonant–vowel variety called babbling. Babbling, unlike cooing, is not so bound to a social interchange and frequently occurs when the infant is alone. However, if an adult speaks while an infant is babbling, the infant will usually stop and wait for the adult to finish before continuing; i.e., it is easy to promote a "conversation" with a babbling baby (Lewis, 1951).

Of great interest is the finding of Lenneberg (1967) that deaf infants are indistinguishable from hearing ones in their babbling, at least through 6 months of age, which strongly implies an endogenous rather than an imitative process. For the evolutionist, then, it seems reasonable to consider babbling the forerunner of linguistic use and, conversely, the sounds of a language are probably dependent to some extent on the range of vocalizations demonstrated in the infant's babbling. In this regard, Brown (1958) speaks of a human "species profile" in that the array of early occurring sounds shows considerable cross-cultural equivalence. Although this need not mean that the child can produce every possible speech sound, he does seem capable of all the rudiments. Similarly, in an experiment with infants of 1 and 4 months of age, Eimas et al. (1971) found that at both ages infants were able to discriminate different phonemic categories, as measured by rates of non-nutritive sucking. They concluded:

The results strongly indicate that infants as young as one month of age are not only responsive to speech sounds and able to make fine discriminations but are also perceiving speech sounds along the voicing continuum in a manner approximating categorical perception, the manner in which adults perceive these same sounds. Another way of stating this effect is that infants are able to sort acoustic variations of adult phonemes into categories with relatively limited exposure to speech, as well as virtually no experience in producing these same sounds and certainly with little, if any, differential reinforcement for this form of behavior. The implication of these findings is that the means by which the categorical percept of speech, that is, perception in a linguistic mode, is accomplished may well be part of the biological makeup of the organism and moreover, that these means must be operative at an unexpectedly early age [p. 306].

A more recent study by Condon and Sander (1974), utilizing neonates as young as 12 hours of age, bears out these ideas; all sixteen newborns gave evidence of being able to perceive adult phonemic and word organization. This finding was judged from sound films and videotapes made of each infant while adult speech, both live and recorded, was emitted in his presence (English and Chinese were used). Upon microanalysis, body movements were found to correspond exceedingly well with phonemic and word boundaries, indicating that infants are "tuned-into" spoken language from the start.

In the same sense, McNeill's (1972) analysis of communication in the famous chimpanzees, Washoe and Sarah, demonstrates that although these chimpanzees were taught to communicate via symbols standing for human words and phrases, they acquired no sense of human grammatical structure. Human infants, on the other hand, display this "knowledge" with their first words, long before an abstract understanding of grammar is possible. McNeill concludes, logically enough, that the human so easily acquires appropriate syntactical usage because of an innate disposition to do so (see also McNeill, 1970). Along with Chomsky (1965), he speaks of innately given "deep structures" which guide the acquisition of syntax and which account for the obligatory nature of a child's grammatical usage.

All this is highly reminiscent of the work of Thorpe (1963) on the development of song in the chaffinch and other birds. In the absence of the adult song, the young chaffinch develops a rudimentary song, recognizable as the species' call but very incomplete. If birdsongs of other species are heard, he will modify his singing in that direction—rarely achieving an adequate imitation. Thus the inner propulsion to sing cannot be denied, but the feedback provided by a con-specific adult is necessary for the full actualization of song. It is also clear that considerable learning occurs before the bird is himself able to do much more than peep, for the songs heard in that period usually influence the form of later singing.

In summary, then, among the ingredients leading to early language are the need to make expressive sounds and an intense social drive to "converse" with others. Further, as in the birdsong, there seems to be a "species profile'' which guides the structure of the emitted sounds. Although this sounds mysterious, language acquisition is inconceivable without some such biological channeling (cf. McNeill, 1966).

Finally, consider the following hypothetical question: Would a group of children, brought up exclusively by otherwise normal deaf-dumb caretakers, and therefore without a common vocal language, proceed to invent such a language? Our answer is yes, because (a) the need to communicate vocally is great; (b) there is a shared interest in the world, and common emotions; (c) mutual imitation would serve to economize phonemic possibilities; (d) if Chomsky's (1965) notion of ''deep structure'' or obligatory grammar is correct, and it appears to be, the grammatical possibilities are severely limited; (e) after about 7 years of age, abstract thought (Goldstein and Sheerer, 1941) would permit the laying out of commonly agreed-upon rules.

Laughter, playfulness, curiosity. The importance of playfulness in human behavior is heralded with the appearance of laughter at about 4 months of age. It nearly always appears as part of social interaction, as when the baby is tickled or lifted high in the air, and there seems little doubt that it is an expression of joy in social stimulation. (The objection is frequently made that such an interpretation is unscientific and ''adultomorphic.'' This objection raises deep philosophical problems which we will not attempt to solve here. However, when I come home and my dog runs to greet me, licks me, and wags his tail, am I not justified in assuming he is happy to see me? Unless we agree to this, further argument will be pointless.)

One need not look far beyond his own experience to realize that laughter is not much transformed over the years, although it is certainly elicited by increasingly sophisticated stimulation. As for evolutionary function, whereas smiling seems in itself to be a mechanism fostering attachment, laughter has a bonding quality only insofar as mutally shared spiritedness binds people together. Laughter seems rather to be one of many emotional expressions that helps a partner evaluate one's emotional-state (cf. Bowlby, 1969). If one laughs, all is well and it is an invitation that play continue. If one cries on the other hand, the partner is signaled to stop what is going on. All this has obviously been ''arranged' phylogenetically, for no baby is taught to laugh or to cry, nor do adults need previous experience with babies to read these signals expertly and immediately. Laughter and crying also have precisely the same signal value in chimpanzees (van Lawick-Goodall, 1968).

As for playfulness, its evolutionary function is apparent throughout Mammalia (cf. Ewer, 1968). Play is a means of learning about one's own capacities *vis-à-vis* the social and nonsocial environment, and it has the great adaptive value of fostering such learning anew in each generation. Naturally enough, it occurs with greatest frequency early in life, in the carefree period when needs are taken care of and protection afforded by adults.

In systems-theory terms, play may be said to operate at the level of a set-goal, with full exploitation and mastery of the living and nonliving environment as its goal. Thus play is closely related to all the other traits that aid in exploring the world, but most especially to curiosity and courage.

It is clear that curiosity, like playfulness, need not be taught nor, probably, can it be taught. As eye-hand coordination matures, at about 6 months, all objects are of interest and are exploited. Presented with wooden cubes and a cup for the first time, most 6-month-olds proceed to fill the cup with the cubes; no prior demonstration is necessary. Similarly, presented with pegs at the side of a peg-board, most 7-month-olds will spontaneously start placing pegs in the holes. Some do this deftly and complete the job on the first try. In some infants unmistakable self-praise follows successful placement, as they smile broadly and look to the examiner or to mother for such acknowledgment.

Anger and self-assertion. As such manipulative abilities begin to flower, obstinacy and "egoism" begin to play a role. This is seen in clear form when the 9-month-old fiercely insists on feeding himself, however unaccomplished and sloppy his technique. Beware the meddling parent, for continued "help" in the service of neatness will frequently bring on a temper tantrum. While such behavior is frequently called "negativism", it is, in fact, positive affirmation of the child's emerging sense of being an autonomous someone.

Thus temper and anger make their first appearance in the service of self-assertion and the need to express the emerging primacy of "me". The adaptive function of anger, then, is clear in that it is usually the best means available of immediately effecting changes in the environment to make it conform with one's own wishes.

Lorenz (1966) has beautifully documented the adaptive value of anger and aggression in fish and birds in a book whose original German title was *Aggression, the So-called Evil.* His point, as is ours, is that a world without anger is inconceivable because of the great adaptive value of such volatile self-assertion. Temper tantrums in the face of parental "guidance" is a case in point.

(We see how our discussion of laughter and playfulness has led naturally into discussions of curiosity and self-assertion. Again and again we come up against the fact that all developmental trends are interrelated, some more obviously than others, and that all may be considered parts of a single macro-feedback system.)

Fear of strangers. A developing fear of strangers and of the strange is yet another example of a developmental trend intercalated with many others.

Newborns through about 3 months of age prefer visual patterns they have seen before, to judge by preferential watching (Lewis, 1969). Similarly, the infant of 3 months shows preference for his primary caretakers to judge by preferential watching, cooing, and smiling (Schaffer and Emerson, 1964). As the infant approaches 5 and 6 months, however, he begins to prefer *novel* patterns over familiar, again to judge by relative amount of time spent watching (Lewis et al., 1967), and in the social sphere he begins to stare more at strangers than at familiar persons (Schaffer, 1966).

After the sixth month, however, there is a decided divergence in reactions to animate and inanimate novelty. Inanimate novelties are rather readily reached for and explored if they are not too unusual. If they are unusual, one can see vigilance and reluctance to touch them. But strange persons almost invariably draw reactions of vigilance, and it is clear that animate strangers are the major source of fear for infants in the second half of the first year (see Chapter 4 for a discussion and graphs of individual differences in the course of the fear of strangers over the first year).

The stranger is particularly fearsome if he is tall (Laser, 1966), or if he is encountered in a strange place, as in a doctor's office (Spock, 1955). That strong attachments are prerequisite for the full-blown fear-of-strangers response seems indicated by the fact that infants raised in orphanages show less fear than do children raised in a family (Mallardi et al., 1961). Also, there is good evidence that the *visual looming* of the stranger is perceived as his most frightening aspect, and blind infants consequently appear to have a reduced fear-reaction to strangers (Freedman, 1965).

The possible phylogenetic origins of the fear of strangers have been discussed by Freedman (1961), who has pointed out that many mammals and birds show similar fear responses to strangers and strange places after they have formed their initial attachments. In carnivores the fear response starts as the young begin to travel farther and farther from the nest (about 5 weeks of age in dogs), whereas in preyed-upon herd animals everything is sped up. Young ungulates are on their feet within minutes or hours after birth, attachment is quickly formed to the mother, and the fear response becomes manifest in a matter of hours or days.

The adaptive value for the young of a species to flee potential predators (strangers) is self-evident and needs little discussion, and the only animals that do not exhibit a flight response have evolved in predator-free environments, e.g., the Galapagos hawk (Darwin, 1839).

Closely related to fear of strangers is the advent of fear of heights which follows soon after the beginnings of motility in animals and humans, and without prior experience of falling. In an experiment by Gibson and Walk (1960), infants who had just started crawling, refused to do so over an apparent "precipice," quite clearly evincing a built-in information circuit that must connect height with vigilance. (Parents, whose infants have crawled to the edge of a bed and tumbled off, may doubt these results, but by putting the same fearless infant at a greater height, such as on a bureau, a substantial visual cliff effect will be seen.) With motility, all animals become exposed to many new dangers as their curiosity and investigative drives take them from the nest, and self-protective counter-drives, such as fear of falling, are necessary to assure survival.

While motility and fear of strangers and heights are related in lower mammals, when a human infant develops its fear of strangers, usually between 6 and 9 months, it simply does not have the motor ability to escape a predator. It can turn or sometimes crawl away, but the main defense is its cry and the subsequent appearance of the caretaker; thus, in human infants in most current societies, the fear of strangers does not serve primarily as defense against predators. Instead it apparently functions to prevent dilution of primary relationships while intensifying bonds between the infant and those already close to him. In this regard, Kovach and Hess (1963) found that the reaction of fright makes bonds between a chick and an imprinted object even stronger, so that this function is also served in lower forms.

There have been a number of alternative explanations of the fear of strangers. Meili (1957) has postulated that such fear is caused by an inability to assimilate the perceptual input. One trouble with cognitive interpretations, however, is that they rarely ask the prior question: Why this particular response and not another?

Spitz (1950) has made a cognitive-psychoanalytic interpretation by attributing the fear reaction to the infant's insight that other people are "not mother," so that the fear reaction for Spitz is a sort of anticipatory separation-anxiety. The simple experiment by Laser (1966) has served to eliminate this overly sophisticated interpretation, for she found that babies are simply more fearful of an adult stranger than of a child stranger who is dressed the same and rehearsed to behave just like the adult. There seems little doubt that it is the stranger-qua-stranger that is feared, and that size adds to the fright.

To summarize, social attachment between baby and caretaker may be viewed as an adaptive, evolved characteristic of hominids, and human mutuality is attained by many mechanisms. Some examples are the desire for physical proximity, the appearance of mutual watching, mutual smiling, mutual cooing, mutual laughter and play; protection of the young when they cry or become fearful may also be viewed as a means by which attachment is increased, as may the very act of time spent together. By late in the first year, when imitation,[2] self-assertive anger, and the first use of words appear, social bonds are normally very strong and the child is an integral part of the

---

[2]Imitation is clearly a magnificent means for the acquisition of all forms of behavior and it becomes an effective force toward the end of the first year. As in sucking, craning the neck to see the face, reaching, turning over, sitting, and standing, the drive to emulate is extremely strong. Only in the human is it carried to such persistent extremes, and it is a comment on psychoanalytic theory that it should be concerned with "anal" play in the second year while imitation, which is flowering, has been largely undiscussed. What better way to work into eventual autonomy than to practice directly an experienced partner's methods of coping with the world?

lives of those about him. He is then ready to start exploring the world, for he has a firm home base from which to operate and to which he can retreat when afraid.

Parent-Offspring Conflict

Much of the foregoing describes the story when things go smoothly in the parent-infant relationship. However, we must acknowledge the universal phenomenon of parent-offspring conflict, as when an infant wishes to continue nursing and when a mother wishes him to be weaned. From a biological view, complete selflessness of a mother with regard to her infant, in any species, is unlikely since they share but half their genes. That is, if care for a particular infant becomes extremely energy consuming, to a point where further successful reproduction is unlikely, evolutionary theory would predict the distinct possibility of maternal rejection so that she might go on with the next brood. The most basic evolutionary principle, it will be recalled, holds that each organism will attempt to maximize his genetic contribution to the next generation; and, as Trivers (1974) has pointed out, evolution has been a matter of balancing costs against benefits. Thus, from the infant's "point of view," he should perhaps like to continue nursing to the exclusion of future siblings, but from the mother's "point of view" (again speaking metaphorically) reproductive success is maximized by weaning and becoming pregnant again.

In the same vein, when a human or baboon adult seeks to socialize its offspring by preventing physical conflict between siblings through appropriate punishment, he is maximizing chances for his own genetic material to enter the next generation, for both offspring are probably equally related to him. It thus behooves the adult to be even-handed. Sibling rivalry, on the other hand, appears to reflect the fact that each sib is seeking to maximize his own reproductive success to the relative exclusion of the sibs; he is, after all, related 100% to himself but shares only 50% of a sib's genes. In general, it would appear that conflict between parents and offspring, if only on the basis of each seeking to maximize his own reproductive potential, is inevitable within all species (Trivers, 1974).

"CRITICAL PERIODS" IN THE DEVELOPMENT OF ATTACHMENTS: THE QUESTION OF ENVIRONMENTAL DEPRIVATION

Varying rates of growth in ontogenetic maturation are well known. So are the embryological findings that normal growth is interfered with depending on *when* an experimental transplant or teratogenic agent is introduced (Willier et al., 1955). Furthermore, there are numerous findings that in postnatal life interference with normal sensory input can cause tissue degeneration and/or the dropping-out of normal responsivity. Here, again, timing is important (Riesen, 1961).

These findings have been of interest to developmental psychologists as models for viewing behavior, and hence the notion that the absence of certain experiences during some hypothetically critical time will yield a behavioral defect. In the sphere of social behavior, Spitz (1945, 1965), Bowlby (1952), and Goldfarb (1955) have all stressed the importance of infants forming attachments sometime in the first year if subsequent behavior is not to be abnormal (described below). Experimental work with isolated monkeys, dogs, and other lower animals has supported this contention by demonstrating that early social deprivation, if sufficiently prolonged, can cause social animals to become permanently maimed in their social interactions (Mason, 1965; Freedman, 1961).

The postulate that there is a critical period for the formation of human attachments was first elaborated by Spitz (1945). He presented evidence from a South American orphanage in which progressive deterioration occurred in 3-month-old infants after their mothers left. "The infants remained in the Foundling Home, where they were adequately cared for in every bodily respect. Food, hygiene, medical care and medication, etc. were as good as, or even superior to, that of any other institutions we have observed [p. 56]."

At the end of the second year, these children had either died (ca. 40%) or else had developmental quotients at the level of severe defectives. This information was first published in 1945, and, as of 1965, Spitz (1965) still held that this wasting away, called marasmus, was due entirely to lack of "mothering." The fact is that the "Foundling Home" was located in a severe protein deficiency belt and that marasmus was and is a major public health problem there, even among home-reared babies (Scrimshaw and Behar, 1961). It is therefore small wonder that no temperate zone worker has ever found such lethal results from lack of mothering.

Facts such as these have cast doubt on the entire notion of the first year as a critical period in the formation of attachments (Pinneau, 1955), but there is nevertheless ample evidence that Spitz's pioneering work was in the right direction. Bowlby's famous monograph of 1952, *Maternal Care and Mental Health,* has withstood the test of criticism and time, and in a reevaluation some 10 years later, Ainsworth (1962) gave the following excellent summary of the results of affective deprivation:

(1) Recovery from a single, brief, depriving separation experience seems fairly prompt and complete with respect to overt behavior under ordinary conditions; there is evidence, however, of vulnerability to future threats of separation—i.e., there is at least one "hidden" impairment that prevents the reversibility from being described as complete.

(2) Relief from deprivation after even fairly prolonged deprivation experiences in early infancy can result in rapid and dramatic improvement in overt behavior and in generalized intellectual functioning; vocalization, however, may be retarded, even

though the relief occurs before twelve months of age, and effects on other specific aspects of intellectual and personality functioning cannot be ruled out until these aspects have been explored in research.

(3) Prolonged and severe deprivation beginning early in the first year of life and continuing for as long as three years usually leads to severely adverse effects of both intellectual and personality functioning that do resist reversal.

(4) Prolonged and severe deprivation beginning in the second year of life leads to some grave effects on personality that do resist reversal, although the effects on general intelligence seem to be fairly completely reversible; specific impairment of intellectual functions has not yet been studied.

(5) The effects of age at the onset and relief of the deprivation experience are undoubtedly important factors in influencing reversibility, but these are not understood in enough detail to set precise limits for a "sensitive phase" of development of special processes.

(6) In general, in the first year of life, the younger the infant when deprivation is relieved (and hence the less prolonged the deprivation experience), the more normal is the subsequent development; yet after the first year of life has passed, the older the child at the onset of deprivation the more readily and completely reversible seem to be the effects of a deprivation of a given duration.

(7) Certain impairments seem to be less readily and less completely reversible than others—impairments in language, in abstraction and in the capacity for strong and lasting interpersonal attachments.

(8) Especially if undertaken when the child is still very young, intensive therapeutic efforts may result in marked improvement of some very severe effects that resist reversal through ordinary relief from deprivation.

(9) Subsequent experiences of insufficiency, distortion or discontinuity in interpersonal interaction may be important in reinforcing impairments that otherwise might have been reversed more or less completely [pp. 153–154].

While these findings are remarkably straightforward, Casler (1961) has chosen to emphasize their shortcomings and suggests perceptual deprivation rather than affective deprivation as the causal agent. Actually, no sharp distinction is possible, for cognition, perception, and affective behavior all work in concert and represent our own somewhat artificial abstractions. In addition, as Ainsworth (1962) points out, in the early months of life perceptual deprivation is equivalent to social deprivation since it is primarily the caretaker who provides the infant with perceptual stimulation.

With regard to critical periods, it is difficult to pinpoint the rising fear of strangers in infants as a natural end to the period in which primary attachments are formed, as Gray (1958) has proposed; but it is also a safe guess, on the basis of the data reviewed by Ainsworth, that for most infants, attachments by 7 months are essential. In evolutionary terms, it is highly adaptive that attachments between human infant and caretaker form by this age so that subsequent development of autonomy, in the newly motile child, may take place relatively unfettered by recurring dependency. Erikson's (1950) surmise that a basic sense of trust or mistrust is established in the first year is a complementary way of dealing with the same set of events.

Erikson (1950) has also proposed that the major theme of the second and third years is the development of autonomy, and few observers would deny that the demand for and insistence on autonomy forms a major aspect of the lives of 2- and 3-year-olds. Nor is there much difficulty in surmising the evolutionary importance of such self-propelling investigations of the environment.[3] But in what sense are these periods critical?

In considering this question, Harlow and Zimmerman's (1959) study of monkeys reared in isolation is to the point. These sensually deprived rhesus infants explored very little, preferring to lie in one spot, and in effect suffered from impaired autonomy. The young orphaned children described and filmed by Appell and Aubry (1951) behaved with striking similarity: They were fearful, they explored very little, and they had to be helped to find out what the world was like. Ainsworth reports other such data, and it seems that this is one appalling way in which events of the first year may affect ensuing development. We can assume further that the manner in which years two and three are negotiated affects the relatively unique developments of the 4-year-old period, and logically each period must to some extent be "critical" for the next.

But it is too frequently forgotten that there are striking individual differences in relation to critical periods, and experimental work with animals provides a helpful paradigm. Ginsburg (1968) has demonstrated that the handling of some strains of mice during a pre-weaning period will exaggerate adult aggressiveness whereas handling another strain will result in unusually pacific animals. In addition, the amount of handling also makes a difference in later aggression depending on the strain of mice used. Since each strain is essentially a single sample of the species' possibilities, it is clear that tremendous variability exists in responsivity to early stress. Breeds of dogs yield similar information (Freedman, 1958), and there is no reason to suspect the same is not true of humans. *Experiences critical for one child may well have entirely different effects for another* (Murphy, 1964), and variability rather than uniformity of response is to be expected within the broad framework of the species pattern, providing the experiences or deprivations are not completely antagonistic to the nature of the species. With regard to this last point, Murphy (1964) has pointed out that individual deprivation discussed by Ainsworth amounts to a species-wide debilitation where individual differences have become submerged by the shocking nature of the general symptomatology.

SUMMARY

The human infant is born with numerous abilities which are actualized through interaction with the environment. To recount a few: At birth, he will turn to models of a human face rather than to a scrambled version of it; he turns to the voice in preference to other sounds; it is also evident that he has

[3]That parental thwarting of autonomy will result in shame, as Erikson holds, has much less to recommend it. The feeling of shame is a common Japanese emotion, for example, yet autonomy in boys is greatly encouraged and considered desirable in that culture (Haring, 1956).

available all the perceptual constancies, and that they are perfected with time rather than learned.

The human infant shares much behavior with other mammals: He cries when uncomfortable, roots and sucks for milk, becomes attached to those around him. Like other mammalian predators, he becomes increasingly motile and investigative even as he becomes wary of potential dangers. He begins to wander farther from the adult caretaker and at the same time plays more with his peers.

Adult caretaking among humans does show substantial uniqueness in that the child is usually reared within a family. However, it is similar to the macaques, for example, in the following ways: At first the adult's role is completely nurturant, but as the youngster becomes more motile and assertive, the parent counters with more flexible guidance; in time (at 1 year in rhesus, 5 or 6 in humans) parents expect the young to start guiding themselves, and may at times actively encourage independence. Also, in both macaques and man, there is a progressive importance to the peer group, as more and more time is spent away from the parent (especially in males).

There are, of course, obvious uniquenesses in the hominid infant: Its relative immaturity at birth, its slow motor development, its complex, extended vocal and visual interaction with the caretaker (including smiling and babbling), its excellent eye-hand coordination and manipulative abilities (at about seven months) and, at about 1 year, its ability to walk erect, to use language, and its developing sense of self or "me."

All the above assumes normal development and average endowment, and it is presented with the expectation, which may in some instances be proved false, that in these behaviors there is relatively little cultural variation.

3
SEX DIFFERENCES

What is the function of sex? The evolutionary answer is that it provides a population with tremendous variability unobtainable in asexual reproduction. Such variability usually makes possible the continuing survival of at least some members of this population under conditions which are lethal to most.

Once introduced into the course of evolution, sexual differences themselves became exploited, so to speak, via secondary sex characteristics. Etkin's (1967) discussion of differences in aggressive potential is to the point:

> A secondary sex characteristic, which may be designated as aggressive potential, is the difference between male and female with regard to capacity for fighting. This type is common among vertebrates. Most prominent among these dimorphisms are differences in size and strength. One of the extreme examples is seen in the seals and related marine carnivores. Elephant-seal males are as much as two and one-half, and fur-seal males ten times as large as their females. Though this is extreme, a difference of 50 percent or so is not at all rare among mammals. In a majority of mammals, the male tends to be bigger and heavier than the female. Only exceptionally, as in the European rabbit, is the female the larger.
>
> Aggressive potential in favor of the male often takes the form of weapons. Horns and antlers are in many instances differentiated between sexes. We are familiar with them in many species of deer. Teeth as weapons are also frequent secondary sex characteristics of mammalian males. We see this in the enlarged canine teeth in male baboons and, in extreme form, in the single large tooth of the narwal. In birds, examples of dimorphism in weapons are fewer, but the spurs of the rooster provide a good one [p. 68].

There are many other considerations in sexual dimorphism, such as the display coloration in males of many species—usually associated with territorial defense and mating. Less dimorphic animals tend to share more tasks, including nest-building, care of young, hunting, and so forth.

An obvious question to ask about highly dimorphic species is, Why are the males rather than the females larger and more aggressive? Bateman (1948), a zoologist, felt that energy investment in the care of young was the crucial issue here. For example, in species where the female invests considerably more energy in care of young than does the male, males normally compete among themselves for females, and the results of selection for colorful plumage, size, aggressivity, and strength in males is usually seen. Conversely, in the few known cases in which males invest more energy in the care of young, as in the phalarope, the reverse is true. Females of this small shore bird species fight among themselves for the right to mate, and it is they who have developed secondary sexual characters to facilitate these activities. They are larger, sport brighter plumage, and are more aggressive than males. After mating, female phalaropes stay at the breeding ground only long enough to lay their eggs, and then leave to form another temporary alliance.

Among most primates, care of the young is largely the female's job, and as Bateman's rule would predict, dimorphism is substantial in these species (see Table 3-1). Only when we study the gibbon and man do we see a substantial reduction in dimorphism, and it is indeed true that in both these species, as opposed to others listed in Table 3-1, there is cooperative care of the young. That is, while males of the other primate species will protect a youngster in danger, only in gibbons and man is there a male and female unit which cares for him, and Bateman's rule thus appears to hold.[1]

The entire issue of differential parental investment in the rearing of young is of great importance, especially as it relates to reproductive success. Trivers (1972) has pointed out, in an extension of Bateman's work, that in most species the reproductive success of females is relatively invariant compared with males. That is, females usually are capable of limited reproduction, and compared with males each female approaches that limit.

---

[1] While dimorphism is reduced in man and gibbon, it is of course not absent, and males of both species are more aggressive, tend to treat other males as rivals, and females still have primary responsibility for the young.

In addition to these data on primates, however, the aggressive nature of our more immediate evolutionary forebears should be considered. The first identified linear relative was *Australopithecus africanus*. These early savanna-living hominids, who according to current estimates were present as recognizable species for about three quarters of a million years beginning 2¼ million years ago, were erect and bipedal, averaged about 4 feet in height, were

TABLE 3-1

Differences in Weight Associated with Sex in Higher Primates[a]

Primate	Male	Female
Baboon	75 lbs.	30 lbs.
Gibbon	13	13
Orangutan	165	80
Chimpanzee	110	88
Man (U.K.)	155	150
	(Height, 67.5 in.)	(Height, 62.5 in.)

Note: The figures are approximate, since they are derived from small samples.
[a]After Campbell (1966).

Males, with their enormous production of gametes, come nowhere near their potential for insemination. They are thus open to varying strategies in order to best fulfill their potential. For example, some male birds are completely promiscuous and attempt to inseminate as many females as possible, whereas others are permanently monogamous and male potential is limited by one female's egg production (Trivers, 1972). In general, since reproductive success has probably been higher in females who chose mates that helped in raising the young, some sort of medium position between male promiscuity and monogamy can be seen in most species. That is to say, a variety of strategies around parental investment of energies in young have been worked out in nature, and most species exhibit a compromise solution.

Typically, this compromise has involved greater mobility and aggression in males, as well as higher mortality. In this latter regard, the males of a species have higher metabolic rates and suffer more from protein deficiencies, and this also appears to be true of the relatively monomorphic species such as man. They are, quite simply, the more expendable of the species. As Trivers (1972) has pointed out, these differential death rates vary with the amount of male investment in the young and have apparently been selected for. The rule seems to be, the less the paternal investment within a species, the higher the relative male mortality. Natural selection can thus be said to

---

predaceous and wielded bone weapons, and apparently murdered their own kind upon occasion (cf. Dart, 1955). On this last point, their upper Pleistocene successors, *Homo erectus,* were fairly certainly cannibalistic. This can be judged from the widely dispersed skull remains whose base (around the foramen magnum) had been broken open as if to better extract the meat inside (cf. von Koenigswald, 1962). It is startling, in fact, to note the common agreement on these deductions among our top paleontologists. While this does not assure correctness, we may note that some present-day New Guinea tribes, who until recently practiced cannibalism, broke open the enemy skulls in the same way, and that weaponry, hunting, and predation certainly characterize the recent hominid adaptation.

have accounted for much of the consistencies one sees in male-female differences across species.[2]

DOMINANCE-SUBMISSION HIERARCHIES AND MALE AGGRESSION

It is, then, a clear-cut finding that the male of most species is the more aggressive sex. In socially organized species, however, counter measures against the constant display of aggression have proved necessary. Dominance-submission hierarchies in which males, especially, reach an "agreement" on their relative toughness vis-à-vis one another, are perhaps the most commonly seen solution, and such hierarchies have proven to be central to the social adaptation of all primates.

A dominance-submission hierarchy is generally defined as a linear or quasi-linear arrangement that determines which animal has preferential access to various aspects of the environment, e.g., food, sitting places, copulation. In newly assembled groups the establishment of a hierarchy may involve considerable fighting, whereas in ongoing primate troops, the dominance relations are implicit in their daily activities; for example, as one animal steps aside to let another pass. Further, the linearity and rigidity of the hierarchy varies with the troop's ecological niche, and it appears that ground-living species are considerably more aggressive than tree-living species. This is probably because terrestrial living offers more dangers from predators and, therefore, high levels of aggressive response have proven necessary. For example, tree-living langurs in Ceylon are less aggressive and exhibit a looser social hierarchy than do their ground-living cousin species. For that matter, chimps in the forest are less hierarchical and form less physically compact groups than are the same animals when in open bush

---

[2]The question of male investment in young (i.e., paternal behavior) is directly related to the question of altruistic behavior. Hamilton (1964) has made a good case for altruism having been phylogenetically selected on the basis of kinship (see also Trivers, 1971). That is, help given to two relatives sharing one quarter of ego's genes is equivalent to help given an offspring where the degree of genetic relationship is one-half. Altruism, then, is seen as an evolutionary development based on natural selection and success in maintenance of one's own genetic material, whether in offspring or kin.

It follows that within any troop of primates, relatives would tend to group together and more readily form coalitions with one another than non-related animals. According to Fiske's (1973) review, this is indeed the case, and since paternity is usually uncertain among primates, such groupings are necessarily around central females. In man, familial grouping is universally present and human kinship systems can be shown to be systematic attempts to maintain genetic lineages and to thereby insure survival of one's genes. Further, since paternity can often be determined in man, and is in fact a crucial issue within many cultures, male lineage is at least as common as lineage traced through females (Fiske, 1973).

country. As Washburn and DeVore (1961) have pointed out, man as a terrestrial primate seems to be more like the baboon and macaque in his social organization than like the genetically closer arboreal great ape because of the selection pressure exercised by a similar ecology.

We know more about the ontogeny of dominance hierarchies among the macaques than any other terrestrial primate, for the macaques are the most widely distributed as well as the most studied genus. While the following remarks may not hold entirely for each macaque species, they do provide a composite picture at the generic level (cf. Southwick, 1963; DeVore, 1965; Jay, 1968).

Jensen (1966) has found that even as infants, macaque mother-son pairs interact differently from mother-daughter pairs in that more aggression and mutual independence are seen in the mother-son pairs. By the first year the male infants, who tend to wander farther from the mother than females, have found each other and have begun to play. If for some reason the youngster persists in his dependency and continues suckling, a few well-placed bites by the mother helps send him out into the world of his peers (Harlow and Harlow, 1966).

Rough-and-tumble play occupies the young males much of the day, and, perhaps because the adult males find this annoying and nip at the youngsters, the young macaque males generally take their play to the periphery of the troop. The female young do not take as much to rough-and-tumble play, and generally remain closer to their mothers as they mature, engaging in mutual grooming and assuming some responsibility for the new infants. All females, young and old, generally remain in the geographical center of the troop.

In time, the rough-and-tumble fun of the males becomes progressively more serious and, during the second year, severe biting indicates that the dominance-hierarchy is well underway. By 3 years, the peripheral males have established a hierarchy of strength and/or courage. To see one of the ways by which this sorting out may occur, one has only to watch Koford's (1963) films of the juvenile rhesus of Cayo Santiago courageously diving from high trees into a shallow lagoon—apparently with the sole purpose of splashing one's playmates. Although no data are reported, there seems little doubt that these displays result in respect, not only from the watching human audience, but among the monkeys themselves, and that they help to sort out the dominance order.

By age 4, the more brave among the juvenile males may make forays into the troop's central hierarchy, where they usually fight first with the females and then with the younger males. Depending upon a number of factors, including the hierarchical position of his mother, the young male finds his way into the dominance-submission order of the troop. He usually finds well-established mature males at the top, and often a coalition of two or three of them appear to lead the troop. The hierarchy is usually fairly linear, with females occupying the lower half.

The problem of intergroup contacts is most interesting and important. Most of our information is based on the Japanese macaques, which are forced into frequent contact, as on the island of Koshima. There the monkey troops develop a dominance order, usually based on size of the troop. Even troops that have just formed from the splitting of a single group show the same rivalrous pattern. That is, former troop mates become "enemies" once the split occurs. However, sustained aggression is rare at either the intratroop or intertroop levels, for somehow each animal and each troop assess their chances and come to decisions *before* a fight. At least this is true in the majority of encounters, although a number of observations have been made of rare but vicious fights between an established male and a challenger; no one, however, has yet reported analogous sustained combat between monkey troops. In fact, the central males usually do not participate in intergroup threats since the peripheral males, because of their position, take the lead in such contacts. Indeed, the theme for young males is the display of courage, while for females it is the care and grooming of younger sibs.

There are many more facts of interest that might be added, but this will suffice as a generalized model for social organization usually seen in terrestrial subhuman primates. We may now inquire if there are not comparable patterns in man.

THE DEVELOPMENT OF DOMINANCE HIERARCHIES IN MAN

Discussion of sex differences in man, even those to be seen in infancy, is inseparable from a discussion of his primate heritage, and more specifically the ontogeny of human dominance hierarchies. A number of studies have been performed at our laboratories which deal with this issue, and they will form the bulk of the present discussion (Omark, 1973; Edelman, 1973; Beekman, 1970; Parker and Freedman, 1971; Freedman, 1973).

Our work began with the common observation that man, like the macaques, frequently engages in intragroup dominance displays, except that among men we tend to use vernacular terms such as "one-upmanship." Such social rivalry appears to occupy the males of the species more than the females, and there is no point in cataloging here examples from everyday life, for by now much has been written on the subject (cf. Freedman, 1967). It is similarly evident that man tends to identify with a primary group (family, city, nation, race, religion), and when intergroup competition arises, as over land, resources, or markets, groups act in concert vis-à-vis one another not unlike macaques, with the weaker group usually giving way to the stronger. Of course, there are enormous differences between monkeys and men, but the basic pattern is undeniably similar and, although all the evidence is not in, it seems to be cross-culturally universal.

How do dominance-submission hierarchies come about in man, and how do they first form? In search of answers, we started by noting that at the local "progressive" school when 3- and 4-year-olds went from classroom to classroom (they were allowed this freedom there), they went alone, or at most in twos or threes. By 5 and 6 years, however, boys invariably moved about in groups of three or more, while girls continued as before in small groups or couples. On the playground, too, we found that after 5 years boys tended to swarm in groups of five members or more, and tended to use the entire grounds as their play area, often keeping in touch as a group through loud shouts and gestures. The girls, by contrast, occupied smaller and less expansive groups, and their games tended to occur in a confined space and to involve repeated rhythmic activity. Boys' games involved unpredictable patterns of movement and a good deal of playful aggression, even as they do among the macaques. Displays of courage seem equally important to human and macaque males, and among both jumping from an "impossibly" high place is a much esteemed game.

In the sandbox, 5- and 6-year-old girls usually sat alongside one another forming sand pies or cakes, with their conversations frequently taking precedence over the activity. Boys were more physically active in the sandbox and more frequently worked on a common project, such as digging two or three tunnels joined at a common point.

When we questioned the children about possible competitive feelings, we found that by 4 years, boys were definitely aroused by the question, "Which of you is toughest?" A typical 4-year-old's response, no matter who the opposition, was "Me!" Girls, on the other hand, were rarely provoked by this question.

By 6 years, however, when asked the same question, boys tended to agree with one another on who *was* tougher. In other words, a hierarchy had been formed. Girls, again, were for the most part less interested in placing themselves in such a hierarchy, although their perception of "toughness" in boys was as accurate as judgments among the boys themselves. The major source of disagreement, naturally enough, was one's own rank in that children tended to see it higher than general agreement would have it. Thus, something of the 4-year-old's egocentrism and push toward alpha-ness seemed to remain at 6 and 7 years and—most probably—forever after (cf. Freedman, 1967).

With regard to facial expressions, it is commonly observed in monkey troops that individuals of lower status demonstrate a "fear-grin" when passing near a dominant; similarly they spend more time watching the dominant animal than he does watching them—a sort of disdain on the dominant's part and its complement, fearful watchfulness on the submissive's part. A straight-on stare, in fact, is invariably interpreted as a threat.

Among our 6- and 7-year-olds, we were able to measure very similar behavior and obtained very similar results. After pairing all possible combinations of high and low dominance boys and girls we found that, as in monkeys (Chance, 1967), low dominance children stare and smile considerably more at high dominance children than the reverse and, consequently, girls smiled and stared considerably more at boys than the reverse. In other words, to be dominant among human children means that the attention of others is on you and deference behavior is shown to you (see section on Smiling, Chapter 2).

We have extended our observations to a number of other culture areas. The results indicate that just about the same differential patterns of play and behavior characterize boys and girls around the world, and it would appear that we are dealing here with "species-specific" behavior. One aspect of this cross-cultural study consisted of observations of and free drawings from 5- to 7-year-old children in Chicago, Kyoto (Japan), Hong Kong, Bali, Australia (Aborigine), Kandy (Ceylon), Pondicherry and New Delhi (India), and in a Kikuyu and Masai village (Kenya). In all the samples, boys were more aggressive, more motile, more intrusive, and more boisterous in their play, although there were cultural differences in degree. Also, boys of every sample more often had themes of action in their drawings, and vehicles were much more frequent than among the girls' drawings. Also, boys everywhere were consistently less neat in that they tended more frequently to burst through the outlines of figures. It should be noted that while dimorphism in Balinese drawings was low relative to, say, Japanese drawings, Balinese boys still drew more vehicles and drew with less respect for boundaries than did the girls.

These findings would appear to bear out what has been said before: that culture teaches with greatest ease that which children will want to learn, as when boys choose to draw more vehicles, and girls choose to concentrate on flowers. That is, we must speak of differential thresholds or biosocial pathways in conceptualizing the fact that boys and girls differentiate in about the same way in all the cultures examined. Put another way, not only does each culture differentially distribute its wares to the sexes, but we must conclude that boys and girls choose and react differently as well.

The fact that boys and girls may be differentially treated as infants, for example, may well depend more on actual differences in their behavior than on the differential expectations adults have for boys and girls. However, in order to substantiate this supposition, our job now is to review the facts of prenatal and early postnatal development of sex differences.

PRENATAL DEVELOPMENT

While it has long been recognized that there are male and female forming hormones in vertebrate embryos (androgens and estrogens), it is only recently that a new and important distinction has been made regarding the action of these hormones. We now know (cf. Harris, 1964) that there are critical periods in the early development of mammals, usually during embryogenesis, when the presence or absence of androgens respectively *permanently* masculinizes or feminizes the brain. Young (1965) called this the *organizational* function of the sex hormones. Later, at puberty, the *activational* function of the sex hormones serves to initiate elaboration of secondary sexual characteristics, as has long been known.

The organizational function will concern us here, for if indeed there is masculinization or feminization of the brain prior to birth, we should expect to find a certain amount of male-female differentiation in behavior perhaps as early as the first days of life, and certainly within the first year.

Figures 3-1, 3-2, and 3-3 represent results of an experiment with rhesus monkeys by Young et al. (1965). Pregnant monkeys were injected with testosterone propionate, a synthesized androgen, which resulted in virilization of all female fetuses. Tests of the early development of these genetic females revealed typical male rhesus behavior with regard to social encounters: facial threats, invitations to play, and rough-and-tumble play were distinctly malelike. Similar injections after birth did not have comparable effects, although in rats analogous behavioral effects occurred with testosterone injections up through 5 days after birth (Levine and Mullins, 1966). In both these studies it appeared that testosterone propionate affected the

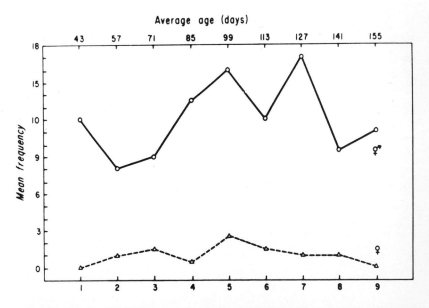

FIG. 3-1 Display of facial threat by female pseudohermaphroditic (solid line) and normal female (broken line) monkeys, plotted relative to age. The abscissa is scaled in successive blocks of five trials. (From Young, Goy, & Phoenix, 1965.)

developing central nervous system in some complex way, probably at the hypothalamic level, to produce the male phenotype (Harris, 1964).

Interestingly, the influences of estrogen on male fetuses are not as marked, which bears out the dictum that among mammals the basic pattern is female, and males are a derivative form. (In birds the opposite situation prevails.) Thus removal of the gonads in mammalian embryos, no matter what the original sex, results in anatomically complete females (Burns, 1961).

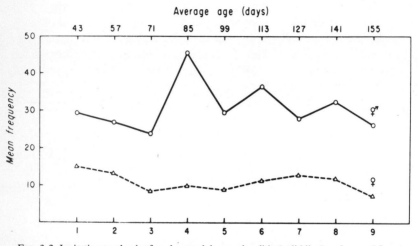

FIG. 3-2 Invitation to play by female pseudohermaphroditic (solid line) and normal female (broken line) monkeys, plotted relative to age. The abscissa is scaled in successive blocks of five trials. (From Young, Goy, & Phoenix, 1965.)

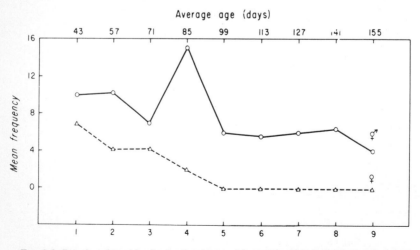

FIG. 3-3 Rough-and-tumble play by female pseudohermaphroditic (solid line) and normal female (broken line) monkeys, plotted relative to age. The abscissa is scaled in successive blocks of five trials. (From Young, Goy, & Phoenix, 1965.)

The same mechanisms appear to be operating at the human level. One source of data are otherwise normal girls who were virilized in utero as a result of their mothers having received synthesized progesterone injections to prevent aborting. (Synthetic progesterone can simulate the action of testosterone and the two are closely related biochemically.) Money (1970) found that in adolescence these girls, like the virilized rhesus, exhibited a number of traits usually considered male, e.g., they were "boyish" far beyond a comparison group. To quote Money, fetal androgenization of girls tends to make for later

> vigorous, muscular energy expenditure and an intense interest in athletic sports and outdoor activities in competition with boys. It is not especially associated with aggression and fighting. It is accompanied by scorn for fussy and frilly feminine clothes and hairdos in favor of utility styles. It is incompatible with a strong interest in maternalism as revealed in the rehearsals of childhood doll play and in the future ambitions for the care of tiny babies. It does not exclude the anticipation of romance, marriage and pregnancy, but these are regarded in a somewhat perfunctory way as secondary to a career. Career ambitions are consistent with high academic achievement and with high I.Q. which tends to be a characteristic of girls with fetal androgenization.

An equally striking source of evidence for prenatal masculine-feminine organization in humans is the not uncommon occurrence of genetic male-pseudohermaphrodites (Stern, 1960; Wilkins, 1965; Money, 1970). Because of a familial recessive gene whose action prevents the utilization of testosterone, the "afflicted" person appears to be a perfectly normal female despite an XY constitution. Massive doses of testosterone are to no avail, so that it has been concluded that there are no binding sites for the male hormones. The presenting complaint most usually involves sterility and the absence of menstrual periods, and only the sparsity of axial and pubic hair may be considered as externally anomalous. Such individuals are mentally normal, distinctly feminine in behavior, and frequently marry before the problem is discovered. Finally, Dawson (1972) has recently summarized the literature on sex hormones and cognitive style and concluded that sex hormones serve to differentiate performance into a male or female direction while social rearing may act in either a contradictory or reinforcing fashion.

Thus, humans, like other mammals, are probably not "psychosexually neutral" at birth as Hampson and Hampson (1961) have claimed. While this notion was in vogue for a while, few researchers would hold to it at present. [See especially Diamond (1965) for a refutation of the Hampson and Hampson conclusions.] In fact, there is now direct evidence from experimental animals that there are sex differences in the secretion of gonadal hormones throughout the prepubertal period (Critchlow and Bar-Sela, 1967), so that we now know that these activating hormones may be present right at birth, differentially effecting behavior.

POSTNATAL BEHAVIOR: DIFFERENCES
IN PARENTAL TREATMENT

A number of studies have found that from very early after birth, human mothers treat boys differently from girls. Thoman et al. (1972) found in a group of primiparous mothers that newborn girls were talked to and smiled at more than were boys. In studies with 3-month-old infants, Moss and Robson (1968) found that mothers were more apt to respond to fretting girls by talking, watching, and offering a pacifier, whereas they were more likely to respond to fretting boys by holding them close or by trying to distract them. Also with infants of 3 months, Lewis (personal communication, 1971) found that mothers vocalized more frequently to girls, and held boys more often than girls. It would thus appear that differential socialization begins right from birth, or at least soon afterward.

In macaque monkeys, too, at least two studies have shown that mothers treat infant males differently than females. Jensen (1966) found, as did Mitchell and Brandt (1970), that mothers were considerably more aggressive with male infants. In the latter study it was also found that male and female offspring present quite different sets of stimuli for the mothers, differences which complemented and made comprehensible the maternal differences in behavior. Male infants, for example, explored the environment more, climbed further, ran and jumped more often, and threatened other infants for longer periods.

This raises the question then, do human infants also present differential stimuli which are sex-dependent? It is with this question in mind that the following sections on neonatal sex differences are presented. It should be noted at the outset of this review that there are many studies which show an absence of male-female differences over a wide variety of traits; the following sections represent only those areas which consistently show differentiations.

POSTNATAL BEHAVIOR: DIFFERENCES IN
IMPOSITION-OF-SELF ON ENVIRONMENT

It is not a particularly new finding that boys are more intrusive than girls, and Mead (1949) reported this as a probable cross-cultural universal in her book *Male and Female*. Her criteria there included such male activity as the tendency to wander farther from a home base, to investigate unknown areas, and lower thresholds for aggressive behavior. Females, on the other hand, were described as generally more accommodating to and more influenced by the environment, a finding that has more recently been emphasized by the numerous studies of Witkin and his associates (1954). In their experiments, they have found that women are more likely to use cues in the environment for the solution of problems, while men are more likely to act on the basis of internal cues.

In what may well be a related item and therefore an indication that these differences are not learned, the author found that neonatal females habituated more quickly to light flashing repeatedly on the eyes (Fig. 3-4). That is, females accommodated to the repeated stimulus while males were still reacting with a blink. Similarly, females of 3 months were found to be less interested in visual complexity and quickly habituated to visual novelty (Lewis et al., 1967; Meyers and Cantor, 1967). Also, if one uses "demand-ingness" as a measure of intrusion on others, Moss (1967) found that 3-week to 3-month-old males were already more demanding of mother's attention than females.

With regard to intrusiveness and investigativeness, Kagan (1971) found that 6-month-old boys typically reached behind a barrier to obtain an attractive object, whereas girls tended to look away from both the barrier and the object. By 1 year, differences in assertiveness are extremely clear, and in

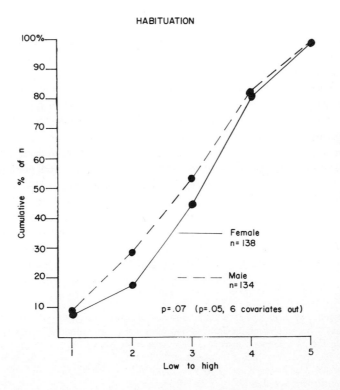

FIG. 3-4 Newborn females stopped reacting sooner to a pen light repeatedly flashed on the eyes.

a well-documented and well-controlled study, Goldberg and Lewis (1969) found that

> . . . girls (of 13 months of age) were more dependent, showed less exploratory behavior and their play behavior reflected a more quiet style. Boys were more independent, showed more exploratory behavior, played with toys requiring gross motor activity, were more vigorous and tended to run and bang in their play. Obviously, these behavior differences approximate those usually found between the sexes at later ages [p. 29].

Brooks and Lewis (1973), using boy-girl twins of the same age (13–14 months), found much the same thing, and so did Messer and Lewis in a study of 1-year-olds (1972). Other investigators, using different techniques (e.g., Maccoby and Jacklin, 1973), have not found stable sex differences, but it does appear fair to say that, in general, females accommodate more readily to environmental impositions, while males tend more to exploit and intrude upon people and objects.

SEX DIFFERENCES IN AFFILIATIVE BEHAVIOR

It is most interesting that in three independent studies, ours, Korner's (1969) and Horowitz' (personal communication, 1970), newborn females exhibited a greater frequency of eyes closed *reflexive smiling* (Fig. 3-5).[3] It may be recalled from our previous discussions (Chapter 2) that smiling is best conceived of as a phylogenetically adaptive trait which fosters interpersonal affiliation, and that frequent eyes-closed smiling seems to herald highly affiliative behavior in later life.

Lewis et al. (1966) have stressed the same theme. They report that at 6 months of age, girls preferentially directed both visual and vocal attention to social stimuli as opposed to nonsocial objects, whereas boys did not make this differentiation; Kagan (1971) reported that this trend continued in tests at 8 months and at 1 year. In more recent work, Lewis (personal communication, 1973) reported that 9-month-old girls appear to know when an adult is addressing them, whereas boys do not yet have this capacity. He has found that boys will often respond with vocalization to two adults addressing each other, but girls respond only when directly addressed! In summarizing his

---

[3]In these, and all other figures on newborn sex differences, two sets of probability values were obtained. In the first set, medication was a covariable, and no probability figures have been presented if differences in medication were also significant. In the second set, six additional covariates were eliminated and, therefore, did not influence these probability values. The covariates were mother's age, baby's age, Apgar, baby's weight, length of labor, and number of previous deliveries.

All probability figures relating to newborn behavior in this and the next chapter were obtained via a multivariate analysis for nonorthogonal data developed by Professor Darrell R. Bock, Committee on Human Development, University of Chicago.

longitudinal studies (3–27 months), Kagan (1971), reported further that 3-month-old girls, but not boys, vocalized differentially to male and female examiners—and that 6-month-old-girls, but not boys, vocalized differentially to a loudspeaker emitting male and female voices (the female voice was preferred). Kagan also included, "The stability of *smiling* from one to two years for girls is one of the most hardy evidences of continuity in the entire study."

Indeed, recent studies on smiling among adults bear out these sex differences. McLean (1970), for example, examined high school and college yearbook photos from 1900 until present and found significantly more smiling among the females. Even when over-all smiling was low, as in the depression years, approximately the same male-female differential was observed. Probably because of the lengthy exposure necessary in early photography, there were but eleven smiling faces between 1900 and 1917 in the college yearbooks, and all were females. Similarly, Wolfe (1971), in a well-controlled study, found that women walking through a train terminal had significantly lower thresholds than men in returning smiles from both a male and female experimenter. Wolfe also found the same differential responsiveness at lunch counters and while purchasing groceries, indicating that women more frequently than men are poised on the threshold of a smile.

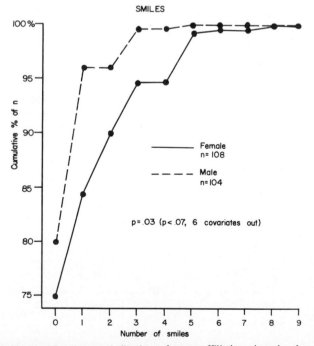

FIG. 3-5 Newborn females gave indications of a more affiliative orientation than males. For one thing, they exhibited more frequent eyes-closed ("reflexive") smiling.

In our twin population, we found girls were significantly higher ($p<.01$) than the boys in *social extroversion,* as reflected in monthly descriptions over the first year (Octant 1a, Table 4-3, and Fig. 3-6). Adjectives, such as smiling, grinning, friendly, playful, and responsive (to people), appeared more frequently in girls' protocols than in those of infant boys.

We also found girls significantly more watchful and fearful of strangers (Fig. 3-7), even as Tennes and Lampl (1966) had reported before us, and it is perhaps not surprising that heightened affiliativeness and heightened fear tend to go together; obviously, both have in common a low threshold for

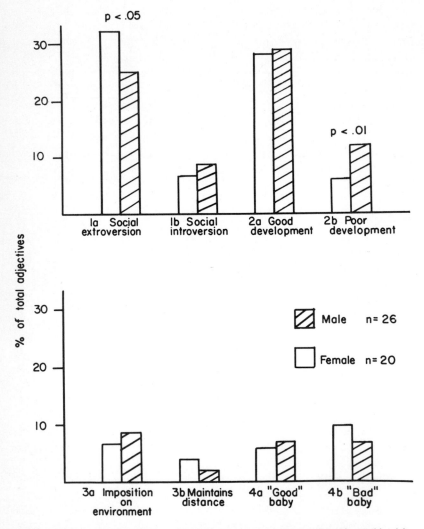

FIG. 3-6 Boys vs. girls, based on adjectives used by observers over 8 to 12 monthly visits over the first year of life (Table 4-3). All children were same-sexed twins.

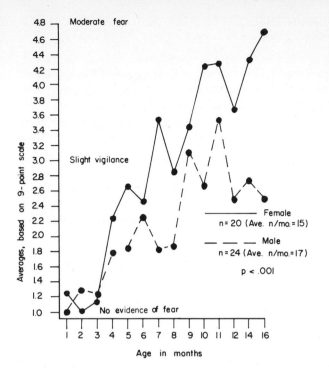

FIG. 3-7 Fearfulness of a stranger visiting at home. Boys and girls in longitudinal study of twins.

social reaction. Similarly, Kagan (1971) found that girls tended to react with more severe fright and inhibition to clay faces at 8 months and 13 months. And Goldberg and Lewis (1969) reported that, at 1 year, girls in a novel situation were more reluctant to leave their mother's side to explore an inanimate environment, revealing a heightened dependency on familiar persons when in an anxiety-provoking situation. From our point of view, it is most interesting that Mason et al. (1959) found similar sex differences among rhesus monkeys in that females were consistently more affected by the presence of a stranger. In the majority of the primate species studied, in fact, females were more prone to exhibit various deference signals, i.e., signs of friendliness or nonaggression (DeVore, 1965; Jay, 1968). One such signal, the fear-grin, is the closest primates come to the human smile (DeVore, 1965).

There are many data from older children and adults that females are indeed more affiliative and more timid than males (reviewed in Garai and Scheinfeld, 1968; Oetzel, 1966; and Goodenough, 1957). The recent findings in infants reported here are important in that they more strongly suggest that these differences are based in human biology.

PREFERRED SENSE MODALITIES
Auditory vs. Visual

Alongside this theme of greater female affiliativeness are considerable data on sex differences in preferred sensory modalities. For example, Kagan has concluded that girls seem to have "a disposition to express excitement through talking," whereas boys are relatively visual. He found that boys of 4 months are equally attentive, visually and vocally, to persons and things, and that their vocalizations appear to be almost random. Differences in girls' vocalizations, on the other hand, tended to be stable, and the vocalization frequency at 4 months correlated with the frequencies found later in the first year (Kagan, 1971). Also, according to Cameron et al. (1967), the relative precocity of the first words spoken by girls correlates significantly with adult IQ. Girls seem thus to be stable in their social vocalization habits from early infancy.

If girls are verbal and auditory, boys are visual. As early as 10 weeks, boys show greater increments in learning to visual reinforcement, while girls do best (as we would now expect) under auditory reinforcement (Watson, 1969). Hull (1967) has found that these two modalities continue to differentially affect the performance of boys and girls through 18 months of age. Further, a whole host of studies, summarized by Oetzel (1966), point to the conclusion that males and females similarly differ in preferred modality later in the life span. Females usually do better at verbal and linguistic tasks, whereas males usually excell with visual-spatial tasks (e.g., taking apart and putting together mechanical devices). Males, in fact, have been found to actually see better and females to actually hear better (Garai and Scheinfeld, 1968), although female cyclicity probably plays a role in these data. For example, Diamond et al. (1972) have found that visual sensitivity in females is poorest during menstruation and rises to a peak at ovulation.

Finally, Kimura (1967) has shown that the right ear and the corresponding left cerebral hemisphere are superior for speech detection; whereas the left ear and right cerebral hemisphere seem to process musical and other nonlinguistic sounds better. She found that females have earlier dominance of the left hemisphere which appears to lend them greater precision and stability in acquiring and processing language (see also Taylor, 1969).

Tactual Sensitivity

In addition to the vocal-visual division, neonatal girls have been found to be more sensitive to tactile stimulation (Bell and Costello, 1964), to have lower pain thresholds to electric currents on the skin (Lipsitt and Levy, 1959), and to be more sensitive to a wet sheet on the skin (Wolff, 1969). In a perhaps related finding, newborn girls were judged more "cuddly" than boys in two different studies (see Fig. 3-8; also Horowitz, 1970); that is, they tended to settle into the investigator's arms more readily than did boys, demonstrating a possible "tactual orientation."

On the strength of this finding, Blanck (1971) did a detailed study of the postures of students in a reading room, and found that females tend to round their bodies into ball-like shapes significantly more than did males. For example, only females had both feet under body, tended to hold the head to one side, or tended to huddle under their coats while studying.

"Orality"

Newborn girls respond more to sweetened milk than do boys as measured by a significantly higher consumption (Nisbett and Gurwitz, 1970), and, in a careful analysis of films of hand-mouth movements, Korner (1972) found that newborn girls engaged more frequently in a "mouth dominated" approach, e.g., the mouth approached the hand; in boys, the mouth did not open until contact was established. In addition, Korner (1969) has found more rhythmical mouthing in newborn girls, even as Balint (1948) had reported more frequent rhythmical clonus of the tongue during bottle feedings. This more frequent "oral receptive" mode seen in newborn girls appears to portend basically different modalities to be seen over the life span. Freedman (1971b), for example, in a review of the different presenting symptoms of preadolescent and adolescent boys and girls who come for

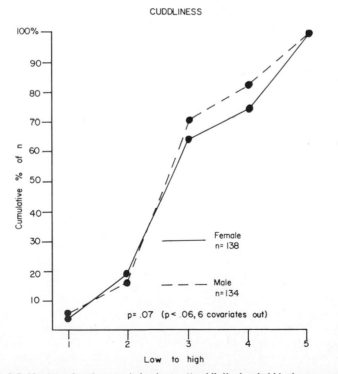

FIG. 3-8 Newborn females were judged more "cuddly" when held in the arms, apparently because they were calmer and pushed-off less from E's body.

psychiatric help, found that whereas boys are more usually referred because of acting-out aggressive behavior, girls most usually present self-punitive symptoms which frequently involve the alimintary system. As an example, anorexia nervosa, the inability to hold down food, is seen in a ratio of about nine girls to every boy.

ADAPTIVE SIGNIFICANCE

If indeed the sexes are on the average thus differentially endowed, what adaptive functions do these differences serve?

Classically, answers to this question should designate how the trait in question facilitates getting an individual's gametes into the next generation. That is, natural selection is "concerned" with survival and proliferation of the genetic material, so that reproductive success and phylogenetic adaptation are seen by zoologists as the same process (Williams, 1966). Certainly this offers immense latitude for the scientific imagination. Wynne-Edwards (1962), for example, has hypothesized that territoriality, the maintenance of a "private" area against conspecific trespassers, is a way of assuring an adequate food suply for at least some members of the species during years of privation. Without it, he points out, an entire species could perish as all would share the minimal food and starve. The majority of "adaptive" explanations center around courtship, mating, and care of the young, however, for the obvious reasons that these aspects of life are most directly related to the success of the next generation.

That brings us back to the first findings that boys, on the average, are more aggressive than girls. We have already discussed the generalization that in a large variety of species, the sex which does not have primary responsibility for care of the offspring (the male in most species) shows the higher aggression. It seems likely that females are most often primary caretakers because of the unlimited male gametic potential (which, in turn, aggression helps realize). There is less point to female-female aggression since her maximum gametic production is relatively low and most females consequently achieve a high ratio of actual offspring to potential offspring compared with males.

Other related adaptive advantages of male aggressivity have been dealt with by Wynne-Edwards (1962), who noted that male aggression is the major mechanism whereby territoriality, with its concomitant advantages, is maintained in a wide variety of species. Similar logic would appear to hold for nonterritorial species that aggressively achieve a dominance-submission hierarchy, insofar as the hierarchy may also facilitate overall survival in times of food scarcity. Further adaptational aspects of dominance-submission hierarchies in primates are discussed by Chance (1967), and we shall add only the following.

In a wide variety of species it has been observed that fecundation is facilitated if the female, who is usually relatively stationary in the sex act, is somewhat fearful of the male; but if the male is fearful or has been defeated by the female, successful mating will almost certainly not occur. For example, in rhesus monkeys it has been shown that males who are submissive to a female will not mate with her unless and until a reversal in relative dominance has occurred (Sade, 1968). There thus appears to have been direct selection within courting species for male aggressivity and social intrusiveness and for relative passivity in females.

Does this apply to the human as well? On the basis of all that has been presented, it would appear so. Even experimental evidence that girls can become as aggressive as boys under the proper reward conditions (Bandura et al., 1963) does not reverse this conclusion. For it is clear that boys, under these same conditions, become even more aggressive. That is, the potential for aggression is certainly available to both sexes, but the human male is more attracted to its display and it is easier to arouse his anger (cf. Maccoby and Jacklin, 1973). It is also clear from considerable clinical material that when a human male is fearful or anxious vis-à-vis the female, it becomes difficult to maintain an erection; and as indicated above, the reverse has no such effect (cf. Fenichel, 1945).

Other aspects of mating behavior appear to be foreshadowed by the finding that newborn girls have lower thresholds to stimulation of the skin by touch. This appears related to the facts that in human courtship males tend initially to be stimulated by visual signals, and females by tactual ones (Kinsey et al., 1948; Kinsey, 1953; Masters and Johnson, 1965). That is, the male becomes sexually aroused distally and the female proximally, and thus, there is reason to believe that such behavior does not blossom suddenly at puberty, but rather that pubertal changes bring into new relief behavioral tendencies already present in the infant and child.

The superior verbal and social skills of females may be related in part to child rearing. If, indeed, primary responsibility for care of children has fallen to females over most of hominid history, and it would appear to be continuous with prehominid history as well, strong social affiliativeness in females must have been fostered. Additionally it was then the female who has taught the child language (language in modern man is acquired between 6 and 18 months), and a low threshold for vocalizing would appear an advantage in achieving this objective (Stevens, 1972).

Finally, the question of greater female affiliativeness, especially as exemplified by lower thresholds to smiling, is of enormous interest. As discussed in Chapter 2, smiling is best considered as a social lubricant, a means of facilitating interaction and establishing interpersonal trust. And it would appear that females are indeed better at this than males. Why? For one thing, the smile may be considered an "appeasement" gesture, even as is the "fear-grin" in other primates.

Given the enormous role of aggression in human history—of tribe raiding tribe and subsequent retribution, of the stealing of women and children and

the murdering of enemy men (as, for example, among the Plains Indians)—
it would appear that women have had to accommodate to new social circumstances far more frequently than have men. As already implied, this history
makes evolutionary sense since the female's reproductive capacities can be
eventualized by any man, whereas males must vie among themselves for that
privilege. It would appear that a lower threshold for appeasement gesturing
in females reflects their relative non-expendability and tends to assure their
survival.

SEX DIFFERENCES IN VIABILITY

What, then, are the facts regarding differences in viability of human males
and females? Trivers (1972) predicts that in species characterized by high
male aggression, many more males than females will be conceived. The best
estimate is that there are between 130 and 140 human males conceived for
every 100 females. By birth the ratio is closer to 106:100, due to higher
spontaneous abortion and still-born rates for males. By adolescence, the
ratio is approximately equal due to higher severe disease and accident rates
among males. Females then proceed to live longer, as they have since
prehistorical times (Birren, 1959), and in the United States they outlive
males by an average of 5 years.

Females mature faster in the uterus and out and, although smaller and
lighter at birth, they are more advanced as judged by X-rays of bone
epiphyses (Flory, 1935), and this remains so through maturity (Tanner,
1961). Consequently, a premature male of the same weight as a female has
less chance of survival (Drillien, 1964). In general, girls are more intact at
birth and males consistently exhibit lower average ratings on Apgar's scale
of viability (Apgar and Hames, 1962) and other signs of neural distress
(Garai and Scheinfeld, 1968). In our own studies, too, there were a number
of indications of greater viability in newborn females. When differences in
elicited reflexes occurred, it was always in the direction of greater female
viability (Figs. 3-9 and 3-10). Newborn males were more tremulous and
more prone to startle (Figs. 3-11 and 3-12), whereas newborn females were
more generally organized and alert as shown by their superior ability to
follow both inanimate objects and the human face and voice (Figs. 3-13 and
3-14).

Beyond infancy, males are more prone to any number of difficulties:
cerebral palsy, learning and behavior disorders, speech problems, mental
defect, autism, broken bones, and much more (see Garai and Scheinfeld,
1968; Kessler, 1966). There is no doubt, then, that as a population, males
are substantially less viable.

The usual explanation of male-female differences in viability is based on
the fact that males have but a single X chromosome, so that lethal recessive
genes cannot be masked as on the autosomes where two chromosomes are

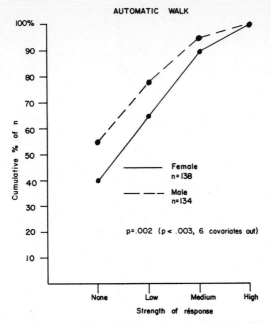

FIG. 3-9 Newborn females exhibited a brisker automatic walk then did newborn males, reflecting their generally greater viability.

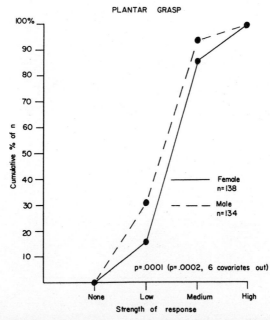

FIG. 3-10 Newborn females exhibited a stronger plantar grasp than did newborn males, reflecting their generally greater viability.

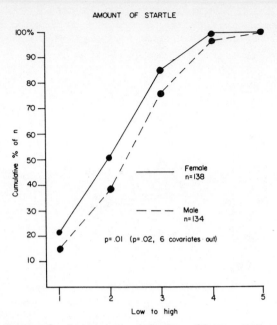

FIG. 3-11 Newborn females gave many indications of better overall organization than newborn males; males startled more frequently.

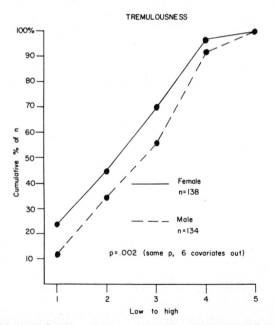

FIG. 3-12 Newborn females gave many indications of better overall organization than newborn males; males exhibited more tremulousness of the limbs and chin.

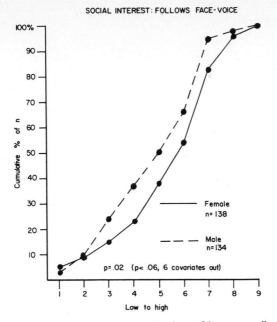

FIG. 3-13 Newborn females gave many indications of better overall organization than newborn males; they exhibited superior visual following of *E*.

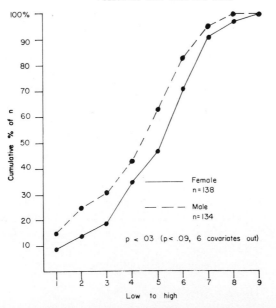

FIG. 3-14 Newborn females gave many indications of better overall organization than newborn males; they exhibited superior visual following of inanimate objects.

involved. In females, each of the two X chromosomes is randomly exposed (cf. McKusick, 1964), and therefore the lethal recessive will be partially masked. While this does indeed seem to account for some of the sex differences, especially in fetal deaths, it is hardly a sufficient explanation for the generalized phenomena described here. In birds, in fact, the male is homozygous for X and the female heterozygous, yet male mortality is higher nevertheless (Trivers, 1972). Similarly, our initial reasoning suggested that the extra physiological steps necessary in the embryonic formation of males might be at fault, but that is not a very satisfactory explanation either. At the risk of bringing up other semi-satisfactory explanations, then, the phenomenon of "genes in balanced equilibrium" should also be considered.

From an evolutionary point of view, one would surmise that the male's greater vulnerability on one front may be transformed into an advantage elsewhere, or else selection would have long ago eliminated so gross a difference in viability. The model for such thinking is a human disease, sickle-cell anemia. This is a gene-controlled disease that causes red blood cells to become misshapen or "sickle-shaped" so that they cannot properly bind hemoglobin. However, it has been shown that while sickling of the red cells reduces viability and can lead to death, it also lends resistance against the malarial parasite that tends to feed on normal red blood cells but that cannot do so in sickled-cells. The sickling phenomenon is therefore present at a high rate in the malarial infested areas of Africa. The general formula is: One sickling gene gives resistance, while two such genes considerably reduce viability. Thus a balance has been struck between its good and bad effects, and geneticists consequently speak of a "balanced polymorphism."

This sickle-cell model, then, suggests a rather obvious hypothesis around greater female viability; namely, the complex traits which we have ascribed to maleness, while tending to lend the species overall viability, nevertheless extracts the price of reduced average longevity in males. That is, traits such as higher aggression, higher exploratory activity, and higher physical courage may require a physiology that has more potential difficulties and therefore one that is more prone to disturbance and disease. As evidence for this contention, Trivers (1972) has noted a number of studies, including some in man, which show the male to have higher metabolic rates and to have greater need for protein than the female.

To repeat, it would appear that most species can withstand reduced viability in males better than in females. As Bateman's rule would imply, where parental investment in the young is substantially greater in females, they must survive for the successful rearing of their young; once fecundation is achieved, however, males are relatively interchangeable.

CROSS-CULTURAL CONSIDERATIONS

A major goal of this chapter has been to demonstrate continuities in male-female differences from a very young age as evidence that such differences are biologically based. While we have succeeded in this task to some extent, it is also evident that a vast literature on social-learning and on cross-cultural comparisons has been severely slighted. Added up, that literature's dominant theme is that the only biologically based male-female differences are the physically obvious secondary sex characteristics and that all others have been imposed through custom and habit by society (cf. Maccoby, 1966). Rarely have the questions been asked, Of what function to the species are the secondary sex differences? What correlated behavioral differences could then be expected to follow?

Margaret Mead has perhaps been the major proponent of the view that male and female roles can vary in all their possible permutations and her studies of three New Guinea cultures (1935) are most frequently cited as evidence for this position. A key to this argument were the Tchambuli, for they were to become the classic case of role-reversal. Tchambuli women were the principal breadwinners and also made all major decisions, whereas the men were engaged in relatively passive pursuits about the home. However, it has been insufficiently stressed that only one generation before, the Tchambuli had been a tribe whose entire organization had pivoted about the institution of head-hunting; masculine pride and the social hierarchy had been completely entwined with this activity. Western intervention had thus deprived them of their major basis for sorting out the male hierarchy, and like the Dani in New Guinea today (Heider, 1970), they had either to immediately reorganize ageless social institutions or to come apart at the seams. Thus, the Tchambuli, by Mead's own admission, were a society in decay, and by today's ethnological standards should have been analyzed in those terms.

The fact is that about 75% of the world's societies are polygynous, 25% male dominated and monogamous, and an infinitesimal fraction polyandrous (Murdock, 1957). The few polyandrous examples always exist under very special circumstances, such as groups in transition who find themselves with too few women (Montagu, 1956). This would indicate that male-dominated power hierarchies are the rule, no matter how lineage may be determined, whether through the male or female line.

We have already pointed out that greater male aggression and motility have been found in children over a wide sampling of cultures. In addition, it would appear fair to state that while a good deal of local variation exists, certain other aspects of the male and female role seem to persist over most of the world. To use Parsons' terms (Parsons and Bales, 1955), the male motif is everywhere more *instrumental,* the female more *expressive,* although the two are always in combination within any individual.

Parsons defines these terms in relating the system of the nuclear family and other societal systems; the instrumental role is considered by Parsons as functionally "external" and the expressive role as "internal" to the nuclear groups. That is,

> the area of instrumental function concerns relations of the system to the situation outside the system, to meeting the adaptive conditions of its maintenance of equilibrium, and instrumentally establishing the desired relations to external goal objects. The expressive area concerns the "internal" affairs of the system, the maintenance of integrative relations between the members, and regulation of the patterns and tension levels of its component units [p. 47].

It would take us too far from the present context of human infancy to extend this discussion, so let it suffice that within the instrumental-expressive dichotomy lie a great array of possibilities, in that the modal men and the modal women of a society can conceivably vary from extreme male-instrumental and female-expressive to near equal combinations of each. However, the evidence is that *reversals* in these male and female modalities within a society is not probable.

Finally, this chapter's message is not that we live in the best of all possible worlds, and that feminist movements are anti-evolutionary. Quite the contrary, it has recently been observed that the entire women's liberation movement may be, at its heart, an unconscious response to runaway population growth and its concomitant pressures. Indeed, if the relative dominance of women rises due to the movement, lowered birth-rates would almost certainly follow. Also, since physical strength now means less in a practical sense, and since peace now seems prerequisite for the national survival of the great states, more women may henceforward rise to alpha positions, such as heads of state.

Thus, we are here acknowledging the importance of social-learning and societal input in the patterning of variation in male and female roles, but we are at the same time emphasizing that societal institutions do not arise, as it were, out of the blue; world-wide consistencies in institutionalized male-female roles appear to reflect phylogenetically adaptive differences in the sexes, differences which may already be seen in their incipient forms in very early infancy.

SUMMARY

We started this chapter by noting a zoological rule: Within a given species, the parent who devotes the most energy to care of the young, whether the parent is male or female, will have less secondary sexual growth and will be the less aggressive of the two. The other parent will devote major energies to rivalry with others of its sex, as it attempts to court successfully. The ratio of dimorphism may vary from such weight differentials as ten times in the fur seals to relatively small amounts in humans.

As in the terrestrial macaques, man tends to form linear dominance-submission hierarchies, and where toughness and aggression determine one's position, males tend to dominate females. This is so since males are apparently born with lower thresholds for aggressive response and they become more involved in competitive encounters. In general, human males of all societies appear to have specialized in "instrumental" roles; human females, in more "expressive" roles.

Concurrently, males have relatively greater manipulative and investigative interests and females relatively greater affiliative interests. Apparently related are the repeated findings that males are better able to engage in visual-spatial manipulations, while females are more auditory and verbal. Experimental studies in relating hormones and cognitive style emphasize the biological nature of these differences, and much of this behavior may already be seen in infancy.

Finally, males of all ages are subject to much higher mortality, disease, and defect. Using the sickle-cell anemia model of "balanced polymorphism," it was hypothesized that reduced viability and the more volatile behavior of males are in balance, with the former as a sort of price extracted from the male of the species.

4
INDIVIDUAL DIFFERENCES IN PERSONALITY DEVELOPMENT

Within any sexually reproducing species there is exhibited wide individual variation with regard to physical structure, physiological function, and behavior. This seems, in fact, the major evolutionary function of sexuality, for in this variation on the species' theme lies the potentiality for adaptation to changed surroundings. Each human infant, for example, negotiates sucking, crying, smiling, vocalizing, grasping, the fear of strangers—all the major evolutionary adaptations—in his own unique way. In this chapter we plan to show that this uniqueness is a result of the actualization of a highly improbable genotype in a highly variable environment. But first, what other explanations of individual differences are there?

SOME PREVIOUS ATTEMPTS TO UNDERSTAND INDIVIDUAL DIFFERENCES

We generally acknowledge two major sources of individual differences in personality—biological structure and familial-cultural milieu. The emphasis in the social sciences has been overwhelming on the environmental sources of variance, and cultural anthropology and neo-Freudianism have joined forces in demonstrating that people are different because they grew up in different environments.

This may be termed the "modern" view to distinguish it from older views which were definitely slanted in a biological direction. Hippocrates, for example, wrote of what today would be called biochemical or hormonal predispositions to temperament: predominance of blood, black bile, yellow bile, or phlegm yielded, respectively, sanguine, melancholic, choleric, and phlegmatic temperaments (Allport, 1937).

Many forms of typology have since been proposed, culminating in the recent systems of Jung, best known for its apposition of extroversion and introversion, and of Sheldon, who claimed that three types of body build—endomorphy, mesomorphy, ectomorphy—were associated with three different personality types. Both of these typologies are "dynamic" in that no individual is a pure type, but rather one combination from a spectrum of possible combinations that can be generated.

Summarizing the typological approach, MacKinnon (1944) writes:

> All typologies are based upon the assumption that personality is characterized by a more or less enduring structure. Typologists may disagree as to the nature of this underlying structure; some conceive of it in psychological terms, others conceptualize it physiologically, and yet others think of it in terms of neural structure. It is not by chance that most typologists have been biologically oriented. Typologists may emphasize different traits and characteristics as most fundamentally differentiating the basic types of personality but on one point they agree, namely, that there are intrinsic traits of personality [pp. 24–25].

WHAT'S WRONG WITH TYPOLOGIES?

The noted biologist, Ernst Mayr, answers this question (Mayr, 1958) with the following argument:

> The philosophical basis in much of early science was typological, going back to the *eidos* of Plato. This implies that the "typical" aspects of the phenomenon can be described, and that all variation is due to imperfect replicas of the type, all variants being, in the terms of Plato's allegory, "shadows on a cave wall." Such typological thinking is still prevalent in most branches of physics and chemistry and to a considerable extent in functional biology, where the emphasis is at the performance of a single individual. The typological concept has been completely displaced in evolutionary biology by the population concept. The basis of this concept is that fact that in sexually reproducing species no two individuals are genetically alike, and that every population is therefore to be characterized only by statistical parameters such as means, variances, and frequencies. . . . Genetic variability is universal, a fact which is significant not only for the student of morphology but also for the student of behavior. It is not only wrong to speak of *the* monkey but even of *the* rhesus monkey. The variability of behavior is evident in the study not only of such a genetically plastic species as man but even of forms with very rigid, stereotyped behaviors such as the hunting wasps. . . . The time has come to stress the existence of genetic differences in behavior, in view of the enormous amount of material the students of various forms of learning have accumulated on nongenetic variation in behavior [p. 351].

The point is that all diploid populations (those with two sets of chromosomes, one set paternal and one set maternal) show a wide range of genetic variation and that no two genotypes are precisely alike (save in identical multiple births). This gives a population greater viability as well as increasing the possibilities for ultimate speciation. The exceedingly slim chances in man, for example, of the same mother and father producing two identical offspring in separate fertilizations can be seen from the fact that each may produce 2^{23} (8,388,608) kinds of gametes. As if this were not sufficient variation, if one additionally assumed that 2% of the genes were heterozygous, a single cross-over between each pair of strands would raise the figure to 8,388,608 followed by 23 zeros, a very conservative figure at that (Stern, 1960).

It is not surprising, then, that the search for a stable typology of personality, if indeed personality has biological roots, is a doomed project before it starts. Let us consider, for example, the genetics which most probably underlie correlations between body build and personality, such as those found by Sheldon and Stevens (1942). This is best illustrated by animal experimentation where the proper matings and controls are possible, but as far as we know the logic holds for all living forms.

Stockard (1931), in his work with temperament and behavior in dog breeds, was able to genetically dissociate behavioral traits from body build by crossing experiments, and dissociation always occurred in the F_2 and back-cross generations, as one would expect from Mendelian models. For example, he was able to take the lethargic and low-slung basset hound and, via the proper matings, produce basset-like dogs with high strung behavioral characteristics. It can therefore be deduced that the lethargic low-slung basset hound was simultaneously bred for lethargy and body build since the two are genetically independent.

In all probability there is an analogous history to the correlations found between human temperament and body build. In the history of human groups there may well have been selective packaging of genes so that today certain body builds go with certain temperaments more often than by chance; but we must assume that with controlled mating studies such correlations might also be reduced or eliminated, and that all combinations of temperament and body build are possible. Sheldon's own data bear this out, in fact, in that he finds no pure "types." In light of modern biological thinking, then, it is safest to assume the potential for continuous variation of behavior rather than a "natural" piling-up into discontinuous categories or types. Science has been described as the making of discontinuities out of continuities and of continuities from discontinuities. Since our aim is to achieve some isomorphism between personality theory and biology, it seems advantageous at this time to stress the continuous nature of variations in both genetic patterns and personality.

Given this point of view, the following definition of personality seems appropriate, and it is approximately what we mean as we use the term: Personality is a Gestalt of species traits, largely related to interpersonal behavior; it varies uniquely for each individual because each genotype and each history is unique. The standard for the comparison of individuals is a composite image of the species, and each person is considered a variation on this basic species theme.

ONE, TWO, OR MANY GENES

Before presenting the data, let us discuss what constitutes a demonstration of genetic cause or influence. Usually, when we talk of genetic influences on behavior, we are talking about the *difference* between two groups, e.g., between two inbred groups, or between groups of fraternal versus identical twins. Such studies usually demonstrate only that genetics is playing some kind of (unknown) role.

The classic Mendelian study, therefore, has much more scientific merit. For here we have the possibility of relating specific genes and specific behavior. Consequently, a number of pioneering behavior-geneticists have striven, through Mendelian studies of fruit flies, mice, and dogs, to duplicate classic studies on structure. What have we learned from such studies?

The problems of the genetics of behavior are precisely those which faced the great geneticist Morgan in the 1920's. For example, while he knew the location of the single gene which caused white eye in *Drosophila,* Morgan estimated that at least 50 unknown genes played a role in *normal* eye coloration. And so it was for every other trait: wing-veinlessness, a single gene; normal veination, probably hundreds of genes, and so on. Classic genetics has thus discovered little about normal structure or normal development.

The same situation holds for behavior. Phenylketonuria is the result of a single recessive gene which apparently causes an enzyme block, which in turn interferes with normal metabolism, and eventually results in mental deficiency. Other mental deficiencies may be traced to various chromosomal trisomies, and with each year new cause-effect relations are found between genetic anomaly and mental defect. The genetics of mental *efficiency*, on the other hand, are vastly complex and hardly illuminated by the aforementioned work. Many more examples are available (cf. Fuller & Thompson, 1960), and it would appear that Mendelian inheritance has been demonstrable only in defective structure or function. Traits that have proved phylogenetically adaptive are invariably polygenic, i.e., they have invariably accumulated a substantial number of supporting genes.

While some will argue against this position, perhaps as a matter of faith in the atomistic methodology of genetics, there is yet to be demonstrated a single gene which accounts for a substantial part of the variance in a normal behavioral trait (cf. Scott & Fuller, 1965). This generality holds as well for two-gene systems, and, as Crow (1960) has aptly stated, beyond two genes one can speak only of "many genes." It follows that developmental psychobiologists who deal with nondefective behavior are invariably dealing with polygenic systems, and the search for a simple genetic system in mammalian behavior is a search for a will-o'-the-wisp.

For these reasons, unfortunately, precise genetic studies of adaptive behavior are at present not tenable; the best we can do today is impute genetic cause for the differences we find between our experimental groups, and the rest of this chapter is comprised of such data.

THE INTERACTION OF CONSTITUTION AND ENVIRONMENT: ILLUSTRATIVE ANIMAL EXPERIMENTS

The author's entire interest in the present subject started with his Ph.D. thesis, an experiment performed with puppies of various breeds. It will be of interest, therefore, to give an extended account of that study as it appeared in *Science Journal* (Freedman, 1967).

The studies that form the basis of this article had their origin on the campus of Brandeis University, near Boston, Massachusetts, in 1953. In the winter of that year the campus mascot, a motley bitch with what looked like a beagle and dachshund background, gave birth to a litter of four. We were not sure who the father was. As graduate students in the newly formed graduate school, Norbett Mintz and I had sufficient time to "play around" and we had the happy notion that puppies might prove enjoyable experimental subjects—as indeed they did.

In considering what we might do with the puppies, we had two previous studies in mind. The first was that of J. P. Scott and M. Marston at Bar Harbor who, in 1950, had suggested that three to eight weeks of age was a critical period in the social development of puppies. Although this was little more than an impression then, it had subsequently turned out to be largely correct within the breeds studied. Secondly, John Whiting, a psychoanalytically oriented anthropologist, had been working with adult dogs and had developed a test to measure their "conscience." This was assessed by the extent to which they remained obedient in the absence of the handler. The test was attractively simple and merely involved a person punishing a dog for eating food that had been forbidden him. The person then left the room and, watching through a one-way glass, recorded the amount of time the animal stayed away from the forbidden food. In this way the extent to which punishment was "incorporated" received a quantitative score.

Our chore became one of using this information in a meaningful study of development, and when the idea finally came to us it seemed the most natural study possible. As clinical psychologists, Mintz and I were aware of the work of the child psychiatrist, David Levy. As a result of his extensive experience with behavior disorders in children, Levy had hypothesized that extreme permissiveness on the part of parents could lead to a psychiatric condition called psychopathy. This is characterized by an abnormal inability to inhibit one's impulses. These people are asocial in that their own desires and wishes always take precedence over those of others. Levy found that in many families which produced such individuals, the parents allowed themselves to become complete slaves to the tyrannical willfulness of the child.

With Levy's work in mind we carried out the following study. Two puppies were to act as "control." One was given to a family which we decided was typically "middle class"—in other words, a home in which the puppy would receive plenty of affection, but would also be restricted to certain areas, prevented from biting, be housebroken, and so on. A second puppy was raised separately in a room by itself, save for the few minutes each day it took to put food in and take the old bowls out. As for the "psychopathic" puppies, Mintz and I decided to enlist the aid of the boys in the dormitories of which we were proctors. The puppies were to have complete freedom in the dormitory. Urine and faeces were to be cleaned up after them. If they wished to climb on someone's bed or lap, they were to be helped up. If they wished to get off, they were helped off. If they wished to sleep in someone's bed, they were allowed that. (If they nipped an ear in bed, one *was* allowed to duck under the covers.) They were not to be punished for any offence. Since the study was to last only six weeks (from three to nine weeks of age), all the students agreed to co-operate.

At nine weeks we had two distinctly different groups of dogs, and this was nicely shown by the "incorporation of punishment" test. Beginning at the ninth week of age and continuing for eight consecutive days, we administered the test devised by Whiting. We placed each pup, which had not been fed for at least four hours, in a room with a bowl of meat at its center. When the pup attempted to eat, the experimenter hit it on the rump with a newspaper and shouted, "No!" After the experimenter left the room, the time to eat was recorded. In this early version of the test the experimenter rushed back in and punished the pup each time it ate.

We found that whereas the home-reared dog averaged 37.5 minutes and the isolate 9.5 minutes between each transgression, the permissively reared pups averaged a lightning 2.2 minutes. By the eighth day of testing, in fact, the permissively reared pups managed to eat all the meat before the tester had a chance to leave the room. He would smack the pup only to have it immediately circle back through his legs for another bite. This happened so fast that we could not measure the time between transgressions accurately and consequently we overestimated the time between transgressions in the seventh and eighth test sessions.

The subsequent history of these two pups was not a happy one.

Although people were initially taken with them because of their uninhibited friskiness, they were passed from home to home as each owner found something else to complain about. They seemed to have become untrainable.

The isolate's behavior was typical of pups raised in this fashion. She was hyperexcitable and initiated contacts only to run when a hand was reached out or when another pup tried to play with her. After the fourth session of testing, however, she calmed down somewhat and was able to learn what was demanded of her. We are happy to report that she subsequently became a beloved and loving pet, and we could not help but reflect that a dog with no experiences with people may be preferable to one with the wrong experiences.

Having become completely captured by the study, we decided to try another experiment. David Levy had postulated that a second class of psychopaths are formed by extreme cruelty or great emotional deprivation in childhood. With this second hypothesis in mind, we raised a beagle from four to nine weeks of age under conditions in which all his contacts with people were negative. Each time he tried to make contact he was either ignored or pushed aside, and it is not surprising that he developed a rather depressed, fearful personality. True to Levy's hypothesis, his performance on the test was like that of the over-indulged puppies, although the average time between transgressions was higher: 8.14 minutes. Again the controls were a home-reared littermate and a littermate kept in isolation. Both quickly learned to stay away from the food and averaged one transgression each 31.13 minutes. Once again Levy's hypothesis, developed from studies of problem children, appeared to hold when applied to puppies.

It was clearly time to do these studies on a larger scale and in a systematic and repeatable fashion, and I proposed such a project for my Ph.D. thesis. After interesting Paul Scott, Chairman of the Division of Behaviour Studies at the Jackson Laboratories, Bar Harbor, Maine, it was arranged that the work be done there.

In the Bar Harbor study, eight litters of four pups each were used. They included two litters each of Shetland sheepdogs, basenjis, wire-haired fox terriers, and beagles. Following weaning at three weeks of age, each litter of four was divided into two pairs which were equated as closely as possible on the basis of sex, weight, activity, vocalizations, maturation of eyes and ears, and reactivity to a startling stimulus. Thereafter, each member of one pair was indulged and each member of the second pair was disciplined. However, because of the numbers involved, this treatment could be given only during two daily 15 minute periods, again from the third to the eighth week of age.

Indulgence consisted of encouraging a pup in any activity it initiated, such as play, aggression, and climbing on the supine handler. As before, these pups were never punished. By contrast, the disciplined pups were at first restrained in the experimenter's lap and were later taught to sit, to stay, and to come upon command. When still older they were trained to follow on a leash. I handled all the pups and tested them individually; they lived with the identically treated littermate in isolation boxes the remainder of the time.

A revised punishment test was initiated at eight weeks of age. As before, when the pup ate meat from a bowl, he was punished with a swat on the rump and a shout of, "No!" After three minutes the experimenter left the room and, observing through a one-way glass, recorded the time that elapsed before the pup again ate. This time the experimenter did not return to the room until the allotted ten minutes were up.

The first breed that went through this experimental rearing and testing was a basenji litter. By the fourth day of testing all basenjis tended to eat soon after the experimenter left the room, the method of rearing having little effect. This was most discouraging, since we had failed to duplicate the results of the pilot experiment, but we decided to carry on.

The second group was a Shetland sheep dog litter and they were equally disappointing, except this time all tended to refuse the food. At least one thing was clear at this point: the breed of dog was a major factor to consider. Second litters of basenjis and of Shetland sheep dogs from our inbred stocks bore this out, for they performed much like the first litters.

The next breed which became available was a beagle litter. We found that their behavior depended upon the way they were reared but, paradoxically, in a direction opposite to our pilot studies. A second beagle litter, from the same mating, performed exactly the same way and so did the two litters of wire-haired fox terriers (Fig. 4-1).

The conditions of rearing were continued over a second period, when the pups were 11 to 15 weeks of age, and all tests were readministered with essentially the same results. At this point we were so fascinated with breed differences that we postponed thinking about the contradictions to our pilot work. Our question now was how could the breed characteristics explain the differences in performance?

It was clear that, during training, beagles and wire-haired terriers were strongly oriented to the experimenter and sought contact with him continuously. Basenjis, by contrast, were interested in all phases of the environment and often ignored the experimenter in

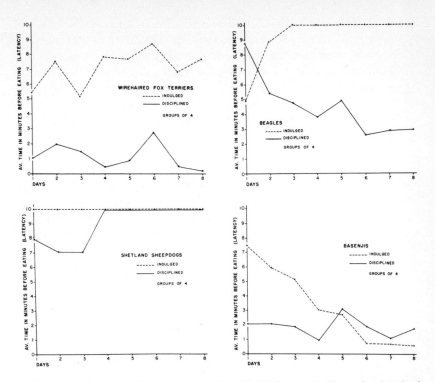

FIG. 4-1 Performance of 8-week-old puppies in "inhibition to eating" test; four breeds of dogs (wire-haired fox terriers, beagles, Shetland sheep dogs, basenjis), raised in two ways (indulged or disciplined). Pups were punished for eating meat in the testing room, after which the experimenter left the room and clocked the amount of time before the pup went back and ate, up to 10 minutes. This was repeated daily over 8 days.

favor of inanimate objects. Shetland dogs showed yet another pattern; all became fearful of physical contact with the experimenter and tended to maintain distance from him. Thus the two breeds that were highly attracted to the experimenter showed behavioral differences as a result of the mode of rearing, whereas the breeds that exhibited aloofness (basenjis) and excessive timidity (Shetland sheep dogs) did not. Apparently it was the strong constitutional attraction combined with indulgent treatment that enhanced the effectiveness of later punishment.

It should be noted that basenjis and Shetland dogs were not entirely unaffected by the differential treatment. The scores of all indulged animals were significantly different from those of their disciplined counterparts on five of ten tests administered. In general, these tests indicated that the indulged pups were more active, more vocal, less timid (although more easily inhibited with punishment), and more attracted to people than disciplined pups. To give some specific examples, the indulged pups soon became more uninhibited in the presence of the examiner, as witnessed by the number of times a pup jumped from the scales during weekly weigh-ins (Fig. 4-2). Further, when the period of testing began at eight weeks of age, indulged pups were found to be more dependent on the examiner, to judge by the greater number of vocalizations when separated from him (Fig. 4-3). Similarly, in the *handling test* (Fig. 4-4) indulged pups were scored as more attracted to and less shy of the examiner.

We now had to reconcile the findings of the pilot studies at Brandeis and the major study at Bar Harbor. In the first we found that over-indulged rearing in the dormitories led to "psychopathic" performance, but in the Bar Harbor work the disciplined animals of all breeds tended to be more disobedient, although this was true of the Shetland sheep dogs and basenjis over only the first three days of testing.

To recapitulate the pilot studies, a regimen of affection and freedom and no discipline produced hyper-active, disobedient pups. A regimen of discipline and no affection likewise produced a disobedient pup, albeit within a depressed and fearful personality. Actually, none of the Bar Harbor findings contradict these "rules."

In the Bar Harbor studies the permissive group was given free reign to express affection, to investigate and to bite, but each time they were returned to their boxes they were under enforced control, as their cries to get out attested. It became clear that they were treated much like normal home-reared dogs in that restrictions were regularly imposed on their freedom.

The disciplined group, on the other hand, received considerably less affection than do home-reared dogs and, in addition, few dogs at home have so much demanded of them at so early an age. When we had initially planned the study we called this group "normal," but very early we changed to the word "disciplined." It was clear that in terms of affection and play they were a *deprived* group and that "disciplined" was only partially descriptive of the treatment they received.

It was in this way that we attempted to resolve the contradiction between the Bar Harbor results and the Brandeis pilot studies and, setting aside any genetic factors for the moment, the general hypothesis still appeared viable: dogs who did not "incorporate" punishment were those reared under conditions of excessive freedom vis-à-vis humans or, conversely, under conditions in which human contacts were largely negative. It is of interest that some of the great trainers of field trial champions, such as Tetzloff and Spandet of the Danish Kennel Club, stress the importance of basing discipline on deeply affectionate relationships between trainer and dog. . . .

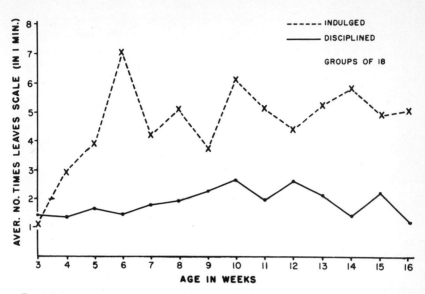

FIG. 4-2 Indulged pups were less inhibited than disciplined pups during weekly weighing procedure ($p < .01$).

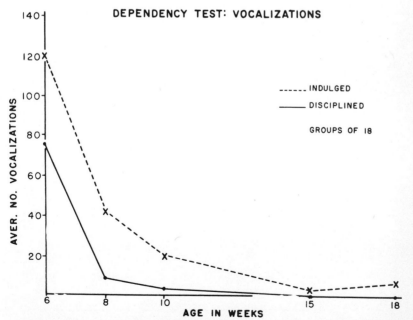

FIG. 4-3 Indulged pups complained by yelping more than disciplined pups when ignored by E ($p < .04$).

For our present purposes, the major point of this study was the clear-cut illustration that phenotype is a result of genetic and environmental interaction. By now, many other examples have filled the literature in the burgeoning new field of behavior genetics, and we shall present but one further study. It was a massive investigation (1968) of mice by a colleague, Joanne Jumonville, at the University of Chicago, and forms a second example of experimentally produced genetic and environmental interactions. One reads of the positive effects of early stimulation in animals, especially rodents: Extra handling and buffeting of infant rats reportedly leads to greater

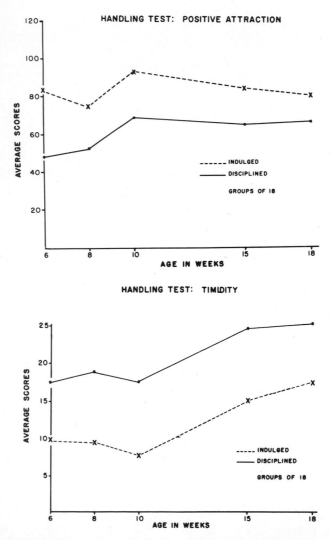

FIG. 4-4 Indulged pups were more attracted to E ($p < .01$) and showed fewer signs of timidity when approached by E ($p < .01$) than disciplined pups.

viability, greater alertness, and improved problem solving in the adult animals (cf. Ambrose, 1969). Analogous studies are now being tried with human infants, and it is therefore important to pay Jumonville's findings careful attention. She found that the "value" of early stimulation varied with the animal strain and the time and amount of stimulation given; there was no overall benefit from extra handling. For example, the same amounts of early handling can either increase or decrease aggression, susceptibility to audiogenic seizures, and rate of weight gain—depending on the strain studied. Table 4-1 shows the effect on weight gain of mouse strains in interaction with amount of handling and sex. As a result of 2 minutes of daily

TABLE 4-1

Mean Weight in Grams at Weaning Age (30 Days)[a]

Strain	Sex	Control	Days of age when handled			
			2–14		2–27	
HS10	M	18.1	16.6		19.6 .01[b]	↑
N		(29)	(36)		(27)	
	F	15.8	15.5		17.0 .05	↑
N		(29)	(25)		(30)	
DBA/2	M	16.5	15.2 .05	↓	15.8	
N		(32)	(27)		(31)	
	F	15.6	13.3		14.0 .01	↓
N		(27)	(33)		(27)	
DBA/1	M	13.8	13.8		12.7	
N		(27)	(28)		(26)	
	F	11.9	12.4		11.8	
N		(31)	(20)		(26)	
C57BL/10	M	14.9	14.7		16.3 .02	↑
N		(32)	(33)		(25)	
	F	14.2	14.1		15.5 .02	↑
N		(34)	(23)		(24)	
C57BL/6	M	15.4	15.0		15.6	
N		(37)	(37)		(20)	
	F	13.5	13.7		13.9	
N		(24)	(19)		(34)	
Ajax	M	15.2	13.9 .05	↓	13.5 .01	↓
N		(32)	(24)		(23)	
	F	14.2	11.9 .001	↓	13.1	
N		(22)	(26)		(26)	

Note: Comparison of 6 mouse strains, 2 handling regimens. Results vary according to strain and handling regimen.

[a] After Jumonville (1968).

[b] Significance figures based on weight comparisons with control animals.

stroking from 2 to 27 days of age, two strains were heavier than their control group and two were lighter; additionally, there were sex-specific effects in the latter two strains and not in the former. Moreover, when handling ceased at 14 days instead of 27 days, still another pattern of results emerged. Thus, presumably equal and beneficial environmental treatments may backfire if the genetic background of the organism is not considered.

The little experimental work available comparing stimulated and non-stimulated human infants is not very promising, perhaps because similar complexities are at work at the human level. In an attempt to find a procedure antidotal to the prematurity syndrome (cf. Drillien, 1964), Freedman et al. (1966) found that kinesthetic and vestibular stimulation of human premature newborns had only temporary effects on rate of weight gain, and little or no effects on the behavioral parameters investigated. These investigators were therefore not impressed with the possibility for changing growth trajectories in human neonates. Perhaps, as Tanner (1961) has hypothesized, a hormonostat for the regulation of growth is set sometime before birth in humans and cannot be modified thereafter.

THE INTERACTION OF CONSTITUTION AND ENVIRONMENT: TWIN STUDIES

Before discussing the data, it is important to understand the differences and the similarities between experimental studies of inbred animals and a twin-study. It is pertinent that behavior geneticists who work with animals have never needed to work with twin animals since inbreeding (laboratory-controlled brother and sister matings extended over some 20 generations) creates as many individuals of a single genotype as one could want (cf. Fuller & Thompson, 1960). The twin method, by contrast, is relatively inconvenient since it involves samples of, at the most, two members of any single genotype (monozygotic twins). These paired samples, the identical twins, are then compared with dizygotic twins, who resemble each other as do ordinary brothers or sisters; i.e., on the average, sibs have 50% of their genes in common.

In a twin study, therefore, one deals with a variety of unique genotypes and seeks to measure whether the paired identical genotypes perform more alike than do the paired fraternal genotypes. The questions one asks and answers are very general; e.g., Does heredity play a role in the behavior in question? Additionally, there is no such thing as a perfectly duplicated monozygotic pair (Price, 1950), so that at the very outset of a twin study one knows that some uncontrolled and uncontrollable factors are present. For example, in the fetal development of identical monochorionic twins, a competition occurs over the common blood supply, and one twin is frequently runted as a consequence. As a result, the birth weights of monochorionic monozygotic twins are as divergent as are the birth weights of fraternal pairs. By contrast, monozygotic twins who develop within separate choria (dichorionic) are highly similar in birth weight. However, two-thirds of identical twins are of the monochorionic type. The embryology of these two types of twins and a typical fraternal pair is illustrated in Fig. 4-5.

We now quote again from the author's article (1967).

The studies of dogs naturally set me thinking about their relevance to man. First of all, I was very impressed by the fact that each breed displayed a unique personality towards myself, and that this uniqueness started with the very first interactions, at about three weeks of age. Is it possible that in puppies so much of their personality is inherited, whereas in humans it is all learned? Or, contrariwise, is the story quite the same, and do human and canid individuals start life along unique pre-programmed lines—and is personality in each case the outward expression of a unique genetic makeup (genotype) acting upon the surrounding world?

The only reasonable way to answer this question, it seemed, was to use the twin methods, as others, starting with Galton and his many successors, had made it clear that the various cognitive skills which make up IQ tests are to a substantial degree inherited; imitation is also an important factor in the acquisition of social traits. How, then, is one to separate mutual imitation of, say, facial gestures from genotypic causation? The answer involved either studying twins reared apart, or else studying infant twins before such mutual imitation might affect the results.

Another problem with studying twins reared apart is the fact that the actual organism is the result of the genotype in complex interaction with the environment. Thus, even if one located a substantial

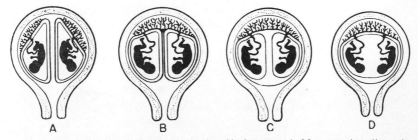

Fig. 4-5 Diagrams of twin pregnancies enclosed in the uterus. A. Monozygotic or dizygotic twins with separate amnions, chorions, and placentas. B. Monozygotic or dizygotic twins with separate amnions and chorions, and fused placenta. C. Monozygotic twins with separate amnions, and single chorion and placenta. D. Monozygotic twins with single amnion, chorion, and placenta. (From Potter, 1948.)

number of identical twins who had been reared apart, there would be no way of ascertaining the extent of environmental effects, unless one also had a group of fraternal twins reared apart. No study to date has undertaken this formidable task, although three very interesting studies are now available in which identical twins reared apart have been investigated.

Since, in any event, I enjoyed working with newborn children, I decided to study identical and like-sexed fraternal twins—before mutual imitation started. From the work of Jean Piaget, we knew this about imitation: Imitation of facial gestures usually starts at about nine months but imitation, of any sort, in the absence of the person being imitated does not normally appear before 14 months or so.

Thus, my assistant, Barbara Keller, and I (see Freedman and Keller, 1963) studied 20 pairs of twins on a monthly basis in their first year of life. The twins were same-sexed pairs born in our three co-operating San Francisco hospitals. All families entered the study voluntarily, and they represented a variety of racial and cultural backgrounds. Keller worked with 11 pairs and I with 9. In an attempt to keep observations objective, zygosity determinations— investigations to discover whether the pairs of twins were fraternal or identical—were not made until after our studies were completed, at which time we found we had 11 fraternal and 9 identical pairs fairly well distributed between us. (Thirteen blood group factors were used.)

With regard to possible biased rearing by parents, they were, of course, as ignorant of zygosity as we were. Parents who ventured an opinion tended to believe their twins were fraternal. By eight months of age our own guessing became rather accurate since we had other twins with which to compare a set, and it is fair to say that we were in doubt about zygosity in only two cases by one year of age. However, the results over the first eight months were similar to those obtained over the last eight months of the first year so that any bias introduced as a result of our knowledge must have been minimal.

Both Keller's group and my own formed similar distributions on all tests and rating scales, suggesting that they are readily duplicable. We each found that within-pair differences were consistently greater among the fraternal pairs on both of our major measures, the Nancy Bayley (1970) Mental and Motor Scales and her Infant Behavior Profile (Figs. 4-6, 4-7, 4-8, Table 4-2).

In what was perhaps the best controlled aspect of the study, we managed to eliminate possible "halo" effects by a procedure in which films formed the basis of judgment. During each monthly visit we had taken motion pictures in which each twin of a pair was filmed separately in the same situations, and the film of each was accumu-

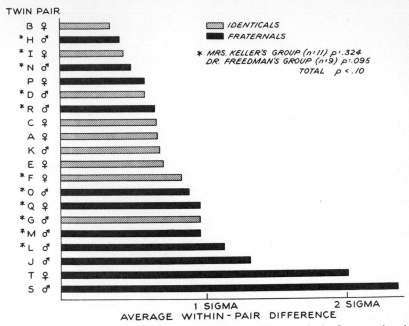

FIG. 4-6 Bayley Mental Scales. Average within-pair differences in the first year, based on 8 to 12 monthly administrations.

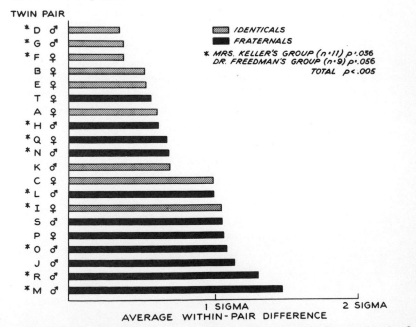

FIG. 4-7 Bayley Motor Scales. Average within-pair differences in the first year, based on 8 to 12 monthly administrations.

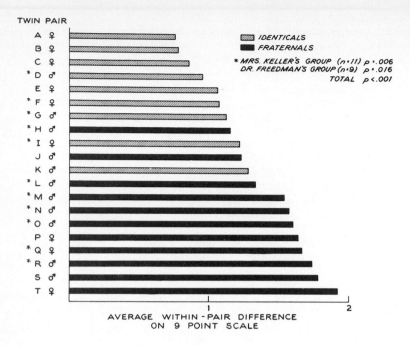

FIG. 4-8 Bayley Infant Behavior Profile, a rating scale consisting of 21 items covering 12 categories of behavior. Average within-pair differences in the first year, based on 8 to 12 monthly administrations.

TABLE 4-2

Nancy Bayley Infant Behavior Profile—Survey of Individual Items

	P
1. *Social orientation:* responsiveness to persons	.005
(1) Does not modify behavior to persons as different from objects	
(9) Behavior seems to be continuously affected by awareness of persons present	
2. *Object orientation:* responsiveness to toys and other objects	.02
(1) Does not look at or in any way indicate interest in objects	
(9) Reluctantly relinquishes test materials	
3. *Goal directedness:*	.02
(1) No evidence of directed effort	
(9) Compulsive absorption with task until it is solved	
4. *Attention span:* tendency to persist in attending to any one object, person, or activity, aside from attaining a goal	.02
(1) Fleeting attention span	
(9) Long, continued absorption in toy, activity, or person	
5. *Cooperativeness:* (Not relevant most of first year)	

6. *Activity:* inactive-vigorous   N.S.[a]
  (1) Stays quietly in one place, with practically no self-initiated movement
  (9) Hyperactive: cannot be quieted for sedentary tests

6.1 *Activity:* level of energy (low to high)   N.S.

6.2 *Activity:* coordination of gross muscle movements for age (smooth functioning to poor coordination)   N.S.

6.3 *Activity:* coordination of fine muscles (hands) for age (smooth functioning to poor coordination)   .04

7. *Reactivity:* the ease with which a child is stimulated to response, his sensitivity or excitability. (May be positive or negative in tone.)   .04
  (1) Unreactive; seems to pay little heed to what goes on around him. Responds only to strong or repeated stimulation
  (9) Very reactive; every little thing seems to stir him up; startles, reacts quickly, seems keenly sensitive to things going on around him

8. *Tension:*   N.S.
  (1) Inert, may be flaccid most of the time
  (9) Body is predominantly taut or tense

9. *Fearfulness:* (e.g., reaction to the new or strange: strange people, test materials, strange surroundings)   .05
  (1) Accepts the entire situation with no evidence of fear, caution, or inhibition of actions
  (9) Strong indications of fear of the strange, to the extent he cannot be brought to play or respond to the tests

10. *General emotional tone:* unhappy-happy   N.S.
  (1) Child seems unhappy throughout the period
  (9) Radiantly happy; nothing is upsetting; animated

11. *Endurance* or behavior constancy in adequacy of response to demands of tests   N.S.
  (1) Tires easily, quickly regresses to lower levels of functioning
  (9) Continues to respond well and with interest, even with prolonged tests at difficult levels

12. *Sensory areas:* preoccupation or interest displayed. (None to excessive.)
  (a) Sights: looking   .025
  (b) Sounds: listening   N.S.
  (c) Sound producing: vocal   N.S.
  (d) Sound producing: banging, or other   .005
  (e) Manipulating (exploring with hands)   .02
  (f) Body motion   N.S.
  (g) Mouthing or sucking: thumb or fingers   N.S.
  (h) Mouthing or sucking: toys   N.S.

Note: Probabilities are from Mann-Whitney one-tailed tables and refer to items in which identical twin pairs exhibit significantly greater concordance than fraternal twin pairs over the first year. In no case was the opposite true.

Each item was rated along a scale from "deficient" to "overendowed," with five steps usually spelled out; a nine-point scale was obtained by adding half steps. The first and last steps are supplied to clarify the items.

[a] N.S. = Not significant.

lated on separate reels. At the end of the study, the filmed behavior
of half of each pair was rated by a group of judges using the Bayley
Infant Behavior Profile. Another group of judges rated the films of
the remaining twins. Again, within-pair differences among fraternal
twins were significantly larger (Fig. 4-9). These differences correlated with our direct ratings, indicating a significant relationship
between the judgments of films and our own observations.

Our personal experiences in the recording of the data showed that
four pairs were so alike that unless our impressions of differences
were recorded immediately it became impossible to do so, since their
personalities tended to merge into a single picture. This merger
could not be ascribed to similar appearance, for there was no difficulty in recording other identical looking pairs who exhibited some
clear-cut behavioral differences. Small wonder then, that even
brothers, sisters, and parents tend often to speak of "the twins"
rather than call each by name, and that identical twins often grow
more and more dependent on each other and may even develop a
common, shared identity (Leonard, 1961).

We have chosen four pairs of twins to illustrate the course of development
over the first 18 months, as measured by the Bayley Mental and Motor

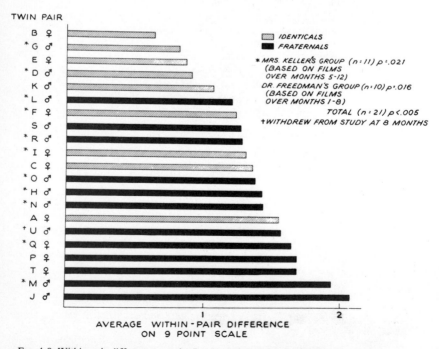

FIG. 4-9 Within-pair differences on the Bayley Infant Behavior Profile, based on 8 consecutive months of filmed behavior (either months 1 to 8, or months 5 to 12).

Scales. Figure 4-10 represents a pair of fraternal twin girls who were consistently dissimilar and Fig. 4-11 an identical pair of girls who were consistently alike; Fig. 4-12 represents a pair of decidedly unalike fraternal twin boys and Fig. 4-13 a pair of identical boys who showed consistent albeit small differences. All scores are standard scores based on Bayley's norms.

It will be noticed that in the identical twins, the twin who did better one month often did worse the next, whereas the fraternal twins tended to maintain consistent performances vis-à-vis each other. The extent of within-pair consistency is indicated by the following: On the Mental Scales, in identical twins, within-pair shifts in who performed better at successive

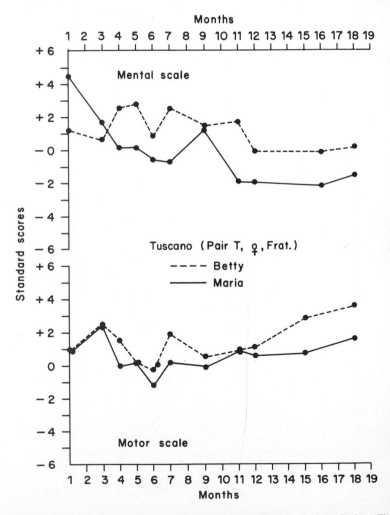

FIG. 4-10 Individual performances on the Bayley Infant Mental and Motor Scales. (These children, fraternal twin girls, are described in detail in the text.)

testing periods occurred in 37% of the tests administered, while fraternal twins switched positions on only 23% of the tests. Likewise, on the Motor Scales, identical pairs switched positions on 35% of the tests compared to 15% in fraternal pairs, and in both cases these differences were statistically significant (Freedman and Keller, 1963).

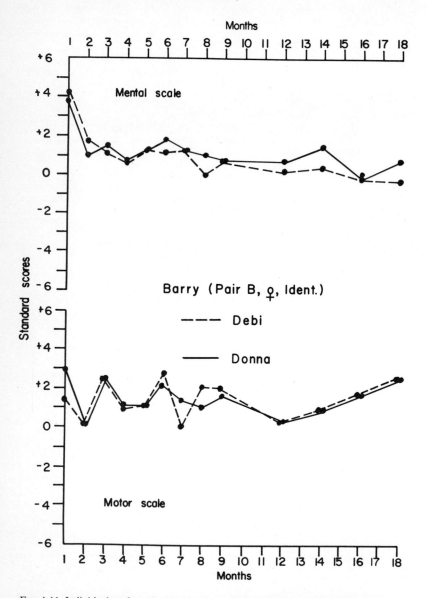

FIG. 4-11 Individual performances on the Bayley Infant Mental and Motor Scales. (These children, identical twin girls, are described in detail in the text.)

Finally, the richest source of material on the twins was the monthly notes recorded by each investigator following a home visit. These monthly notes were independently coded at the end of the study, and an adjective list (Table 4-3) was developed from the coding. The list was arranged into four groups of opposed themes, or eight octants: social extroversion vs. social introversion; good development vs. poor development; imposition of self on envi-

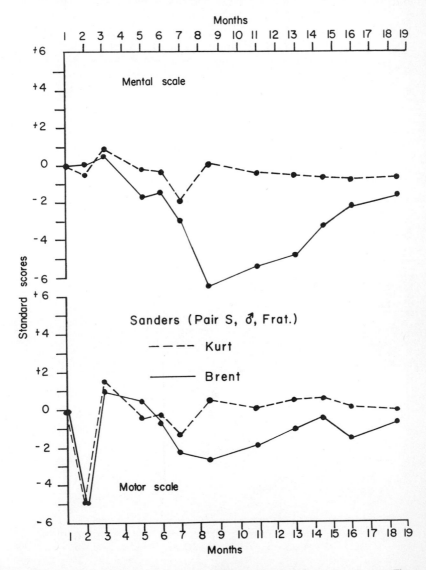

FIG. 4-12 Individual performances on the Bayley Infant Mental and Motor Scales. (These children, fraternal twin boys, are described in detail in the text.)

ronment vs. withdrawal from the environment; and "good" baby vs. "bad" baby. A count was then made of the adjectives used in describing each child after each home visit, and, as before, identicals ranked considerably more alike than fraternals, i.e., they tended to be described within the same octants ($p < .01$).

As can be seen from Table 4-2, among the items on the Infant Behavior Profile found to be significantly more concordant within identical pairs are

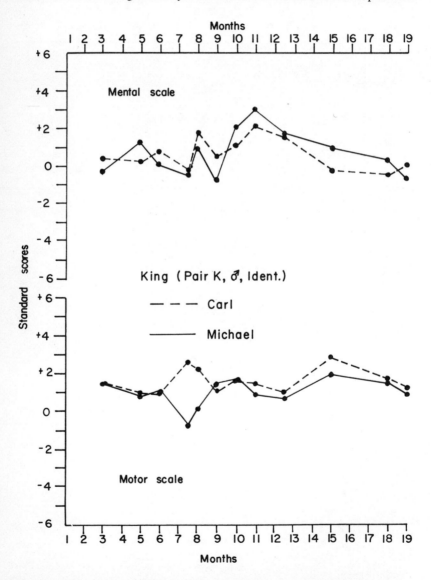

FIG. 4-13 Individual performances on the Bayley Infant Mental and Motor Scales. (These children, identical twin boys, are described in detail in the text.)

TABLE 4-3

Adjectives Used Spontaneously by Child Development Experts in
Describing Films of Infants over the First Year

1a Social Extroversion	1b Social Introversion
smiling	unrelating
grinning	unsmiling
happy	watchful (people)
outgoing	sober
friendly	intense
eyes sparkle	serious
joyous	solemn
playful	frowning
responsive (people)	sad

2a Good Development	2b Poor Development
alert	dull
attentive	unresponsive (objects)
responsive (objects)	inattentive
motorically advanced	distractible
well-coordinated, gross motor	motorically somewhat retarded
well-coordinated, fine motor	uncoordinated
	awkward
bouncy	passive
active	inactive
highly mobile	

3a Imposition of Self on Environment	3b Maintains Distance from Environment
determined	fearful
energetic	distrustful
impulsive	hesitant
excitable	inhibited
investigative	withdrawn
tenacious	timid
uninhibited	wary
robust	cautious
vigorous	dependent

4a "Good" baby	4b "Bad" baby
quiet	unhappy
placid	tense
relaxed	cranky
easygoing	fretful
pleasant	irritable
accepting	demanding
phlegmatic	cry-baby
content	angry
unexcitable	tantrums

social orientation (*p* < .005) and *fearfulness* (*p* < .05). Social orientation, during the first 5 months, was scored on the basis of visual fixation of the experimenter's face and on social smiling (*p* < .05, months 1–5); it would thus appear that these very earliest social behaviors have a demonstrable genetic component.

In order to check these findings, we conducted an additional small-scale study. We compared attending, smiling, and vocalizing in three pairs of dichorionic identical twins and four pairs of fraternal twins on a *weekly basis,* from birth through 4 months of age. As before, zygosity determinations were made after completion of the study. Figure 4-14 indicates that the identicals were, once again, substantially more alike than the fraternal pairs over this crucial early period in which initial contacts with another human being are being made.

Additional corroboration for this comes from a study by Reppucci (1968). She presented a series of visual stimuli to ten identicals and ten same-sexed

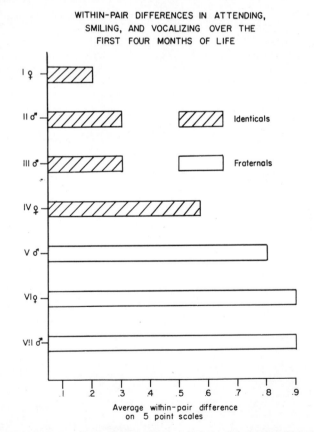

WITHIN-PAIR DIFFERENCES IN ATTENDING, SMILING, AND VOCALIZING OVER THE FIRST FOUR MONTHS OF LIFE

Average within-pair difference on 5 point scales

FIG. 4-14 Attending, smiling, and vocalizing to mother and to the experimenter were each scored separately on 5 point scales, and the scales averaged over the first 4 months of life. Average number of home visits was 10 (range 7–14).

fraternals at 4 months of age and found that the identicals were significantly more alike than the fraternals in amount of smiling to one of her stimuli, a three-dimensional mask. It thus appears fair to say that the smiling response of infants is a stable and readily demonstrable reflection of genotypic differences.

It will also be noted in Table 4-2 that identicals were more concordant than fraternals in their fear of strangers response ($p < .02$). Figures 4-15 and 4-16 represent the course of *fearfulness* from 6 months to 12 months for each child in the study, and, while some of the identical pairs were very similar over time on these ratings, fraternals never were, nor did any *two genotypes exhibit a similar pattern of fearfulness.*

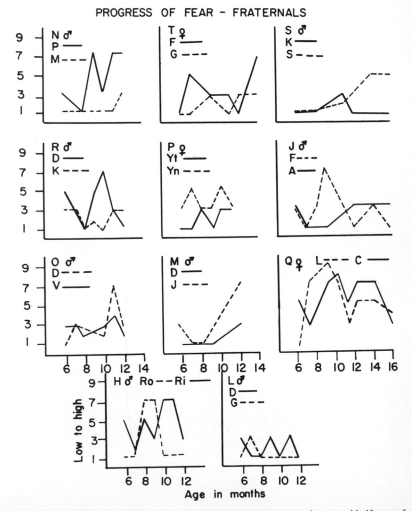

FIG. 4-15 Fraternal twins' fear-of-strangers reaction at home, over the second half-year of life. Based on ratings of the Bayley Infant Behavior Profile.

To summarize, much of the variation in early human behavior, as in puppies, is dependent on genetic variation. The basis for this conclusion is the fact that infants with identical heredity are, on the average, more alike than fraternal sibs over the first year of life.

It is of great interest that approximately the same order of differential concordance is found in studies beyond infancy as those found over the pre-imitative first year. This suggests that mutual imitation within older twin pairs is probably not a confounding factor as is sometimes claimed.

A good deal of research on inheritance of intelligence is summarized by

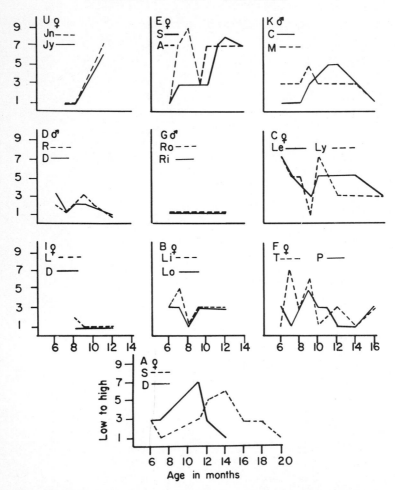

FIG. 4-16 Identical twins' fear-of-strangers reaction at home, over the second half-year of life. Based on ratings of the Bayley Infant Behavior Profile. Although showing considerable within-pair variability, identicals vary significantly less than fraternals ($p < .05$).

Erlenmeyer-Kimling and Jarvick (1963). In the 52 studies summarized, the closer the biological relationship between two individuals, the closer are the intelligence test scores, with environmental differences apparently playing an important but subsidiary role. Although the degree of concordance in studies of personality is rarely as great as in studies of intelligence, Vandenberg (1967) reviewed fifteen twin-studies which have used various personality questionnaires and found greater concordance among identicals in each study.

In the remainder of this chapter, we will attempt to spell out what this means in terms of individual development.

THE ROLES OF CONSTITUTION AND ENVIRONMENT WITHIN INDIVIDUALS: CONTINUITIES VS. DISCONTINUITIES IN ABILITIES AND PERSONALITY

At the population level, the solution to the problem of "how much" heredity and "how much" environment is a statistical one, and elaborate formulas, however problematic, have been calculated to answer this question (cf. Fuller and Thompson, 1960).

On the other hand, the question of heredity and environment within individuals simply cannot be dealt with. How can one disentangle heredity from environment within you, or me? Where does heredity stop and environment begin? Indeed, as pointed out in Chapter 1, these questions are answerable only when asked of populations. Psychology, however, is for the most part an ideographic science, and a usual way for the heredity-environment issue to appear is via the equation of "nature" with continuity of a trait or ability, and "nurture" with its discontinuity.

At first blush this may seem reasonable. If a trait persists over a lifetime, is this not evidence for its biological base? Consider, however, that certain behavior emerges for the first time at puberty, such as deepening of the male voice; this is certainly under genetic control but must nevertheless be termed noncontinuous. On the other hand, there are behavioral characteristics that an individual may exhibit over a lifetime although they are not primarily of genetic origin, such as hyperactivity and lowered IQ in children of extremely low birth weights.

Thus continuity vs. noncontinuity, *per se*, tells us little about the relative contributions of nature or nurture. Nevertheless, there is some point to the common view that if *normal* traits appear early, in the absence of a proximal cause, and if they persist over time, genetic origin is implied. This is, in fact, the logical basis of the "isolation" experiment used extensively in ethological studies of lower animals (cf. Lorenz, 1937). That is, if an animal is reared or hatched in isolation, behavior which it thereupon exhibits is considered "innate"; for example, most birds eventually fly whether or not they have contact with other birds. While ethology has been interested in species differences rather than individual differences, the same logic should hold for within-species variations. It is therefore of substantial interest to consider the evidence available with regard to the persistence or nonpersistence of differences in human traits from early infancy.

Infancy Tests

With regard to abilities, it is a well-established finding that, the extreme of the distribution aside, there is little predictability from scores on so-called intelligence tests in infancy to scores beyond 3 years of age (Anderson, 1939). In the Berkeley longitudinal study, for example, a 30-year follow-up yielded only one substantial correlation with performance in the first year. In females only, precocity of vocalizations in the first year correlated at about .80 with Verbal IQ at age 26.

There appear to be many reasons for this lack of continuity. For one thing, tests before 2 and 3 years and those after these ages depart radically in what is being measured. Infant tests, naturally enough, are almost entirely nonverbal and certainly require no abstract thought. Sensory acuity, eye-hand coordination, and physical precocity are the major ingredients of high infant scores. Beyond 18 months, verbal ability rises in importance, and beyond 5 years the ability to work with abstractions is the major ingredient (cf. White, 1965). Additionally, after 3 years of age, the average child's motor capacities are so complex that no one has yet devised a test for these years comparable to the infant tests in range of assessment. For example, no test examines dexterity and success in children's playground games.

The follow-up data in our twin study are similarly discontinuous. While some of the infants who scored very high or very low on the Bayley Scales did so again on the Stanford-Binet at 5 and 6 years of age (Fig. 4-17), the overall correlation between IQ and the first year Bayley scores (averaged over at least eight administrations) was extremely low ($r = +.33$ with the Mental Scale and $+.13$ with the Motor Scale).

Personality Scales

With regard to "personality," the attempt to assess continuities via our present rating scale categories or check lists of traits have been only minimally successful, and the "meaty" individualized aspects of personality descriptions have invariably been lost. Reports by Kagan and Moss (1962) and Schaefer and Bayley (1963), in separate longitudinal studies of about 30 years' duration, are to the point. Schaefer and Bayley found that the most stable dimensions over the years were "active, extroverted vs. inactive, introverted" behaviors, while Kagan and Moss found consistency from the preschool years to adulthood in the aggressive behavior of males and in the passivity and dependence of females. The latter finding is borne out by Honzik (1964) and Macfarlane (1964), who found greater consistency among females over the years on an independence-dependence dimension,

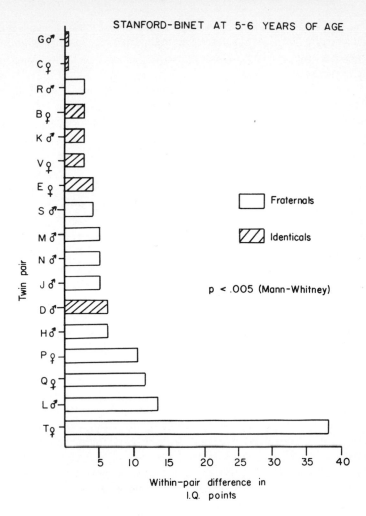

FIG. 4-17 Within-pair differences on Stanford-Binet at 5 or 6 years of age.

and by Bayley and Schaefer, who report relative stability among females on an active-passive dimension. While these findings are interesting, particularly from the point of view of evolved sexual dimorphism, they reflect group differences and not individual differences. How does one assess continuities in the progress of individual lives?

Without doubt, a major problem in assessing continuities in individuals has been the fact that maturational changes affect the total organism; that is, there is constant reorganization as new nodal points in development are attained (Goldstein, 1963). In systems theory terminology, set-goals change over time. For example, toddlerhood, adolescence, and parenthood necessarily involve considerably different sets of phylogenetically evolved adaptations; since the organism's viability depends on its ability to achieve organization in terms of *all* forces acting on it, whether exogenous or endogenous, there is a continuous repatterning of personality in the service of attaining current set-goals.

For somewhat the same reasons, *prediction* of personality from performance in infancy has also met with minimal success (Benjamin, 1959; Escalona and Heider, 1959; Fries and Woolf, 1953). Since each genotype is highly unique, and since the history of interaction with the environment further individualizes the organism, we simply do not have an accurate means of predicting social behavior.

It is not surprising, therefore, that Macfarlane (1964) is more impressed by *changes* in people than by *continuities* in their behavior over the 35 years her growth study has been active. It is her view that the most interesting aspects of personality are those which are essentially not predictable, e.g., how someone may deal with an emergency. That such behavior is difficult to predict is borne out by the work of MacKinnon (1948) and his O.S.S. colleagues during the Second World War in which, after extensive personality assessment, they were notoriously unsuccessful in predicting what people would do in various emergency situations.

Murphy (1964), however, has taken a middle ground. She reports in a major study in which over 60 children were seen from infancy through prepuberty, that ''over half the children changed markedly in one or another aspect of functioning . . . children showing most continuity had greater developmental balance and less vulnerability in infancy, and were growing up in environments which were relatively homogeneous, stable, free from traumatizing vicissitudes, and congenial to the child's natural style of development.'' Conversely, children showing least continuity were subject to greater physical and environmental instability. Murphy was also impressed with the individual styles of coping which, whether continuous or discontinuous over the years, tended to be unique for each person.

Finally, the strongest evidence on the side of continuity of personality comes from a study by Neilon (1948). She contacted, in late adolescence, the subjects Shirley (1933) had studied over their first 2 years of life. General personality descriptions were made of these young men and women without knowledge of what they were like as infants. These descriptions were then given to a number of judges to see how well they could be matched to the descriptions reported at 2 years of age. Matching was well above chance so that at the global level of personality description it was possible to demonstrate continuity from 2 through about 18 years of age.

Longitudinal Studies of Twins

Our own studies of twins, which span a shorter segment of time (10 years), tend to corroborate the findings of Neilon. The following description, summarizing an examination of films taken from birth through 5 years, is an illustration of what our studies have yielded.

> Arturo and Felix, a pair of fraternal twins, showed striking dissimilarity in their thresholds to smiling as early as two months of age. At that age, Arturo would smile with his eyes closed to the stroking of his cheek, a soft voice, or the tinkle of a bell. Felix rarely smiled but, by contrast, was alert and unusually observant. At nine months, when confronted by a stranger, both seemed equally uncomfortable. Arturo, however, tried to smile despite his fear, while Felix simply kept his eyes from meeting those of the stranger. At the five and one-half-year follow-up, the persistence of these differences in interpersonal approach was striking. Although both appeared equally anxious, Felix exhibited only one full smile during the entire interview, while Arturo smiled constantly over the entire time. Such striking differences were never seen among identicals and we must conclude that different genotypes were ultimately responsible.

Because of the promise of such observations, a matching study modeled after Neilon's was performed with six pairs of fraternal twins (only fraternal twins were used, since the written descriptions of identicals were never as rich—an artifact, apparently, of the fewer contrasting traits within identical pairs). Each judge worked with six individual children (as if they were singletons) and was asked to match working notes written at 5 and 6 *months* of age with subsequent reports written at 18 *months*, 5 to 6 *years,* and 10 *years* of age. The results were much the same as Neilon's: Matching at the various ages was accomplished at well above chance levels, with some children proving much easier to match-up than others. All in all, we can say with confidence that unique and persisting trends in personality can be discerned as early as the first months of life, and in some infants, from the first weeks of life.

Illustrative Case Histories

An inquiry into the life histories of identical and fraternal twins has much to teach us. First there is the question of continuities vs. discontinuities, which all longitudinal studies try to answer. But additionally, since we can here trace two individuals of the same genotype growing up (as in identical twins), and contrast them with the growth patterns in differentially endowed children (fraternal pairs), there is hopefully much to be learned about how a genotype actualizes itself through the life-span.

Case histories are often faulted because they are descriptive and not experimental, but it is from such observations that new ideas may emerge. Goldstein's (1963) holism and his notions of concrete and abstract thinking, for example, emerged from his extensive work with individual brain-injured patients. In the same vein, then, when the facts of the present cases bring up points of theoretical interest, the flow of the cases will be interrupted for appropriate discussions.

Four longitudinal studies of twin pairs, two identical and two fraternal, will be presented from our pool of twenty. These cases were chosen not only because they are interesting and fairly representative, but because we have their complete developmental records from 1 month through 10 years of age. All were seen, tested, and filmed on a monthly basis over the first year of life and on a bimonthly basis from 12 through 18 months. They were subsequently studied and filmed several more times, including visits at 5 and 10 years of age. These are the same four twin pairs whose first year Mental and Motor graphs appeared as Figs. 4-10 through 4-13.

Case 1. Betty and Maria Tuscano, dizygotic twin girls (Pair T, Figs. 4-6 through 4-7).

Betty and Maria Tuscano are the third and fourth children of an Italian-American "middle-class" family. Mother was a bookkeeper before marriage, father a semi-pro baseball player, now a meat-cutter. Both had had high school educations and were members of large families, most of whom were fishermen. This was a most affectionate, open-hearted household, with frequent visitors, and the two older brothers (6 and 8 years) were, from the start, very pleased with their new sisters. Although the family was practicing Catholics, the pregnancy was a "mistake", and mother, who was rather eager to return to work, did so before the first birthday of the twins.

The twins are uniquely interesting for a number of reasons, but perhaps mainly because the child who was later clearly superior in intelligence had the most difficult start in life. Maria was born first in a normal cephalic presentation, and was judged totally viable. She weighed 7 lb-4 oz and her 1-minute Apgar rating was 10. Betty, at 7 lb-13 oz, arrived 5 minutes later and was a breech presentation; as is rather common in breech birth, she had a substantially lower Apgar rating of 6 because of her blue extremities and labored breathing. After 30 minutes in an Isolette with a CO_2-O_2 mixture to stimulate breathing, she was judged normal. However, as we will see, Betty appeared to spend much of her first 3 months of life recovering from the trauma of this breech birth. Other than this, the only other unusual note in the hospital record was, "Maria is a voracious eater."

The following excerpts are taken from notes on the twins over a 27-month period:

> *1 month, 1 day.* Mother calls Maria "The big one," and Betty "the little one." I never heard her use their names. There are clear differences between Maria and Betty. Maria has large eyes which take in all the people in the room. Mother says that she is very

"nosey" and "always enjoys seeing what others are doing." When she becomes hungry, her arms and legs flail back and forth as she cries. She slurps the bottle down 4 or 5 times as fast as Betty.

At first Betty was not interested in me at all, but as I talked to her she began to focus. After a minute or so she began to follow me, but only within a few degrees, and she lost interest quickly. Her iris is centered rather low so that one can see white on the upper side. (This is termed the "sunset" sign by neurologists, but its significance is unclear.) Betty was near sleep throughout her feeding. She would awaken, suck a little, and then go off to sleep.

3 months, 1 day. Maria continues to be louder when hungry, is hungry more often, and slurps the milk down a little quicker than Betty. She has large round blue eyes and keeps them open and fastened on me. Betty, on the other hand, does not stare intently but tends to look off into the distance. You can get her attention and she will look at you and smile, but never with the concentration or awe of Maria.

By 4 months, Betty seemed fully recovered from the presumed trauma induced by the breech presentation and began exhibiting some trait differences vis-à-vis Maria that were to be seen thereafter. As when first seen, Maria continued to be highly social, but in a quiet, passive way.

4 months, 7 days. Mother says that Maria is probably suffering from the aftereffects of shots received the previous day, but when I bent over and spoke to her, she smiled. As I continued to speak, she smiled more and more and began to vocalize and to move her hands and feet. It was not long before she was a completely different girl, extremely happy, and always on the verge of a smile. This happy demeanor continued for the rest of the afternoon and, unless I was out of view, Maria did not take her eyes off me.

Betty was active from the start, waving her arms and legs, but she did not focus on me for any length of time. When I whipped Betty over my head, she began to laugh and squeal with delight. When I did the same with Maria, she startled. Mother says that father plays roughly with Betty but does not do so with Maria because of this differential reaction. Later when mother gave the girls a sponging, Betty crowed, squealed, laughed out loud, and made sounds I did not think she was capable of. Maria just smiled silently. Betty is generally somewhat expressionless, even looks a little fierce, but when she is stimulated she can brighten and become enthusiastic. Maria is described by everybody as soft, sensitive, people-oriented, and very ready to smile.

By 5 months of age, Betty's general developmental progress was exceeding Maria's to a substantial degree, a difference that was to persist throughout the study period, and probably throughout their lives.

> *5 months, 0 days.* There is a big change this month between Maria and Betty. In the test, Betty is the most alert and advanced in that each object presented to her is of great interest. She tries to grab the objects and hold on to them. She changed the rattle from one hand to the other and, for the first time, smiled readily at the examiner. She is a very sturdy, bouncy baby, responds with a smile to rough play. Maria is softer, more placid, sinks like a sack in your arms and still smiles sweetly, as she has done since the third month.
>
> There were no complaints from Betty when by herself on the settee, whereas Maria cried when similarly placed. Mother corroborates that Maria complains in order to be picked up. She stopped crying when placed near the kitchen where there was much activity, even as she had quieted when placed near people as early as the second month. Maria pays very little attention to the objects presented to her and appears predominantly people-oriented. Betty is more people-oriented than before, but retains a strong interest in objects.

As can be seen from performance over the first year and a half on the Bayley Mental and Motor Scales (Fig. 4-9), Betty was substantially more successful than Maria after the first 3 months. By 9 months of age, the division between the girls' abilities and behavior was so pronounced that the question of abnormality was raised about Maria.

> *9 months, 0 days.* I am struck by the persistence of the difference between Betty and Maria. Betty continues to crawl all over the floor, to smile very little, but to respond hilariously to rough play. Maria does not move around but sits in one spot rocking, and when you approach her she smiles.
>
> In the last two visits, Maria has exhibited rocking behavior and a continual rhythmic movement of her hands, the right hand in particular. When sitting alone on the floor, the behavior is unfortunately reminiscent of stereotypic movements of mental defectives. However, when in contact with me or her mother, she does not do this, but smiles and plays interestedly with the toys I give her.
>
> Although she smiles very often, Maria does not seem to give the message that she is getting to know you. She seems to smile because her eyes fixate your eyes. She is not interested in contacting you or in pursuing the relationship any further, as if the smile itself is sufficient. Betty, by contrast, has a strong outgoing tendency, although

she has a chronic pout and still only laughs when treated roughly. She creeps after people, watching them all the while, and creeps after objects in an attempt to get them. Maria seems to be in her own world and simply acknowledges objects and people as they enter her sphere.

When the girls were about 11 months, mother, a very active woman who preferred the business world to homemaking, decided to return to work. It was clear from Betty's reaction that this was a very unhappy point in her life, and she took it much more personally that did Maria. Films were made of each girl performing in the same situation throughout the study. In the analysis of films taken at 12 months, the following comments were made[1] :

Films—12 months, 0 days. In this situation, with mother gone and strangers in the house, Betty is extremely tense and seems introverted, shy, and unhappy. Maria, on the other hand, deals fairly happily with the strangers. It is as if Maria's relatively shallow interpersonal mode is an aid here, whereas Betty's deeper involvement makes for greater unhappiness. She looks depressed and seems to be thinking "nobody loves me" and "why did they leave me?"

Betty's relative unhappiness and moodiness in strange circumstances was illustrated again at 18 months of age, when the family came to the hospital for filming in a standardized situation.

Films—18 months, 5 days. This is an interview between Dr. F. and the girls, one at a time. Maria looks at Dr. F. the entire time smiling coquettishly, is quick to say no if she feels she can't do something, and is apparently content to have others do it for her. Betty is intent upon doing tasks for herself, and obviously gets pleasure in their accomplishment. There are interesting differences in the forbidden lollipop sequence. [This is a test of frustration tolerance: A lollipop or cookie is laid on the table, and the child is told to wait, up to 5 minutes, until the experimenter has finished writing.] Although Maria was persistent in trying to get it, she simply waited when told "no," apparently without being personally hurt. Betty was very hurt when told "no," and began to cry. This sensitivity to rebuff is reminiscent of Betty's depression during the twelfth month visit and is in marked contrast to her great self-confidence at other times.

[1]The films were analyzed by Peter Druian, Louis Fourcher, Robert Marvin, and the author in the following way: The films of each pair were projected side by side for each month, from 1 month through 5 years, and then discussed. The films for any month were then reshown if there was a point of disagreement or an unresolved question. Once consensus was achieved, the analysis was recorded, in front of the group, by the author. Any further objections, deletions, or additions were then added as a postscript.

The 27-month visit reveals the usual theme with mother present. Betty exudes self-confidence and ability; Maria engages only in social "basking."

> *Films—27 months, 17 days.* This was filmed in the home. Each girl was presented with the testing kit. Maria takes a completely undifferentiated approach: each toy is drawn from the box and tossed somewhere close by, then the next toy is brought out, looked at briefly, and again tossed aside. Betty is completely oriented toward what she extracts from the kit, and when she finally finds something that interests her—a scissors—she tries to cut a piece of crayon with it; the rest of the time was spent in attempting to master this task. Once again, Maria seems to be mainly aware of the people in the room.

At 5 years, 5 months, another interview is filmed in the hospital, and what happens is now familiar:

> *5 years, 5 months.* Maria's transparent coyness and superficial interest in the examiner make all the viewers laugh. She smiles constantly at the interviewer, flirts with him, and is completely unperturbed when she can't understand his questions or if she fails on a task. It's as if she is completely optimistic that things will take care of themselves; in fact they do, for she builds a very high tower although the blocks are precariously placed. Betty is once again moody, tense, and socially inhibited. In fact, she seems near tears, so that the balloon-busting sequence was saved for the end (a balloon is blown-up by the experimenter and the child is asked to burst it with a pin). In contrast to Maria, she built a tidy, very well done little tower. All of Betty was inside, and very little of her came out during this interview. All of Maria is worn on her sleeve, and she has become the unreflective, sweet, little darling. One would guess that this behavior is greatly rewarded in her family because she wears it now so effortlessly. Betty seems to have suffered, and her sensitivity to rebuff appears to have had a cumulative effect. In short, she strikes one as smart, moody, and too frequently feeling "nobody loves me."

Maria's Stanford-Binet IQ at this time was 67, suggesting a diagnosis of mental retardation as a possibility. However, since the correlation between IQ at 5 years and later achievement is not very high, we were not too worried. However, at the age of 9 years, 11 months follow-up, she scored at the same level on the Wechsler Intelligence Scale for Children (WISC). Her full scale IQ was 68, performance 68, verbal 74. Betty's full scale IQ was

113, performance 96, verbal 126. Maria had, in fact, been placed in a class for mentally retarded children 6 months previously. Here are excerpts from that report, written by a clinician[2] who had not seen the girls before.

> *9 years, 11 months.* Betty is a slim, self-assured girl with a pretty and expressive face and a very mature-sounding manner of speaking. She was very cooperative during our work together, but rather remote. She seemed to be bright and competent in many areas. During testing, she was a somewhat careless worker and would get a little impatient when she couldn't do something. She seems to have little patience with incompetence—her own or that of anyone else. I wondered what her real feelings about her sister Maria are, although she stated that they get along well. However, Mrs. Tuscano commented that Betty is very critical and doesn't give Maria a chance to talk.
>
> Maria is an overweight, slow-moving girl who has great difficulty communicating. Her overall behavior suggests a level of development comparable to about a 5-year-old. Although when we first started working together she was timid, she quickly relaxed and became friendly and affectionate, reminiscent again of a younger child. She tried extremely hard on the various tasks presented to her, but had great difficulties and needed much and constant reassurance. She is painfully aware of her limitations, and her pleasure upon succeeding is very great. (In order for her to experience success, it was necessary to go down to very elementary tasks.) She would often comment anxiously, "That's hard," and I think that phrase is a dominant theme in her life.

In summary then, Maria and Betty have exhibited striking differences from one another from the fourth month through the subsequent 10 years of their lives. Most clear are the differences in overall mental and motor abilities, but certain personality differences have also persisted. Maria's relatively complete surrender to the social circumstances of the moment, the ease of her smile, and the relative ease of expressing "surface" affection, have distinguished her consistently. Betty, by contrast, was relatively aloof from the very earliest months, and her threshold for smiling has been consistently high; she has to be stimulated to joy. Also, the subtheme of her moodiness, which was first seen at 1 year when mother went off to work, has been noted on most visits since then; since 1 year of age, she seems to have vacillated between great self-confidence and the feeling that "nobody cares for me."

---

[2] All follow-up material at 9 and 10 years of age was gathered by Mrs. Natalie Hirsch.

As for Maria's retardation, there is no reason to believe it has any special etiology, such as early brain damage, since our records are excellent and complete in this regard. It is, however, unusual to have so wide a spread (45 IQ points) within the same family (Honzik, 1957), so that undiagnosed brain damage cannot be completely ruled out. Interestingly, if at birth one had predicted which of the twins had a greater chance of retardation based on neonatal data, Betty, with an Apgar rating of 6 at birth, her subsequent drowsiness, and neurological sign ("sunset" eyes), would doubtless have received the nod.

The Tuscano girls, then, are examples of substantially un-alike fraternal twins who, while showing average differences for fraternals over the first year, grew more and more apart thereafter. Our second case is a pair of monozygotic girls who have exhibited about average similarities and dis-similarities for an identical pair. Like other identical pairs, they are enor-mously similar, but upon careful observation persisting subtle differences may be seen. In this pair, such differences were first noted at 3 months, and, as in the Tuscano twins, they have persisted throughout their subsequent lives.

Case 2. Debi and Donna Barry, monozygotic girls (Pair B, Figs. 4-6 through 4-17).

It should be pointed out again, at the outset of this case history, that it has been much more difficult to describe the individuality of identical twins. Friends, relatives, and parents often begin to think of "the twins" as a single unit and, in fact, the twins often begin to think of themselves in the same way (Leonard, 1961). One way around this problem of description has been to view films of the twins independently, and to describe each as if he were a singleton. However, this has been a help and not a solution, and when one returns to a comparative description of the two, uncertainty reappears; one must then again face the fact that there are no consistent and definite boundaries as between fraternal pairs.

Donna and Debi were born 20 minutes apart and in that order; they weighed 5 lb-11 oz and 5 lb-4 oz, respectively. Both received Apgar ratings of 10, and there were no complications of birth. They were first children; the pregnancy was "unplanned"; father, 27, is an engineer with a B.A. degree; and mother, 23, has had 1½ years of college. The parents are third genera-tion Jewish-Americans. It was very soon clear that this was to be a mother-dominated family:

> *2 months, 3 days.* The most noticeable person in this household is Mrs. Barry. She seems always running from room to room, asking questions, or offering me something to eat or drink. The children are swamped by mother's intentions for them. What they do is not as important as what she would like them to do. She acts as if each child were on a precipice and that her job is to prevent its fall.

Neither child looked at me for any length of time (which is the minimal relationship necessary for "cooing" and "smiling"), although Donna did look and smile briefly. However, she was distracted when I left momentarily, and I could not reestablish this connection with her. On the other hand, both watched mother rather intently as they took their milk from the bottle. Both tended to cry when put down, and both scored almost identically on all tests.

In summary, I cannot say very much to differentiate the girls; they merge one into the other. Both were frequently red-faced and irritable and, although they watched their mobiles and looked at their dolls, they did not focus on people with much interest.

By the third month and thereafter, both girls were showing an interest in people as well as objects, and they continued their near parallel development.

3 months, 1 day. The pleasant surprise was that both babies were not crying but were very interested in me, smiling and cooing almost immediately. This was in marked contrast to the red-faced squalling infants of the previous two visits. They vocalized at my unsmiling face, and cooed and smiled with particular interest when I began talking and smiling. They showed moderate interest in all objects presented to them, turned toward sound, and looked from one object to another. There was practically no difference in any aspect of their behavior.

Analysis of films taken during this visit added a few details the experimenter did not originally notice:

Films—3 months, 1 day. There is very little difference this month, although there is some. Mother made both babies cry by her jabbing the spoon into the mouth as she was feeding them, but Donna spent more time with her eyes open looking around the room, especially at the camera, whereas Debi reacted to the discomfort of the situation by closing her eyes, and crying. Similarly Donna turned her head to avoid the spoon, whereas Debi just complained by continuing to cry. Perhaps Donna is the better "coper" of the two.

This proved a good example of the value of a filmed record, for Donna did indeed turn out to have some advantage in this regard. By the fourth month, Donna showed a greater empathy for people, exhibiting both stronger attachments and stronger fear of strangers. This difference seen at 4 months for the first time was seen again on many occasions over the next 10 years.

4 months, 0 days. Donna is larger than Debi and aside from that there are very few differences to be noted. The picture consists of *a* baby and not two babies. This baby smiles a good deal, follows objects well, exhibits a minimum of grasping, grows restless toward the end of the hour, and is then prone to cry; furthermore, it exhibits visual recognition of the mother more clearly than any other child in the study has done by this age. There was but one point of difference: Donna arched her back inviting mother to take her from the visitor, and a differential recognition of author and mother definitely took place. Later Donna cried in my arms and quieted down immediately in mother's arms. On the other hand, mother says the same can occur with Debi although she did not exhibit this during the visit.

While there was therefore some uncertainty that Donna was more affected by a stranger than Debi, by 7 months this difference became quite clear.

Films —7 months, 0 days. All agree that Donna was more involved with mother in what must be described as a joyous encounter, and that she was also more fearful of the stranger. Debi, for her part, looked blankly a good deal of the time, both at mother and at the stranger, although she showed wariness when with the stranger. In fact, when Donna has a blank look, which she has less of the time, she looks almost exactly like Debi. In the social situation with mother, Donna got so involved that she started imitating the mother's pat-a-cake in a rather precocious onset of imitation. Debi was more distant when mother pat-a-caked and just watched.

Again, at 9 months, 4 days, from analysis of films:

Debi's smile to the examiner is always partial and has to be called ambivalent; Donna's is full, and she obviously is totally absorbed in the encounter. This now seems to be the only point of clear differentiation, for they performed nearly identically on all tasks (with a slight edge to Donna). Both also tended to mouth the toys offered, and neither showed any fear of strangers at this time (both male and female strangers were introduced on this visit).

The slight edge to Donna on the Bayley Mental test items, noted here, continues to be mentioned thereafter, and is reflected in the graphed results of the Bayley test from 9 through 18 months (Fig. 4-10).

Both trends, Donna's edge in problem solving and her somewhat greater social involvement, are apparent in notes made at the eighteen-month visit to the hospital. These comments were made by Mrs. Barbara Keller, who had not seen the Barry twins before. It is therefore especially noteworthy that they are consistent with what had been noted before.

18 months, 13 days—Hospital playroom. As soon as the Barry family arrived for the test, both girls began exploring, climbing on chairs, looking around the reception room in a very busy, active fashion. Mrs. Barry and Debi went into the interview room, leaving Donna with a secretary in the reception room. Donna occasionally called for her "mommy" and after about 10 or 15 minutes became very unhappy, crying quite loudly. Mrs. Barry immediately left Debi with Dr. F. in the interview room and came out to Donna. During all of this, Debi occasionally looked up from the test when she heard Donna, but did not call back; she also accepted her mother's leaving the room with a pleasant glance and no fuss. Donna frequently called "mommy" or "Debi" in a loud voice during her test. Donna seems to be a bit more dependent on her mother and to be more involved with people generally than is Debi, although they are both very friendly, responsive children.

Both were very anxious to get to the forbidden cookie (the experimenter forbade taking the cookie until he was finished writing), but here again the strongest response came from Donna. Debi kept reaching for it, her eyes on Dr. F.'s face, but with no fussing. Donna began to cry in a very hurt way, still reaching for it, and continued to cry hard until she got it.

Both girls are beautifully coordinated as far as large-muscled activities go. They both walk very well, balance well on one foot, and manage the stairs, but both show less well-developed hand coordination. They use a rather clumsy whole grasp, rather than a thumb-forefinger grasp when putting the small blocks in the box with a hole. Donna, nevertheless, managed to complete the pegboard, and her tower was built a bit faster than Debi's. Donna also performed at a somewhat higher level on both the Gesell board and the Bayley board than Debi did, but both girls made similar mistakes. Finally, both are very verbal children, with a fairly large number of recognizable words, but here again, Donna seems somewhat ahead of Debi.

At 5 years, 3 months, we can still recognize Debi and Donna. These excerpts are from a report made by a co-worker, Natalie Hirsch, who was seeing the twins for the first time and who had no previous information about them.

Debi was more active than Donna, more curious about her surroundings, more individualistic, "shrewder" in her judgment, and also more self-sufficient. Donna seemed warmer, more dependent, more accepting and more outgoing. Donna seemed to take pleasure in pleasing other people, whereas Debi seemed less concerned about this, and while very friendly, was also somewhat aloof.

If one wishes, one could emphasize these differences, yet it is the similarity in appearance, behavior, and ability which is most striking about the Barry twins. They seem rather to be minor variations of a dominant theme. (The Stanford-Binet Intelligence Scale was given, and Donna's IQ was 140 and Debi's 137.)

At 5 years, 5 months, when the twins came to the hospital to be filmed, Mrs. Barry confided that she had a troubled relationship with Debi and asked me to recommend a clinician who would help "straighten her out." It was my unspoken opinion that mother had exaggerated Debi's relative aloofness into a personal rejection of herself, and that she had succeeded in dividing these very similar girls into a "good" one and a "bad" one. Therapy, however, was not undertaken and, at the most recent testing, it appears that this unfortunate situation still prevails.

Mrs. Hirsch tested the girls again, when they were 9 years, 7 months, at which time Debi scored a full scale IQ of 126 (verbal 129, performance 118); Donna's full scale IQ was 123 (verbal 131, performance 110). Mrs. Hirsch's report follows:

9 years, 7 months. Both girls are very friendly and both seemed very interested in me. In extended conversations, I learned that Donna would like to be in the same class as Debi but Debi likes being in a different classroom. Both said they like being twins, that they get along well, and that they spend much time together. However, each girl seems to have her own special friends. Of the two, Debi was more outgoing this time. She talked constantly, usually about herself, but in a sharing way. Her main themes were her father, whom she mentioned frequently, and animals, of which she is very fond. Donna was just a little less talkative and slightly more reserved. Her special interest is art. According to Donna, she does well in school, volunteering that, "I got some A's, Debi didn't." This was apparently meant to inform and did not sound at all competitive.

The drawings of a house, tree, and person which each girl made are most striking in their similarities in terms of style, size, and placement on the paper (all drawings were done individually). However, Donna's drawing of a girl is more curvy and "feminine" to the point of being a caricature, and this probably accounts for her reputation as being more "artistic."

In the Thematic Apperception Test, Donna's stories were slightly more imaginative; she invented names of people and places and indicated some empathy for other people. Debi's were bland and conventional, usually of the once-upon-a-time type. On the intelligence tests, their performances were extremely similar.

Donna may do a little better here, while Debi does a little better there, but the slight differences seemed random. In short, the similarity of these twins is much more striking than their differences.

Despite this, it is clear that Mrs. Barry sees sharp differences between the two girls. Her relationship with Donna is much better than with Debi. She characterized Debi as the stubborn individualist, and Donna as very easy going. The "stubborn" qualities she described for Debi were not all evident during the interview, and I suspect that the mother has a great deal to do with bringing this behavior about. She did, in fact, add that Debi gets along fine with most people.

This pair, then, illustrates a number of points. Most striking, perhaps, is the overall, massive similarity in rates of development and in personality, undoubtedly reflective of identical heredity actualizing itself in a common environment. Furthermore, these similarities persisted despite decidedly different treatment by mother who, by the time the twin were 5 years, clearly preferred Donna over Debi! (Father, incidentally, tended also to favor Donna, but not to the same degree.) This discrimination was based on an actual though subtle difference in interpersonal warmth which was first seen at 5 months, when the warmer, more empathic Donna gradually became the "good" one, the more aloof, independent Debi the "bad" one.

This case also illustrates a problem in the prediction of behavior. One might assume that Debi's self-concept would suffer relative to Donna's because of these differential parental attitudes. However, there is already evidence that the very traits for which she is resented, her aloofness and independence, help her to better weather emotional storms (as at the 5-year visit to the hospital), and this may in the long run work to her advantage. Prediction is indeed a tricky business.

The next case, a pair of fraternal boys, illustrates yet another issue: How the same environmental deprivation may have different effects upon different organisms. Here, two boys of different genotypes were reared with minimal parental stimulation. The differential reactions to the "same" deprivation are exceedingly complex, and depend, at least in part, on the unique coping techniques available to a particular child.

Case 3. Kurt and Brent Sanders, dizygotic twins (Pair S, Figs. 4-6 through 4-17). In our sample of 20 pairs of twins, only two pregnancies were planned. This was not one of these two, as Kurt and Brent were the fifth and sixth children of a mother and father still in their twenties. The others were 8, 7, 3, and 2, and only the last was a girl. The first two boys were by a previous marriage of the mother.

The parents were high school graduates. Father had worked as a postman and was now a fireman. Mother is of Irish and father of Portuguese descent. The latter part of the twin pregnancy was marred by jaundice, and both Kurt and Brent were yellowed when born, particularly second-born Brent. Apgar ratings were not available but presumably would have been less than 10, somewhat lower for Brent than for Kurt on the basis of his substantial jaundice. This condition was not wholly unexpected since mother had been anemic in three previous pregnancies and had suffered two miscarriages as well.

Both boys were rather apathetic on the first home visit at 1 month, 5 days, and slept much of the time. Even when the bottle was removed neither protested nor made an attempt to retrieve the nipple. Their apathy seemed matched by the mother's. She openly admitted that little attention is or will be paid to the twins as long as they sleep or are quiet. At month 2, it was clear that she had been serious. Note also the long-term trend, starting here, of Kurt's more rapid developmental progress.

> *2 months, 6 days.* The most striking thing about the visit was the lack of contact between either of the parents and the twins. They have four other children and mother pointed out, during the long interview, that she did not know answers to various questions simply because she had spent very little time with the babies. The father cannot tell the children apart although the mother can. She associates her two youngest children with one twin and the two oldest with the other, and via these associations, she is able to distinguish the two boys. I have trouble telling them apart and could not do so after two hours there.
>
> Mother feels that Kurt is more alert than Brent and asked if I did not think so too. My impression is that possibly Brent sleeps more, but both tested almost identically. Both boys followed the red ring quite well, followed the pencil minimally, and tended to be uninterested in other objects or in the experimenter. I found that I had to hold them and talk at least 5 minutes before they would fixate on me for any length of time; then, when put down, they lost interest immediately.
>
> The children were given a bath, and both cried when they were exposed naked to the cool air. The first into the bath tub was Brent who cried louder and for a longer period than Kurt, who after a while quieted and relaxed. This, and the fact that Kurt seems to be awake more, are the two major differences between the boys.
>
> In summary, here are a pair of children who will have to make an impact on their parents via their own endogenous natures to get any attention. Mother seemed to feel somewhat guilty over her lack of active interest and said, ''Twins should be first children, not fifth and sixth.'' As for differences in the twins, Kurt was less tense, less irritable, and possibly more alert.

5 months, 0 days. Both boys have a sort of dreamy, sleepy look, even when fully awake. Kurt vocalizes more, but tends to do so to himself rather than to anyone. He and Brent, however, had a "conversation" for a period of time. Besides being heavier, Kurt is more robust and apparently more resistant to disease; Brent had been sicker than Kurt earlier in the month when both had been ill. Mother notes that Brent fusses more when he is hungry and usually awakens earlier, demanding the bottle. However, when it comes to actual eating, Kurt tends to finish the bottle more quickly, whereas Brent dawdles.

Again, despite these differences, there is great similarity in that both boys are somewhat dulled in outgoingness, interest in objects, and goal directedness as compared with the norm. They behave as if they are being reared in some darkened, isolated hut. Mother stated again that she has made it a policy not to play with them for fear of their becoming spoiled and too demanding.

6 months, 1 day. Kurt was awake and beaming when I came in. He had a beautiful smile and was constantly in motion, with his arms and legs kicking. He could not quite lift himself to a sit while holding onto my fingers, and he was very loathe to reach for objects offered him. Mother assured me, over my shoulder, that this was because they pay practically no attention to him and offer him no playthings.

While Brent is quite as alert as Kurt and seems to look with interest at all persons, he does not smile as broadly nor as often, nor does he show as much spontaneous movement of arms and legs. He, too, was reluctant to reach for objects, and could not raise himself to a sitting position.

7 months, 4 days. Both boys are developmentally slow and perform at the Bayley norm of approximately 5½ months. The most striking thing about them is the fact that they seem to have had fewer learning opportunities than any of the other children in the study. Although they are now not isolated since the cribs are in the front room, they simply are not played with very often. Kurt, in particular, appears very bright and very interested in people, and it would follow that he should do far better on the tests than he did. Neither boy turns over and their spontaneous activity consists of getting up on all fours and rocking. Kurt reaches readily for all objects presented to him, Brent somewhat less readily. Kurt holds onto them more fiercely and several times expressed his disapproval by yelping when an object was taken away. Kurt also enjoyed ringing the bell and banged it continuously. Brent did not exploit the bell nor the rattle, and neither boy did well in retrieving an object that fell from his grasp. Brent's smile is less infectious, and one comes away with the feeling that Kurt is the real charmer of the two. This impression is helped along by the fact that Kurt protests when put down, indicating he likes being played with. However, mother says that Brent will cry if Kurt is picked up, and a precocious jealousy appears to be developing. In general, Kurt comes across as the stronger personality and Brent as the sweet, placid, introverted twin, with both personalities muted because of minimal stimulation.

Then came the most unforgettable visit of all, at 8 months, 22 days:

8 months, 22 days. When I went into the house a surprise awaited me: A vast gulf had appeared between Kurt and Brent in the 7 weeks since the last visit. Kurt was crawling after objects while Brent lay in his playpen, on his back, not moving. I tested Kurt and he was extremely eager to exploit all the playthings offered him. He crawled toward objects out of his reach and persisted until he reached them. He was constantly trying to retrieve the toys I had replaced in my bag. He banged a good deal, and he clearly enjoyed exploiting objects for their noise value. It will not be long before he will be walking since he can take stepping movements now when held by his hands. He started crawling a few days ago and he is going marvelously well at it already. Before testing Brent, Mrs. Sanders warned me that he would not accept any of the materials offered. It was incredible but it turned out to be true. None of the objects, ranging from blocks to rattle, was accepted. Brent simply lay on his back or on his tummy with his hands clenched. I played with his palms and finally got him to accept a peg which he dropped immediately. He held onto my finger briefly but not long enough for me to pull him to a sitting position. When he was placed in a sitting position, he held it briefly and then fell over. Nevertheless, he smiled constantly. Brent thus scored at a 1 or 2 month level on the Bayley test, but it appeared that his refusal of objects involved some sort of an inhibition rather than disinterest. When I picked up Kurt, Brent let out an obvious cry of jealousy, rolled over on his stomach, turned his head away, and put his thumb in his mouth. Mrs. Sanders says this is a familiar sequence.

Here we have expressed in dramatic form the full complexity of the heredity × environment interaction. It seems reasonable to assume that the initial differences in ability and rate of maturation favored Kurt, and that Kurt consequently was in less need of parental stimulation to maintain a steady developmental pace. For example, he was able to enrich his own environment at 7 and 8 months by crawling among his sibs, whereas Brent could not do this as yet. Brent thus suffered a considerably greater setback from parental indifference. This coupled with his precocious jealousy suggested that he had actively withdrawn from competition with Kurt over this period. He may well have been angry and hurt at Kurt's emerging mastery and popularity and could only express this by refusing to do anything. Fortunately, by 11 months, he was clearly on the road back, (see his Bayley Mental Scale results, Fig. 4-12) and, although mother had not been visibly perturbed by his regression, I felt relief.

Brent continued to improve at the 14½-month visit, while Kurt continued to develop along the lines previously seen: outgoing, jovial, and without an ounce of shyness. Of the 40 children in our study, Kurt proved the least fearful of strangers, having shown only brief wariness to a male stranger at 9 months.

> *14 months, 12 days.* Kurt walked right up to me and smiled broadly. He is a huge baby, who toddles around with his arms bent at the elbows. Brent does not walk yet, was quite shy, and hid behind mother for the first half-hour I was there. He had his eyes on me constantly, however, from his position behind mother.
>
> I tested Kurt first. He turned out to be quite demanding, and when I took a toy away from him, I had to substitute another quickly or he bawled. Brent squealed when things were taken from him but he was quick to turn to something else. This is probably directly related to their experiences with one another, for Kurt takes everything Brent has and Brent has little recourse but to look elsewhere. Brent is fragile, delicate, less able to get about, with rather poor over-all coordination.
>
> Kurt vocalized very complex sounds and imitated "thank you" when told to say it. Brent vocalized less and in high-pitched squeaky sounds. On the Bayley test, Kurt generally tested at his age level, and in some items went higher; Brent tested at the 11-month level. Nevertheless, Brent's progress has been steady; he crawls very well, stands, and is reported to have taken a step while holding on.

At the visit to the hospital playroom at 1½ years, aside from the major continuities, some new developments were apparent: Brent was developing a temper, and Kurt showed some signs of being very sensitive to adult disapproval. This report is by Mrs. Keller who saw them for the first time.

> *18 months, 17 days—Hospital playroom.* The differences in appearance between Kurt and Brent are so great that they do not seem like twins but like an older and younger brother. Brent has an immature, babyish face while Kurt looks like a little boy instead of a baby. Brent walks like a 1-year-old, standing very wide based and still very unsteady. This was particularly noticeable when he was pulling a wheel toy on the floor. He pulled it to him, then stood with feet widespread, rocking a bit, obviously wishing he could walk backwards, but unable to do so.

Brent was more wary of the situation and dependent on his mother than was Kurt. He looked frightened when he came into the testing room, but relaxed after Dr. F. boosted him in the air and put him down on a little chair. He was much more annoyed than Kurt at being forbidden the cookie, and mother volunteered afterwards that Brent generally reacts more severely to frustration.

Brent responded to many of the test items by throwing them fiercely to the floor. This seemed to be true mostly of those he did not understand. With the car, for example, his immediate response was to throw it, but after Dr. F. demonstrated rolling it across the table, he rolled it too. Similarly, he showed no comprehension of what to do with the doll when it was taken apart, and threw the head violently. Dr. F. picked it up and gave it back to him whereupon he poked his forefinger inside the head, chewed it a bit, and then lost interest. His hand control is still very immature and he uses his palms more than his fingers. Kurt looked at Dr. F. frequently for approval during his testing, and, in general, he showed a good deal more social involvement than did Brent. At one point during the motor tests, when Dr. F. playfully clapped his hands, he burst into tears apparently believing he had done something wrong.

It may be instructive to pause here and consider these developments in the context of the heredity-environment debate. Certainly Brent's jealousy vis-à-vis Kurt is attributable to his being constantly bested by his brother, and to that extent it is environmentally induced. On the other hand, the emotion of jealousy and the need for retribution seem to characterize all members of the species and must, therefore, be a product of our evolutionary past. Brent's flaring temper has undoubtedly been brought on in part by unfavorable comparisons with Kurt, but there is little doubt that anger *per se* is an evolved trait, possibly homologous at the phyletic level (Lorenz, 1966). Further, one cannot reasonably hold that all members of a species are equally endowed with a potential for jealousy, anger, shyness, or extraversion or that environmental circumstances alone account for differences in such behavior, for there is always individual genetic variation on panspecific traits. Thus we are back to our definition of personality as a unique variation on the basic species' theme, and to the equation:

$$\text{Environment} \times \text{Genotype} = \text{Phenotype.}$$

Given data such as these, one can only make a best or "most reasonable" guess as to the major source of phenotypic differences. It does seem reasonable to attribute the differences in jealousy and temper tantrums primarily to the circumstances of Brent's being second-best in everything, whereas Kurt's relatively rapid progress and the differences in introversion-extraversion seem primarily attributable to genotypic differences. No proximal cause seems to account for these differences, and they have persisted since the earliest months.

By 25 months, Brent had become very task-oriented and had finally caught up with Kurt on the Bayley Scales. However, personality differences have persisted, as this excerpt from the analysis of films indicates:

> *Films—25 months, 0 days.* The main difference between the boys seems to be that Kurt is oriented to the camera and the cameraman the entire time. Both are presented with the toy box and left to exploit it as they will. Brent turns his back to the camera and spends his time putting blocks into the cup, sitting stiff-legged all the while. Kurt spends a good deal of his time walking back and forth, jovially pointing, looking, or making noises at the cameraman.

At 4 years, 10 months, another surprise awaited us. Brent was coming into his own and had become quite an imaginative child. He appeared to outshine Kurt, now, in that he had a greater facility for creating fantasies and novel concepts.

> *4 years, 10 months.* Kurt has changed remarkably little, save for being bigger and older. He is known as the "smiling Irishman," outgoing, warm, and completely involved with the visitor. His drawings are big, robust, and fill the page. Brent, however, is a big surprise. He has flowered; he is now interested in everything, sensitive, rather bright, nicely verbal, and very cute. He appeared relatively independent in that Kurt was concerned with what Brent was drawing, but Brent was content to work on his own. His drawings were collections of detailed things he would then name. Apparent scrawls became tents, sails, or houses. He is an interesting boy now, with many subtle unknowns and with complex ideas. On the other hand, Kurt is outgoing, straightforward, and leaves one with no question marks. The Stanford-Binet was given, and the IQ's were comparable and above average (Kurt 111, Brent 107).

Several months later, the boys were brought to the hospital playroom for filmed interviews, and it appeared as if Kurt, despite his outgoing, devil-may-care appearance, was quite worried about letting go. During the separate interviews, each boy was presented with two inflated balloons and a pin and asked to puncture the balloons:

> *5 years, 2 months—Hospital playroom.* Brent immediately punctured both balloons and, indeed, seemed to enjoy it. Kurt, however, was extremely reluctant and told me quite openly that he was afraid. Finally, he punctured only one whereupon his face grew beet-red. It was my impression that he considered this a punishable offense.

Brent built a very sturdy tower of blocks with a broad base. When I said, "Now you can build anything you wish," he proceeded to space out the blocks in a very interesting design. Kurt built his tower straight up, and when asked to "build anything you wish," he refused and voluntarily started to put the blocks away. He thus appears to be developing considerable reluctance to express himself freely, at least in some areas.

Finally, independent testing some 4½ years later yielded a full scale IQ of 119 for Brent (performance 124, verbal 111) and a full scale IQ of 119 for Kurt (performance 114, verbal 120) on the WISC. Mrs. Hirsch, the tester, had not known anything of their previous history.

9 years, 7 months. Brent and Kurt are part of a large family of children living in a run-down, but warm house, out in the country. They are both attractive boys, but look and act unalike. For one thing, Kurt is a little taller. He is also more socially adept and outgoing, and he kept up a conversation between test items although he worked intently during testing. Brent, though friendly, is quiet and reserved, more serious, solemn, and hard-working.

Both boys stated they got along well with each other, and from what I observed, they had a very cooperative, companionable relationship. They seem to have many complementary qualities, most especially Brent's relative introversion and Kurt's extroversion.

During the interview, Mrs. Sanders characterized Brent as precise and definite, and said he wants everything to be perfect. Kurt is more socially oriented, likes attention, clowns around, and is the loudest in the family. Brent likes solitary activities, such as reading, and watching TV, and is not very active. Kurt is extremely active, moving about all the time. Mother said the boys get along well when with each other or in a group, but with just one other child present, they become competitive. On intelligence testing, both boys received the same overall scores, but there was an interesting difference in their relative strong points—Brent excelled on a performance task, Block Design, while Kurt excelled on the Similarities subtest, which involves verbal and reasoning skills. This appears to square with the fact that Brent spends much time on compulsive, solitary activities such as putting together puzzles, whereas Kurt is more socially and verbally active. Both boys were above average in virtually all areas of testing; the only relatively large difference was the one noted.

Summary. It was apparent from the start that Kurt and Brent were reacting to the same environment in radically different ways, based largely on the fact that, as fraternal twins, they are differentially constituted. Brent suffered more from his mother's anemic pregnancy than did Kurt and appeared less physically viable thereafter. All diseases hit him harder, his development was slower, and he had difficulty expressing himself in all ways over the first 2 or 3 years. At one anxious point in the first year (at the 9-month visit), Brent looked like a defective child; he grasped nothing that was offered him, stiffened his body when lifted, and could manage only a wan smile. An unusual regime of parental nonattention and a robust, fast-paced brother were probably at the root of this development lag, but as Brent developed the ability to crawl and to enrich his own life, these symptoms evaporated.

Kurt also flowered only after he was able to get about, starting at about 7½ months, and he has remained a robust, active, even jubilant extrovert.

At 3 years, Brent's strengths first became visible. He was better able to concentrate on puzzles than Kurt and was less inclined to shift aimlessly from task to task. By 5 years, in fact, the term "compulsive absorption" was used to describe Brent, but there was an interesting, if not creative, imagination also. Kurt, by comparison, had been a straightforward, loving, jovial soul from the first year, whose major worry at 5 seemed to be how to keep out of trouble and in the good graces of adults. At 9½ years, these descriptions were still reasonably applicable. The boys were about equally bright, although they exhibited somewhat different strengths, and seemed to be getting on very well in this youngster-filled home.

One might wish to make a case that the poorer physical status of Brent at birth was somewhat causative of his slowed development, and that an accident of birth rather than differential heredity is a more reasonable explanation of the differences observed. However, in the Tuscano twins we have already seen that the infant with the more difficult birth eventually far outdistanced her sister, so that this is not a sufficient explanation.

The next case, too, demonstrates the inadequacy of causal explanation based on relative viability at birth.

Case 4. Carl and Michael King, monozygotic boys (Pair K, Figs. 4-6 through 4-17). Carl, who was born 6 minutes after Michael, was a breech delivery with an Apgar rating of *one*! After Michael's uneventful delivery (his Apgar was 9), the cervix clamped tightly around Carl's feet and cord, and he was delivered with a heart beat but not breathing. The attending pediatrician saw him 10 minutes later and noted that "respirations had started, but were irregular, shallow, and the infant was cyanotic." He was suctioned and oxygen was delivered by mask, whereupon he slowly responded. It was about 1 hour before there were movements of the extremities and the respirations were satisfactory.

Yet, as we shall see, Carl is later judged the more vigorous of the two, with no visible sequelae whatsoever. Thus, birth trauma, while often a convenient explanation of differences, is rarely an adequate one.

The King twins were monochorionic, and Michael weighed 6 lb-9 oz. and

Carl, 6 lb-7 oz. Save for a bifid left ear lobe on Carl, these boys looked extremely alike, and one could not speak of the smaller or the bigger, as in most identical pairs. As a result there was much confusion over who was whom in the early weeks. Later, behavioral differences frequently provided the clues.

The parents of the King twins are Afro-American, and there was a brother 1½ years old at the time of the twins' birth. Father was 28, with a degree in engineering, and mother had attended a chiropractic school for 2 years beyond high school. To say immediately what will later become apparent, mother was a remarkable woman. At 36, and with two marriages behind her, she was mature, warm, philosophic, and had a questioning mind. There was much loving and affection in this family, although from the very start it was clear that there were also moments of considerable tension between the parents. Nevertheless, a visit to this house was nearly always a happy experience.

The first home visit was at 2 weeks of age and, as expected, Michael was more alert, cried more lustily, and had more vigorous movements. He tended to push his way to the top of his crib and cry after he got there. Carl tended to sleep most of the time, and was always found where he had been placed.

By 1 month, however, both he and Michael were very alert, and both were reported as smiling occasionally. Both followed moving objects and people very closely, but Carl seemed particularly interested in people. (This was a trend that was to continue over the next 10 years of the study.) The analysis of the film footage emphasized Carl's outgoingness; thus, the baby with the difficult birth seemed actually to be doing better.

> *Films—1 month, 0 days.* Michael cries a great deal in the bath and there are no indications of interest in the outside world. By contrast, Carl takes a long look at the cameraman or camera, and during feeding he looks in mother's direction. Carl seems more outgoing and less concerned with his own states. Michael, by contrast, is more tense and more prone to get upset.

On the next visit Carl had obviously continued his rapid emergence, although there were many more similarities than differences between the two:

> *2 months, 13 days.* Michael is now 9 lb-15 oz, compared to Carl's 11 lb-2½ oz. Mother immediately noted to me that Michael is now quiet and cries very little, and that Carl makes all the noise, eats more, and is physically more mobile. I gathered that she was rather proud of Carl's size and the fact that he has turned over three or four times to Michael's once.

Films—2 months, 13 days. The only difference we can agree on is that, in the bath, Michael is considerably more tense than Carl, keeps his hands fisted and out of the water, and holds his body stiff and straight. Carl, by contrast, sits with his hands dangling in the water and seems completely relaxed. Aside from this, both are interested in looking and passively taking in what's around them. The reaction to the removal of the bottle was almost identical—neither protested but just lay waiting for it to be replaced. Mother stroked the cheeks of both boys but neither smiled, and there is no strong fixation on a face as yet.

Michael and Carl were frequently confused with one another at home in these early months, and in the analysis of films at 4 months, we had similar problems.

Films—4 months, 0 days. Carl cried while being fed by spoon, while Michael took to it quite well. However, after Carl quieted down, the boys became extreme similar, and the four observers began searching for differences, largely in vain. We agreed only that Carl is somewhat more active than Michael. Otherwise, we could agree only on similarities. For example, both babies are passive and seem to take things in with their wide eyes and open mouths. Both generally accept what mother does to them; when she took away the bottle at the experimenter's behest, there was no visible protest, and they simply waited with mouth poised for the bottle to be restored.

By 5 months, both boys were becoming highly social, with Carl a bit more demonstrative:

5 months, 0 days. Carl is interested in looking at me, and he frequently arches his back to get a better look or to invite being picked-up. Michael, however, first became interested after I picked him up, and he then worked his way up to my face and put his nose against mine. Social interest has thus definitely set in, but with some differences in style.

At 6 months, what had been a moderate difference since 1 month erupted into a sharp one. Carl was now clearly more ebullient and outgoing:

6 months, 1 day. I noticed immediately that Carl was quite rambunctious; he spread his arms and arched his back, in his baby jumper, in an obvious invitation to pick him up. Michael, however, was collapsed in his jumper, droopy-eyed, and looking toward Carl constantly. Carl smiles and vocalized more readily, and his eyes dart to all who enter the room, inviting them to play. Michael simply watches.

Later, when the children were put on the floor, Michael was much livelier and the differences tended to evaporate. Both got up on their hands and toes as if to stand, but could not quite do it. Both were very interested in anybody talking, and they eyed that individual and smiled occasionally while watching. Both seemed very healthy and bouncy, with Carl somewhat more energetic.

Carl tended, thereafter, to receive higher ratings for extroversion and vigor, but Michael was always close behind. Michael became somewhat more subdued than usual as he underwent a period of fear of strangers at 8 and 9 months, but Carl exhibited similar behavior from 10 to 12 months, and was then more subdued than Michael.

The films taken over this period were summarized as follows:

Films—8 months through 12 months, 17 days. In general, Carl was more exuberant than Michael when with mother or strangers. Nevertheless, both would be at the outgoing end of an introversion-extroversion spectrum. Both are active and motorically precocious; both like being nuzzled and both smile frequently. They are extremely responsive to mother's affectionate kisses and highly affectionate themselves. At one point mother, their older brother, and a new puppy were all mutually engaged in what could be called a "love-in." It was this total joy in sociability that was by far the most impressive aspect of these films.

At 15 months, 1 day, another trend based on already familiar differences became evident. Michael's relative unexcitability became an advantage on the tests, for he was better able to concentrate on directions and complete tasks.

15 months, 1 day. When I came into the house, Carl ran toward me with his arms wide open wanting to be picked up; Michael, as usual, just watched. Carl was extremely active throughout the visit because of his hyperactivity he did not concentrate on test problems and did not do well. Michael was much more placid, looked carefully at each presented item, and while he did roam about during the tests, he followed directions very well and eventually performed well on the Bayley Mental Scale (Fig. 4-13). Carl, as usual, did better on the Motor Scale. Another differentiating characteristic was that Michael immediately set out to give me all his toys, and when he ran out of toys he gave me his blanket. Carl was only interested in direct contact with me. Carl's smile came easier and he has a hearty laugh. Michael smiled, stopped the smile, and then smiled again, as if he was not sure whether he should. Mother bathes all three boys together and she says Michael often ends up watching, while Carl and their older brother have themselves a riotous time.

20 months, 3 days—Hospital playroom. (Notes by Barbara Keller who had not seen these children before.) Both the King boys show a great amount of persistence; they really have minds of their own. They are both very active and move around a good deal during the testing, climbing off and on the chair, walking around the room, etc. This is somewhat more true of Carl than of Michael.

On the other hand, Carl was not as interested in the tests as was Michael. For example, only after he knocked the Bayley Board to the floor did he become interested in it; then he quickly placed 7 blocks correctly.

Michael seemed to be more motivated by the test items and achieved a somewhat higher Mental Scale score (Fig. 4-12). He grinned and waited for each peg as Dr. F. handed it to him, placing each one instantly. He felt, examined, and poked at the doll. He was very precise in such tests as placing the small cubes in the box or the larger cubes in the cup; he used his left hand most of the time.

Mother feels that Michael is now a cuddler and a mamma's boy, whereas Carl prefers to go his own way and is like his older brother in this respect. Carl also has temper tantrums if he does not get what he wants; he is quick to investigate all new things, and is often scolded as a result of these investigations.

There were no surprises at 3 years, 1 month, when both were tested at home with the Stanford-Binet. Each achieved a mental age of 3 years, 5 months, and we quote from the report:

3 years, 1 month. It wasn't too long before Carl dropped his suspiciousness and smiled at me, but Michael continued to furrow his brow. After a while I asked them if they remembered me, and Carl nodded yes. Carl didn't take long, then, to come over. He showed me a banged thumb; I stroked it, and then he showed me another bruise on his forehead. These and a scratch on Michael's cheek became the differentiating landmarks for the afternoon. Mother says she still mixes them up. Actually their behavior was sufficiently different vis-à-vis me so that I had little trouble. After Carl's initial direct approach, Michael came over and slowly but surely became dependent, insisting upon sitting on my knee. It was he who cried when I left, ostensibly because he wanted a pair of scissors in my toy-bag, but apparently because he became dependently attached within this short period. This trait seems due to family alignments: Mother says Carl and older brother team-up, leaving Michael on his own; when father is home, he is usually with the former two while Michael clings to mama.

Michael appears to have the edge in imagination. As he drew, he announced dragons, ghosts, Indians, and he had men jump from the paper at Carl to scare him. His speech, too, was filled with fantasy.

The boys came to the hospital playroom at 5 years, 6 months, for testing and a filmed interview. On the Stanford-Binet, Michael's IQ was 110, Carl's 113.

5 years, 6 months. Despite the similarity in test results there were some clear contrasts in behavior. Michael had his eyes on Dr. F. much of the time, concentrating on directions and the interchange. Carl, by contrast, seemed to take nothing seriously and was on the verge of being a "ham" the entire time. Unlike any other interviewee, Carl changed posture continuously, lying down, sitting, standing. Only during the balloon popping segment did Michael start moving as freely, and there he tried popping the balloon while Dr. F. was still blowing it up! Both boys were obviously excited by this segment, and both laughed hilariously at each bang. It was as if Michael saw this as permission to let himself go and yielded to it completely, whereas Carl seems perpetually loose and needs no excuse. One gets the distinct impression that they could quickly become a "terrible twosome" in a permissive situation, and mother confirms this. She told of a recent run-away party from school which Michael led; he is apparently better at *planning* mischievous escapades.

As with the other pairs discussed, the King twins were tested with the WISC some 5 years later by Mrs. Hirsch. Carl achieved a full scale IQ of 108 (verbal 106, performance 108); Michael's IQ was 120 (verbal 114, performance 122). This was her report:

10 years, 2 months. Carl and Michael are rather small, very good-looking boys who were dressed alike; both wore "natural" haircuts. They look very much alike, and the easiest way to tell them apart was by superficialities, such as Carl's chipped tooth and a small scar on Michael's cheek and nose.

In discussing how they spent their time and what they liked, it was interesting that both boys used pronouns "we" and "us" rather than "I" and "me." This was most noticeable with Carl and he seems more dependent on the twin relationship than Michael. The boys seem very close and both agree that they usually get along well and like to play together. Both stated that they had difficulty in getting along with their older brother at this time. Carl was more passive, less verbal, and less self-confident. He drew hesitantly, and several times erased the head of the figure and started over. He giggled nervously over difficult test questions. Carl's story to the first TAT card (boy and a violin) indicates his feeling of inadequacy and lack of competence in coping with what seem to him the very demanding tasks of daily life. He commented: ''The boy says, Well, how am I gonna play it? I've never seen it before and my music teacher says I have to play it by tomorrow.'' Michael's personality characteristics are not really very different from Carl's, but relative to Carl, he is much more assertive and self-confident. During testing he worked much faster and seemed more sure about the result of his efforts. On the WISC, Michael scored slightly and consistently higher than Carl on most of the subtests, and this seems to be reflected in their school achievement as well. The older brother commented that Michael was smarter, and Mrs. King says that she now feels closer to Michael, implying that his success at school pleases her greatly. One final comment: Although there are differences in personality and functioning between Carl and Michael, they are a matter of small degree; while not described in detail here, the similarities substantially outweigh the differences.

While this last report is unsatisfactory because of its brevity, it does appear that the years have not been entirely kind to Carl. He has gone from an ebullient, joyous infancy through a rather impulsive early childhood, to what now appears to be a low self-concept around competence and skills. Without doubt there are still times of joy for Carl but, given mother's emphasis on the importance of school achievement, the more competent Michael seems to have become her favorite. Interestingly, signs of Michael's greater competence were already visible at 15 months when his more subdued approach permitted greater concentration on objects and more success on the infant tests. Carl, by contrast, was then more of a social being. Now, at the age in which competence is all important for self-concept (cf. Erikson, 1950), Carl appears troubled, Michael relatively confident.

However, if the investigation of lives in progress has taught us anything, it is the folly of prediction on the basis of present performance. Certainly, within these broad outlines, some things like basic temperament or style of approach seem to persist over time, and so they have with Carl and Michael. But who could have predicted to the present system of forces involving school, mother, and self-concept? As already discussed, attempts at such prediction have been largely unsuccessful, probably because there are too many factors which feed back upon each other and continuously change the context.

Discussion. What is there to learn from these case histories? By and large the cases speak for themselves, but minimally they engender a respect for the strength of genotypic factors in the production of the phenotype. The level of intrapair differences is so enormously expanded in fraternals that, despite overlapping distributions on most measures, one gets the impression of two qualitatively different phenomena from the written histories of fraternal and identical pairs.

As mentioned at the outset, the distribution of intrapair differences on the Bayley Infant Behavior Profile (Fig. 4-8) reflects our personal experiences with regard to the four most alike pairs of identical twins, pairs A, B, C, and D. In each of these pairs, the personalities tended to merge into a single picture after a few hours and, unless our impressions of differences were recorded immediately, it became impossible to do so later. This merger could not be ascribed to greater physical resemblance, for there was less difficulty in recording other identical-looking pairs, such as the Kings, who exhibited more clear-cut behavioral differences.

However, even the King twins, who fall into the category of rather unalike identical twins, were frequently confused with one another. Often our expectation based on past experience with them was not fulfilled and we would feel momentarily bewildered. For example, it was not unusual among identicals for superiority on a particular task to switch around from one visit to the next (see also Burlingham, 1952). Fraternal children invariably contrasted more clearly, usually from the earliest months; as already mentioned, the reports of a fraternal pair were much easier to write.

Given the fact that fraternal intrapair differences were greater, and assuming this is for the most part accounted for by genetic factors, what is the source of those differences that did appear within identical pairs? We have already discussed Price's (1950) injunction regarding possible biases in twin studies on the basis of an unequal fetal blood supply in monochorionic identical twins. In addition to this possibility, Jinks (1964) has gathered much of the enormous literature on nongenetic influences in gametic transmission, and it is clear that nonchromosomal materials in the gamete are often unevenly distributed so that an early zygotic split, as in twinning, is bound to result in partial nonidentity of the cytoplasmic halves. Further, since different physical locations in the uterus may result in somewhat different placental circulation and nutrition, we can only marvel that our identicals were as similar as we found them.

Finally, it should be pointed out again that fraternal twins are a somewhat biased control group since, on the average, they share 50% of their genes. Unrelated infants should, of course, provide even greater contrast.

HEREDITY AND ENVIRONMENT: A HIERARCHICAL VIEW

Given the above evidence, there can be no reasonable doubt that there is genetic mediation of variations in intelligence and personality. In order to avoid misunderstanding, however, it should be emphasized that the phrase genetic mediation does not in any way imply *fixity* of a trait, for the phenotype changes as the combination of heredity and environment changes. In fact, this state of affairs assures us that the heredity-environment controversy will never be resolved, for its solution would involve the impossibly difficult task of subjecting each genotype to a random sample of environments. Additionally, there will always be the possibility that some novel unsampled environment will extract highly novel phenotypic changes from the genotype under study.[3]

Bateson (1972) has presented a hierarchical view of the built-in and the acquired which is most useful, and which does not make the mistake of opposing genome and environment. In Bateson's schema, human behavior forms a continuous hierarchical series ranging from conscious choice, to ontogenetically adaptive habit patterns, to fixed behavior patterns. (Note that, logically, even conscious choice must be represented at the DNA level or how else could one account for species differences in this behavior? Similarly, malleability of behavior is not equivalent with absence of genetic determination.)

Each step in the series is involved and is based on the preceding steps. Conscious choice, for example, is facilitated and dependent on the ability to form habit patterns in that habit frees the sensorium so that appraisal and choice might be made. That is to say, if it were not for our daily habits, each move would require conscious decision and, solely on the basis of energy requirements, the organism as we now know it could not survive.

Similarly, if the expectancy for tens of thousands of generations is the same, as for example in depth perception, there would be no need to learn the details of the task anew each generation. Again, on the basis of energy savings, it is a sensible system in which most aspects in the acquisition of depth perception are encoded in the genome, as indeed they must be (see Chapter 2).

Bateson's schema allows one to additionally posit transitional stages, as between habit and gene-encoded information. Some habits, such as disgust with fecal matter, may be easier to acquire than others because the genotype is sufficiently encoded in this direction to lower the threshold for acquisition. Thus, while not all cultures or individuals exhibit this trait, most do.

With such differentiations as these in mind, Fourcher (1968) examined a single sequence of behavior filmed in the course of our twin-study. It was a balloon-bursting sequence filmed (at sound speed) at 5 years of age. He did a frame-by-frame analysis of each child's behavior in this sequence which lasted approximately 2 minutes. It went as follows: The experimenter and child sat facing each other; the experimenter blew-up a balloon, tied it,

---

[3]The statistical term, heritability (H), is subject to the same logic (cf. Jensen, 1969). Without bothering with the formula, it is sufficient here to note that H refers only to the relative stability of the average expected environment. When the effective environment becomes more variable, H goes down, and when it becomes more stable, H rises.

opened a safety pin, and handed the balloon and pin to child while suggesting that he burst the balloon. After the first balloon was burst, the sequence was repeated.

The results appeared to bear out the hypothesis that behavior which is more reflexive, more fixed, will also be more concordant within identical twin pairs: (1) The reflexive reactions to the burst balloon, i.e., *startle intensity* and *startle length,* were significantly more concordant within identical pairs than within fraternal pairs ($p < .05$). (2) Nonintentional movement, i.e., *number of times the child was in locomotion, the number of changes in posture,* were of intermediate concordance ($p < .07$). (3) Behavior prejudged as socially motivated and of the set-goal variety, i.e., the *number of changes in orientation vis-à-vis the experimenter,* was completely idiosyncratic ($p < .36$).

While admittedly suggestive, these are not sufficiently strong data to back so important a point. It is therefore helpful to find that a similar hierarchy has been suggested by Vandenberg (1967) in a comprehensive review of twin-studies beyond childhood. As shown in Table 4-4, almost 65% of the twin-studies which utilized measures of *primary abilities* exhibited significantly smaller differences within identical than within fraternal pairs. At the other end of this arranged hierarchy, only 32% of the *personality* measures differentiated identical from fraternal pairs at the same levels of significance.

As suggested above, skills and abilities that aid the organism in coming to terms with situations that have been relatively invariant throughout evolu-

TABLE 4-4

Number of Measures in Each of Six Psychological Areas Which Gave
Evidence of a Hereditary Component[a]

	Area of measures	No. of measures	No. significant at .05 level or better	Percent measures showing significantly greater concordance within identical twins
a.	Primary mental abilities subtests	17	11	64.7
b.	Motor skills	14	8	57.1
c.	Perceptual tests	16	8	50.0
d.	Cognitive and achievement tests	18	7	38.9
e.	Sensory and musical	24	9	37.5
f.	Personality test scores [b]	28	9	32.1
	All measures	117	52	45.3

[a] After Vandenberg (1967).
[b] One could arrange a hierarchy within this single category, varying from tests of temperament which show high heritability (e.g., social introversion) through tests such as the Rorschach which invariably yield low heritability.

tion (e.g., perceptual constancies and primary cognitive abilities) should most probably be fixed and unmalleable. Consequently one would expect that they would exhibit substantial test-retest reliability within individuals and high concordance within identical twin pairs. On the other hand, since the social universe changes each generation, great malleability in social behavior has evolved, and tests which tap into this area would tend to have low test-retest reliability and low intra-twin concordance. With this in mind, one may view Table 4-4 as an hierarchical ranking of categories of behavior according to increasing degrees of ontogenetic flexibility, and it would appear that the ordering itself has come about through natural selection. That is, it is most reasonable to assume that the genome is equally active at all levels of the hierarchy, but that it has produced greater or lesser fixity in behavior as a result of phylogenetic selection.

In the same vein, a recent twin-study of the development of language in 2- and 3-year-olds (Fischer, 1973) yielded evidence for "deep" vs. "surface" structures in language. Measures were taken of vocabulary, sentence imitation, sentence comprehension, sentence production, word inflection, and phoneme discrimination; only word inflection did not yield a significantly high heritability score. An hierarchical arrangement of heritability was hypothesized by Fischer for the remaining factors, but the n was too small for any clear-cut decisions. Fischer points out that these results nevertheless support Chomsky's (1965) formulation of deep and surface structure and his idea of grammatical universals:

> According to Chomsky's 1965 formulation of a generative grammar, the addition of inflections to a string is a late occurrence in the transformational history of the derivation of a sentence. Inflections are the result of the application of surface structure realization rules, and are highly variable between natural languages. Rules for inflection usage may not be part of the universal grammar, and not part of the innate equipment Chomsky feels the language learner brings to his task.

Such an hierarchical view may or may not hold up with time, but we can reassert with logical certainty that heredity and environment are inseparable within individuals. Further, there is evidence for this assertion in current studies of twins: When the number of twin subjects in a study is low, as in our own studies, only composite scores and those based on repeated administrations have yielded significant within-pair differences between identicals and fraternals. But as the number of pairs is increased, more and more individual items differentiate identicals from fraternals. In one of the largest twin-studies to date, Nichols (1966) has collected data on 850 pairs, and an enormous number of items were found to be significantly "heritable." These included a large number of trivial items, such as whether or not one bleaches one's hair. This trend is so strong that it appears reasonable to project infinite instances of significance were an infinite number of twins tested. In other words, *every item of behavior has a genetic component residing somewhere within it.*[4]

If this view is correct, it bears out Hebb (1953) who insisted that, in the final analysis, all behavior is best thought of as 100% acquired and 100% inherited. It would indeed appear that as far as explanations of individual differences are concerned, science has artificially separated heredity and environment, and it now faces the essentially impossible task of putting them together again.

[4]The question of the *extent* to which a behavioral trait is inherited versus the extent to which it is acquired is basically an unsolved problem. This is usually dealt with by calculating a heritability (H) score based on within-pair differences of identical versus same-sexed fraternal twins. Unfortunately, this method is more often than not misleading (e.g., the high H in bleaching of hair). The answer to this seeming absurdity must lie in the analysis of what probably went into the finding: Presumably women of certain hair colors bleach with greatest frequency, and it makes sense to assume that the genetic component entered at the level of hair color. More often such an analysis is not possible, and we are left simply with an understandable score of heritability.

5
GROUP DIFFERENCES

Cultural anthropology has changed popular thought as few sciences have done in the past. We know, as did no earlier age, that the uniqueness shown by a nation or tribe is due largely to a lifetime of learning and social interaction within that given milieu. One can see on film the Balinese boy, Karba, growing from a universal infancy into a withholding, muted, graceful, expressionless child, a typical Balinese[1] (Bateson and Mead, 1942).

But was it a universal infancy? This is a reference to the very real possibility that the Balinese gene pool is unique in the world as a result of its specialized genetic history, and that Balinese are therefore somewhat uniquely constituted; and that not every child can achieve, say, Balinese grace given a Balinese upbringing. This somewhat touchy subject has received little attention, probably due to the spectre of racism, but hopefully that period is passing.

Let us first consider the genetics of the situation. In the evolutionary sense, all people are related since at some remote stage in their history they had common ancestors, and the Adam and Eve story is allegorically correct.

Thus, Harrison (1964) writes:

> So far as some particular population is concerned, its past size, if all individuals were unrelated, would have to have been far greater than it actually could have been since

[1] As an aside, the present author and Gregory Bateson recently visited the highland village of Bajung Gede in Bali and met Karba, who is now the village priest. I was struck by the fact that Karba was, even now in his forties, a contained and rather expressionless person, but this was in contrast to his more outgoing fellow villagers, and in very sharp contrast with the lowland Balinese (e.g., those of Batuan) who are decidedly outgoing, albeit graceful and dignified. It would appear that Karba, upon whom so great a theoretical point rested (''culture determines personality''), may be a constitutionally reticent individual.

> every individual has two parents, four grandparents, eight great-grandparents, and 2^n ancestors n' generations ago. Assuming that on the average there have been four generations per hundred years, an individual would have 2^{40}, or approximately a million million ancestors a thousand years ago if there had been no consanguinity. It seems probable that the total population of the world in the tenth century did not exceed 200 million, and it was very much smaller in yet earlier times [p. 158].

This reasoning which renders all men relatives also makes it clear that, in the history of any closed cultural group, there has been considerable inbreeding. This, together with the "founder" principle, i.e., the dependency of the gene pool on the founding generation, leads to the irrefutable conclusion that the gene-pool (the available alleles) is unique for each such population. In addition, there is the fact that different cultures may emphasize different mating tracks so that, as in the development of domestic breeds, unique cultural selective processes may lead to uniquely organized genotypes (Ginsburg and Laughlin, 1967).

Let us spell this out with a hypothetical example. Suppose there are two Polynesian islands, several hundred miles from each other, each populated by groups of five hundred persons with several islands similarly populated within this several-hundred-mile expanse. On Island A the people are friendly and outgoing; on Island B they are shy and retiring. Let us suppose the founding populations of each island were single families and that friendliness or shyness differentially characterized these two families. Let us suppose further that these characteristics were at least partially based on inherited temperamental differences, an assumption for which there is considerable evidence (cf. Chapter 4). It is not difficult to imagine that those Polynesian institutions which are conceivably affected by temperamental differences (e.g., public ceremonies) would take on a unique cast on each island. It seems highly likely, in fact, that it is such processes which help give rise to new cultural forms.

One implication of this reasoning is that the culture developed by an isolated group is particularly adjusted to the gene-pool of that group; that is to say, the culture developed by any homogeneous people must reflect the unique biology of that people—as, for example, its temperament.

There have been few actual data in this area, but it is now well known that Ghanda babies of Uganda are born with greater skeletal maturity and more developed motor abilities than comparable groups of European infants (Geber and Dean, 1966). In addition, Warren (1972) has reviewed lesser-known studies of sub-Saharan African groups; ten of twelve of these studies concluded that the African infants were more advanced motorically than Caucasian samples or Caucasian norms. The same pattern is seen in black-white comparisons in the United States (Curti et al., 1935; Knobloch & Pasamanick, 1958; Bayley, 1965; Walters, 1967).

The African and Afro-American infants appear generally to retain this relative precocity through the second year, or until the tests become progressively more dependent on speech, and when gross motor items are no longer used (e.g., how well a child plays ball, leaps, and jumps rope are never part of an IQ examination). The Caucasian children subsequently do better, largely due to greater facility with verbal abstractions. The usual interpretation of the switchover at age 3 is that there is less chance for African and Afro-American children to apply verbal abstraction in their environments (e.g., Geber & Dean, 1957), although Jensen (1969, 1973) has presented a reasonably good argument that gene-pool differences may be behind these test differences.

In another comparable study of 100 Mayan infants in Chiapas, Mexico, Brazelton et al. (1969) have reported that these babies were substantially different from a Caucasian sample in temperament and coordination throughout the first year, again starting with data obtained immediately following birth. For one thing, the Mayan neonates exhibited almost none of the normally occurring spasmodic movements so common in Caucasian newborns, and maintained smoother gross motor movements throughout the first year.

Our own work has concentrated on newborns, before they have had social contact with their mothers, in order to better assess the possibilities of gene-pool differences between relatively isolated populations. Thus far, this work has involved testing with the *Cambridge Neonatal Scales* (Brazelton and Freedman, 1971) within seven ethnic groups, as listed in Table 5-1.

TABLE 5-1

Ethnic Groups Administered Infant Behavioral and Neurological Scales

Ethnic group	Place	Predominant socioeconomic class	n	Tester(s)
Chinese-American (2nd through 5th generation)	San Francisco	Middle	24	D. G. Freedman N. Freedman
Japanese-American (3rd and 4th generations)	Hawaii	Middle	41	D. G. Freedman N. Freedman
Navajo	New Mexico, Arizona	Lower	36	D. G. Freedman N. Freedman
Afro-American	Chicago	Lower	84	J. Kuchner J. Durfee
Predominantly Hausa	Northern Nigeria	½ Lower (public hospital) ½ Middle (private hospital)	22	D. G. Freedman
European-American (2nd through 4th generation	San Francisco Hawaii, and Chicago	Middle	65	D. G. Freedman N. Freedman J. Kuchner
Australian Aborigine	Darwin, Australia	Lower	17	D. G. Freedman J. Callaghan

Note: The criterion for all but the Afro-American group was four grandparents of the same ethnic background as baby. Skin color alone was used as the criterion for Afro-Americans.

CHINESE-CAUCASIAN DIFFERENCES

The first study, a comparison of Chinese-American and European-American newborns, was reported in *Nature* by Freedman & Freedman (1969) as follows:

> Twenty-four Chinese-American and twenty-four European-American newborns were examined while still in the nursery. The Orientals were largely of Cantonese background. All families were middle class and the bulk were members of a pre-paid health plan (Kaiser hospital, Table 5-2). Table 5-2 summarizes the potentially

TABLE 5-2

Comparisons of Potential Covariables
[after Freedman and Freedman (1969)]

	Chinese-American	European-American
Mean age and range in hours (N.S.)	32.75 (7–75)	33.27 (5–72)
Initial state (rated 1–6, from deep sleep to very alert) means (N.S.)	3.58	2.79
Distribution of sexes[a]	11 male, 13 female	11 male, 13 female
Mean birth weight in grams [b] ($p = .05$)	3,194.33	3,447.91
Mean Apgar [c] rating at 5 min after birth (N.S.)	8.86	9.00
Mean hours of labor (N.S.)	6.08	5.77
Medication during labor [d]	16 received systemic drugs	13 received systemic drugs
	8 received only local anesthetic or none	11 received only local anesthetic or none
Mean age of mothers (N.S.)	26.70	26.66
gmean number of previous pregnancies (N.S.)	1.83	2.41
Hospital	16, Kaiser Hospital, San Francisco	20, Kaiser Hospital, S.F.
	5, Chinese Hospital, S.F.	4, Lying-in, Chicago
	3, U.C. Medical Center, S.F.	

[a]There was no significant interaction between race and sex.

[b]When weight is treated as a covariable it does not affect ethnic differences.

[c]A rating of viability; based on heart rate, colour, respiration, tonus, and crying. Optimal score is 10.

[d]Although systemic drugs significanty lowered Apgar ($p = .02$), automatic walk ($p = .02$) and tonic deviation of the head ($p = .02$), statistical treatment indicates that these drug differences did not affect ethnic differences.

important covariables other than ethnic group, and we see that none could have accounted for the ethnic differences presented here.

The behavior scales (Brazelton and Freedman, 1971) consisted of twenty-eight general behavioral items rated 1–9 and eighteen standard neurological signs, frequently used to screen for neural damage, rated 0–3.[2] The twenty-five general items may be somewhat arbitrarily arranged into five categories as follows: (1) temperament – five items; (2) sensory development – three items; (3) autonomic and central nervous system maturity – eight items; (4) motor development – six items; (5) social interest and response – six items. As will be seen, any single item may overlap categories (e.g., lability of skin color can reflect temperament as well as autonomic maturity).

All testing was done during September and October, 1968. Each test session lasted between 30 and 40 minutes. Testing was performed in the newborn nursery by the author's wife as the author watched, and scoring was done immediately afterwards in a room next to the nursery. Apart from a reliability sample which was marked independently, scoring depended on verbal agreement between the testers.[3]

A multivariate analysis of variance indicated that, on the basis of total performance, the two groups were decidedly different ($p = .008$). Further analysis indicated that the main loading came from the group of items measuring temperament, and those that seemed to tap excitability/imperturbability ($p = .001$). While the following discussion is based on mean ethnic difference on the distinguishing items, it should be emphasized that

[2] The author is aware of the many more exacting techniques available for measuring newborn behavior. These include the optokinetic nystagmus technique for measuring the amount of visual arc discriminated (Gorman et al., 1959), photography of pupillary movement (Wickelgran, 1967), cardiac acceleration rates and respiration changes transferred to an EKG console (Lipton & Steinschneider, 1964), mechanized measure of headturning (Papousek, 1967); certainly many more mechanized measurements can be and probably will be devised. However, a decision had to be made: We could either measure a few behaviors with sophisticated equipment, or else tap a wide spectrum and rely on the examiner's judgment as the major source of measurements. We chose the latter route because we indeed wished to tap as wide a spectrum of behavior as possible in these initial studies. We look forward, however, to further studies of ethnic comparisons using techniques such as those mentioned.

[3] As a reliability check, twenty-one cases have been scored independently by the author and Mrs. Freedman over the various ethnic groups they have tested together. Only two items reported in this chapter, *consolability* and *following the face-voice*, achieved a Pearson r of less than 0.65. The correlation in these items was 0.49 and 0.52, respectively, due to the occurrence of large discrepancies in a few cases. These items were retained since they had achieved correlations above 0.90 on a previous reliability sample. Overall, the average correlation was 0.82, the twenty-fifth percentile $r = 0.88$, and the seventy-fifth percentile $r = 0.70$.

We cannot leave the subject of reliability without stating Bock's (personal communication, 1970) somewhat unorthodox but sensible view. He points out that, due to high variance, inherently unreliable items would be unlikely to differentiate two comparison groups. The very fact that an item does so is *prima facie* evidence of its reliability.

there was substantial overlap in range on all scales between the Chinese and Caucasian infants.[4]

The European-American infants reached a peak of excitement sooner (rapidity of build-up, Fig. 5-1) and had a greater tendency to move back and forth between states of contentment and upset (lability of states, Fig. 5-2). They showed more facial and bodily reddening (Fig. 5-3) probably as a consequence. The Chinese-American infants were scored on the calmer and steadier side of these items. In an item called *defensive movements,* the tester placed a cloth firmly over the supine baby's face for a few seconds. While the typical European-American infant immediately struggled to remove the cloth by swiping with his hands and turning his face, the typical Chinese-

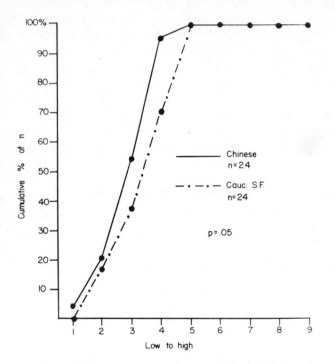

Fig. 5-1 Rapidity of build-up. A rating of how quickly the infant reaches a state of excitement from the initial state.

[4]Inasmuch as the following basic items were significantly different among ethnic groups, they were statistically "eliminated" from all our analyses: age of infant, Apgar rating, mother's age, number of previous pregnancies, length of labor, and presence or absence of systemic medication. All probability values on graphs in this chapter were calculated with these covariates eliminated.

Also, since in this type of test there is the possibility of systematic biases developing in individual testing technique, despite attempts to avoid it, some of these differences may be artifactual. We will, therefore, confine the following discussion only to those items which conform with our actual experiences during testing. In other words, in addition to their statistical significance, our subjective confidence is quite high in all findings reported here.

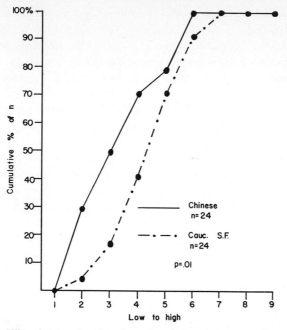

FIG. 5-2 Lability of states. A rating of number of state-changes over the entire test.

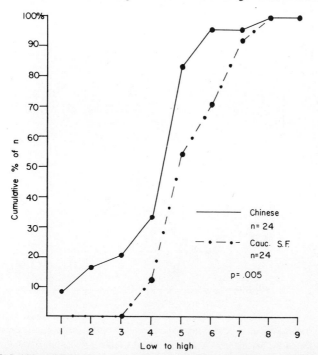

FIG. 5-3 Lability of skin color. A combined rating of number and strength of skin-color changes.

American infant lay impassively, exhibiting few overt motor responses (Fig. 5-4). Similarly, when placed in the prone position, the Chinese infants frequently lay as placed, with face flat against the bedding, whereas the Caucasian infants either turned the face to one side or lifted the head (Fig. 5-5). Inasmuch as there was no difference between the groups in the ability to hold the head steady in the upright ($p = .91$, pull to sit), this maintenance of the face in the bedding is taken as a further example of relative imperturbability, or ready accommodation to external changes. (Another possible explanation for these differences involves the obvious difference in nasal bone structure between Orientals and Caucasians, with the average Caucasian nose considerably larger.) In an apparently related item, rate of habituation, a pen light was repeatedly shone on the infant's eyes, and the number of blinks counted until the infant no longer reacted (shuts-off). The Chinese infants tended to habituate more readily (Fig. 5-6).

There was no significant difference in amount of crying, and when picked up and consoled, both groups tended to stop crying. The Chinese infants were, however, often dramatically immediate in their cessation of crying when picked up and spoken to, and therefore drew extremely high ratings in

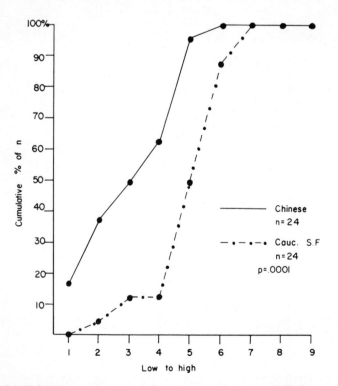

FIG. 5-4 Defensive movements. A cloth is placed firmly over the infant's nose, and the energy expended and the success of his attempts to remove it is rated.

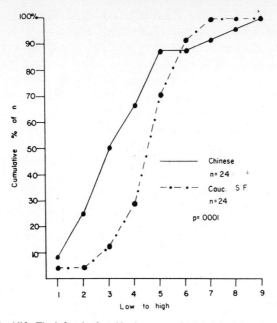

FIG. 5-5 Head lift. The infant is placed in the prone with hands at either side of the head, and the height of head lift is then rated.

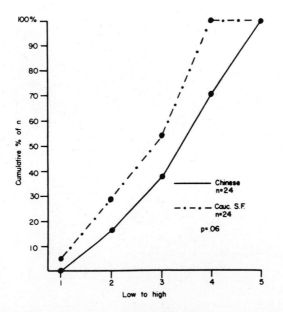

FIG. 5-6 Habituation. A pen light was shone on the infant's eyes at about half-second intervals, and the number of reactive blinks counted. When blinking ceased, the infant was said to be habituated.

consolability (Fig. 5-7). The Chinese infants also tended to stop crying sooner without soothing (self-quieting ability, Fig. 5-8).

To summarize, the majority of items which differentiated the two groups fell into the category of temperament. The Chinese-American newborns tended to be less changeable, less perturbable, tended to habituate more readily, and tended to calm themselves or to be consoled more readily when upset. In other areas (sensory development, central nervous system maturity, motor development, social responsivity), the two groups were essentially equal.

There is some evidence that similar differences characterize these two ethnic groups at later ages as well, although the data are far from conclusive. Green's (1969) study of nursery schoolers in Chicago provides evidence for similar temperamental differences at 3 and 4 years of age. The study, which was an attempt to compare children's use of space in a Chinese-American and European-American nursery school, concluded that European-American children spent significantly more time in approach and interaction behavior, and that Chinese-American children spent more time concentrat-

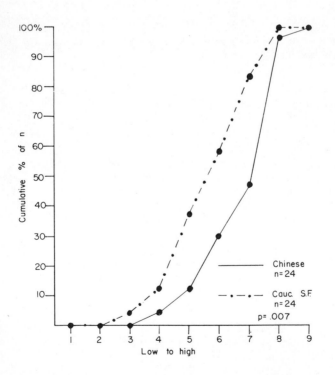

FIG. 5-7 Consolability. The ease with which a crying baby can be consoled, ranging from a hand on the stomach while in the bassinet to rocking in the arms while speaking softly.

ing on individual projects. More revealing than her quantitative findings, however, are her comments:

Although the majority of the Chinese-American children were in the "high arousal age," between 3 and 5, they showed little intense emotional behavior. They ran and hopped, laughed and called to one another, rode bikes and roller-skated just as the children did in the other nursery schools, but the noise level stayed remarkably low and the emotional atmosphere projected serenity instead of bedlam. The impassive facial expression certainly gave the children an air of dignity and self-possession, but this was only one element effecting the total impression. Physical movements seemed more coordinated, no tripping, falling, bumping or bruising was observed, no screams, crashes or wailing was heard, not even that common sound in other nurseries, voices raised in highly indignant moralistic dispute! No property disputes were observed and only the mildest version of "fighting behavior," some good natured wrestling among the older boys. The adults evidently had different expectations about hostile or impulsive behavior; this was the only nursery school where it was observed that children were trusted to duel with sticks. Personal distance spacing seemed to be situational rather than compulsive or patterned, and the children appeared to make no effort to avoid physical contact [p. 6].

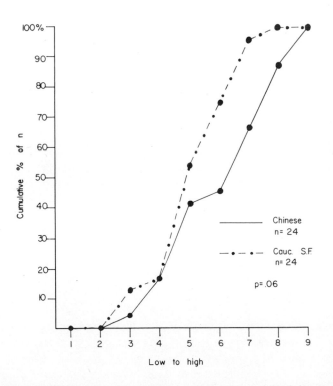

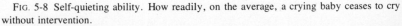

FIG. 5-8 Self-quieting ability. How readily, on the average, a crying baby ceases to cry without intervention.

It is common observation in public schools of San Francisco's Chinatown that the Chinese children there are similarly restrained and rarely fight over toys; we have made similar observations in nursery schools in Hong Kong and Shanghai. Further, my wife has spent considerable time observing in San Francisco schools and has noted much the same differentiation there throughout the public school years. Also, in some work we were doing on stereotypes among high school students, San Francisco Chinese saw their Caucasian counterparts as "flying off the handle" with slight provocation, as being gauche and without sensitivity for the feelings of others, and as generally difficult to "be with." Caucasian students reversed these so-called stereotypes in their comments on the Chinese: Orientals were cool or unemotional, were hard to get to know, hid their feelings, tended to stick together, but were also difficult to be with.

As the work on LeVine (1966) indicates, the streotypes one people have of another rarely misses the mark altogether, and often the picture is agreed to by those being stereotyped. Disagreement, he points out, is largely in the value dimension, with each people usually believing their own traits to be good and the other's bad.

While there is substantial cultural continuity between the Chinese communities in Shanghai, Hong Kong, San Francisco, and Chicago, the fact that Chinese newborns already show a disposition toward nonexcitability and accommodation to external change leads logically to a genetic hypothesis with regard to these Chinese-Caucasian differences. On the other hand, it must again be pointed out that any phenotype is subject to change, depending on the interaction of the genotype and environment. A recent study conducted by Kuchner (1973) indicates that the presumed Chinese-Caucasian differences in temperament is no exception to this rule. In a study conducted in Chicago, Kuchner observed Chinese and Caucasian newborns in their families from birth through 5 months of age, focusing upon mother-infant interactions. All families were upper middle-class. In her initial report of this ongoing study, she states that while many of the differences on the Cambridge Scales reported above were also exhibited by the newborns she studied, relatively few differences were to be seen in mothers' attitudes toward the infants. All mothers, whether Chinese or Caucasian, had become "Americanized" and formed a more or less homogeneous group.

On the other hand, Kuchner found that Chinese mothers interacted less with their infants than did the Caucasian mothers, even as Caudill and Weinstein (1969) had reported for a group of Japanese mothers in Japan, who were compared with a group of American Caucasian mothers. However, Kuchner suggests that the reason for this finding among her groups is that the Chinese infants were, on the average, less evocative. In her preliminary analysis of five Chinese and five Caucasian babies matched for sex and birth order, Caucasian babies changed state more frequently, had longer average active periods, spent more of the diapering time active or fussy, spent less time asleep or crying and more time in an awake, alert state. These differences follow rather directly upon the differences found in temperament at birth, and they seem adequate to account for the differential interactions between mothers and infants. Thus, while the process of ''Americaniza- tion'' may achieve a common end point in the child-rearing attitudes of mothers of different ethnic groups, child-rearing practices may nevertheless differ because of differences in the infants themselves.

There can be no doubt, therefore, that heredity and culture interact as a feedback process, and that each contributes to the other in a multitude of ways. This chapter is not intended then as an argument for genetic deter- minism; rather its intention is to put into question explanations based solely on cultural determinism.

OVERALL ORIENTAL-CAUCASIAN COMPARISONS

The geographic and historical links between Japan and China are clear, but the Oriental origin of American Indians is a surprise to some. It is, however, fairly certain that the Navajos, an Athapaskan Indian subgroup, descended from a migratory Asian people who came to rest in Northern Canada before 200 B.C. Migrating into the area, now the United States Southwest, by about 1400 A.D., the Navajos mixed to some extent with the Pueblos and other established descendants of earlier Asian migrations. To this day, some words in Navajo are nearly identical with present Chinese, and many more can be connected with primitive Sino-Tibetan languages (Shafer, 1952).

Thus, a gene-pool hypothesis is supported by the fact that all the new- borns of Oriental background differed from the Caucasian sample on the very same temperamental items as in the Chinese-Caucasian comparisons. The combined Oriental groups (Chinese, Japanese, and Navajo, $n=101$) were compared with an expanded European-American population ($n=65$) on the same items reported above, and save for *lability of skin color* (Fig. 5-9), the same contrasts persist. (This exception was largely due to the Navajo sample and will be discussed below.)

The most frequently posed alternative to a gene-pool hypothesis is that diets may be a more important causal factor. However, when one considers the fact that the Navajo were all of lower socioeconomic level, and the Chinese and Japanese of middle level or higher, and that diet among the Navajo was in no way comparable with the other groups, one is hard put to explain these results at the nutritional level.

If these differences between Orientals and Caucasians do involve differ- ences in respective gene-pools, how and why has this come about? As we have already said, culture and temperament may be thought of as two aspects of a complex cybernetic system in which each has contributed to the other in a multitude of ways. If there were substantially different founding populations for these two human racial groups, we would expect rather different developmental pathways to emerge at both biological and social levels. This would be so even if there were steady communication at both genetic and cultural levels, between Caucasian and Oriental populations, since once developmental pathways are set they become conservative and tend to maintain direction (cf. Waddington, 1954).

What do we know about the founding populations? In a controversial but nevertheless well-documented section of his book, Coon (1962) has noted that at the stage of *homo erectus*, some 360,000 years ago, Oriental and Western subgroups were already distinguishable one from the other, and many of the details of Peking man's skull, for example (Sinanthropus), demonstrate substantial continuity with current Oriental features. To quote Coon (1962), "Were one to enlarge the Sinanthropus brain by about 300 cc., reduce the brow ridges, shorten the palate, and reef in the zygomatic arches by about 15 mm., it would be hard to tell this specimen from a modern Mongoloid . . . [p. 447]."

While few argue with Coon's descriptions, his assertion of localized evolution from erectus to sapiens has been roundly criticized, since it appears to pose separate speciation for eastern and western hominids, an unlikely set of events to be sure. However, if one allows that genetic exchange was occurring more or less continuously between the eastern and western races of *Homo erectus*, it is likely that each helped the other advance into the sapient form. In addition, one must remember that the terms erectus and sapiens are arbitrary and have been superimposed on a gradual process of change.

It thus appears that there was a pre-sapiens subgrouping of Oriental and Occidental hominids, in forms akin to their present differentiation, and that an East-West division in gene-pool goes back over 360,000 years, although it is most likely that the gene-pools were not so isolated that they could not contribute one to the other.

While we do not offer it as proof for these contentions, our results with the newborn tests are consistent with this notion of partial genetic isolation. On the one hand, the substantial overlap on almost all scales speaks for the basic similarity of all gene-pools thus far sampled. On the other, we found that each of the six ethnic groups was unique in some respect or another. Of the 48 items on the *Cambridge Neonatal Scales*, 30 significantly differentiated ethnic groups at a probability of .05 or less, and 9 of these items were significant at the probability of less than .0001. That is, despite substantial overlap in scores, *averages* tended to vary significantly.

If one then accepts the notion of different average gene-pools with regard to temperament in Oriental and European populations, are there any culture correlates of consequence? A full answer would itself involve a complete work, so let us just note some obvious initial ideas. A number of scholars (cf. Chiang, 1960; Nakamura, 1964) have commented on the polarity in Eastern and Western art with regard to the relative primacy of nature as opposed to egoistic man. In Western tradition, at least as far back as classic Greece, the heroic male abounds in both sculpture and painting. By contrast, there is nothing of that tradition in Chinese and Japanese art. In Chinese traditional painting, for example, men and women are frequently reduced to stick figures dotting the rising mountains of village China. Nature itself is primary, and human figures are merely part of the landscape. When human figures are the central theme, they are formalized and most often contemplative. That Japanese art has some of the same flavor is not surprising (cf. Nakamura, 1964), but it is perhaps surprising that Navajo poetry and philosophy (their art is strictly religious) similarly stresses the continuity and harmony between man and nature, and expresses suspicion at attempts to tamper with "natural ways" (cf. Gorman, 1973). Their greatest and most persistent philosophical conflict with the white world is just this issue of tampering with nature and its presumed sinfulness.

We must, then, conclude this section with a number of questions. Is it possible that the temperamental differences noted between Oriental and Caucasian populations in our studies are bound up with these cultural differences? If so, is it a general phenomenon, and does the average temperament exhibited by a group and their culture invariably fit with one another? Are there notable exceptions? What of the inevitable variations within an ethnic group? These questions, in effect, are proposals for further research since only in that way can they be answered satisfactorily.

NAVAJO SAMPLE

The Navajo infants exhibited two outstanding differences from all other groups: a tendency for the entire body to become red when excited and to remain that way for much of the examination (Fig. 5-9), and a remarkable absence of any leg support reaction (Fig. 5-10), or automatic walk (Fig. 5-11). Note, also, the high kyphosis (Fig. 5-12) which reflects the rather collapsed posture when Navajo babies were pulled to the sitting position. Finally, low ratings on *crawling movements* and *passive movements of the lower limbs* (Fig. 5-13) again reflected the lack of tension and the remarkable malleability of the lower limbs. (Highly malleable lower limbs may be related to the fact that "congenital hip" is very common among the Navajos [U.S. Public Health Service, 1969], possibly because of weak muscling around the hip joint.)

While there are no figures on the rate of motor maturation in Navajo infants, Dennis (1940) reported that the average Hopi infant walked at 14½ months; this is approximately 2½ months later than the European-American average, and 3½ to 4 months later than African and Afro-American averages. Judging by the malleability of the Navajo's lower limbs, we would predict similar later walking for them.

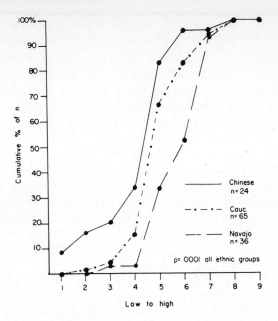

FIG. 5-9 Lability of skin color. The Navajo infants showed unusually high and persistent reddening of the skin when crying.

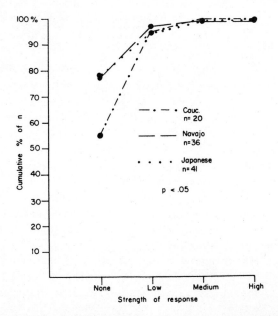

FIG. 5-10 Leg-support reaction. An infant is held under his armpits with feet touching the table. Very few Navajo infants attempted to stiffen their legs to support the body, while among other groups this was an average reaction.

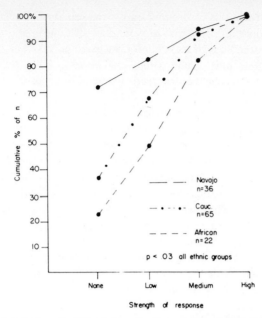

FIG. 5-11 Automatic walk. When held under the armpits so that the feet are on a surface, most neonates stiffen their legs and then start stepping. African neonates exhibited higher and more stepping than average, while most Navajo infants exhibited no walking at all.

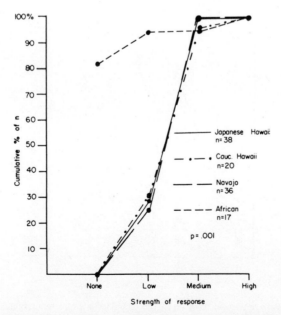

FIG. 5-12 Kyphosis. When pulled to a sitting position, the average neonate's back becomes rounded, and this is called kyphosis. African neonates tended to hold their backs erect. Variations in African n are due to the fact that these scales were introduced after the start of the African study.

The question arose in the Dennis study, and remained unresolved, as to whether cradleboarding of infants or gene-pool differences was the basis for the observed differences in Indian and Caucasian norms. The present data tend to confirm Dennis' feelings that cradleboarding has little effect on motor behavior and that the observed differences are probably rooted in genetic differences.

In addition to these low scores in lower-limb adequacy, Navajo newborns were rated lowest of all groups on vigor, muscle tonus, irritability, and on reaction to a pinprick. In other words, they were judged on the passive, nonreactive side of items in which such a distinction was possible.

This brings up the commonly heard speculation that the subdued emotionality commonly observed in Navajo youngsters is due to an infancy on the cradleboard. This frequently expressed notion, however, seems to reverse the actual situation. It appears instead that Navajo babies are suited physically and temperamentally to the cradleboard in that they are more likely to *permit it* than highly active and complaining babies. The more accurate statement is that cradleboarding probably represents a marriage between cultural practice and infant constitution.

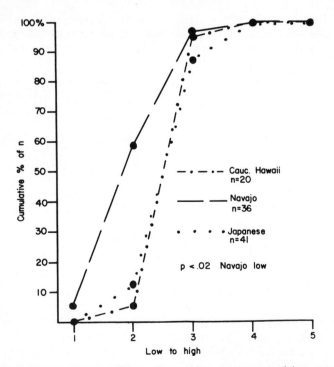

FIG. 5-13 Passive movement of legs. The examiner attempts to straighten and bend the limbs, noting rigidity vs. malleability; the legs of Navajo newborns were extremely flexible.

JAPANESE-AMERICAN SAMPLE

Caudill and Weinstein (1969) carefully studied Japanese and Caucasian mothers and their infants, between 3 months and 1 year of age, and noted that the Japanese infants cried and vocalized much less than the Caucasian babies. Although the babies were never observed at a point where these differences did not exist, the authors nevertheless attributed the differences to differential handling by the mothers. On the other hand, we have already noted that crying Japanese-American newborns were very easy to quiet and tended to console themselves quickly (although not quite as rapidly as did the Chinese-American and Navajo babies). Given that appproximately the same behavior is present at birth, a gene-pool hypothesis cannot be ignored. While it must be true that mothers of different cultures differentially reinforce their babies' behavior, we must again point out that cultural norms and biological predispositions appear frequently to act in concert.

Caudill and Weinstein (1969) also found that 3- to 4-month-old European-American infants were so much more active than a comparable sample from Japan that virtually all of the Caucasian cases are above the median and all the Japanese cases below it. The authors explained this striking difference in environmental terms, involving some of the equally striking differences in maternal treatment and infant living conditions.

But, as LeVine (1970) points out: "Whether this result is accounted for in environmental or genetic terms, such a major difference in gross activity level at three to four months must be taken into consideration in attempting to assess the impact of subsequent child rearing practices. In other words, even at this early age, we cannot assume a behaviorally constant organism across these two populations [p. 576]."

We can only agree, and if one turns to Fig. 5-14, it may be seen that as a newborn population the Oriental group exhibited significantly less spontaneous activity than either the European-American or the African babies. The evidence thus becomes very strong, once again, that gene-pool factors are primary. LeVine, in fact, concluded that if we cannot assume a behaviorally constant organism "for middle-class Japanese and Americans, are we safe in assuming it for any other pair of populations of diverse origin?"

Yet another aspect of the Japanese-American babies is that they were the most consistently tremulous group and also exhibited considerable spontaneous startle. (Orientals as a group were the most tremulous. See Fig. 5-15.) Perhaps as a consequence, or else due to a common cause, following with head and eyes was also significantly depressed (Fig. 5-16).

While we are not sure how this syndrome actualizes itself beyond the newborn period, the observations of Dr. Marshall, a private pediatrician in Hawaii, are suggestive. He has informed us that the Japanese infants in his

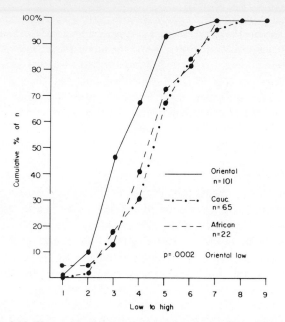

FIG. 5-14 to 5-19 The combined Oriental group (Chinese-American, Japanese-American, Navajo) compared to the combined Caucasian group (Chicago, San Francisco, Hawaii). The results closely parallel the findings of the first study (FIG. 5-1 to 5-8).

FIG. 5-14 Activity. The combined Oriental group exhibited significantly less spontaneous activity than the other two groups.

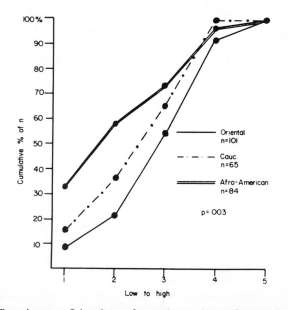

FIG. 5-15 Tremulousness. Orientals were frequently tremulous, Afro-Americans rarely so.

practice react much more severely to their first immunization shots at 3 months than do his Polynesian patients, and that the Japanese babies exhibit more fright on subsequent visits, thus indicating remarkable memory and remarkable sensitivity. Similarly, in our work with twins we have found that infants who were easily startled in the neonatal period later exhibited a greater fear of strangers than their sibs; our interim hypothesis is that higher levels of tremulousness and startle among newborns may reflect a congenitally lower threshold to vigilance reactions.

NIGERIAN SAMPLE

Geber and Dean (1966) reported a number of reflex responses reduced in Ghanda infants (Uganda) when compared with the infants of Caucasians living in Uganda; similarly, in our North-Nigerian sample, the Moro response and the Babinski reflex were relatively muted (Figs. 5-17 and 5-18). However, Geber and Dean's findings that African infants are born nearly a month more mature than Caucasian infants (ergo the reduced reflexes) cannot be confirmed. To judge by our sample, admittedly removed from hers by over 1000 miles, the Nigerian infants seem rather to be specifically precocious in the motor area, most particularly in their excellent ability to

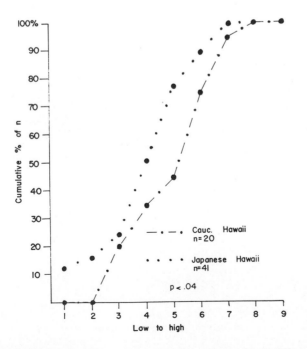

FIG. 5-16 Following with head and eyes. Japanese neonates did not follow as closely inanimate objects moved across the visual field.

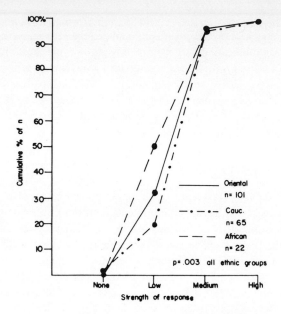

FIG. 5-17 African neonates had a relatively reduced Moro response and Caucasian neonates had a relatively high response. The response was elicited by a sudden drop of the head-end of the bassinet.

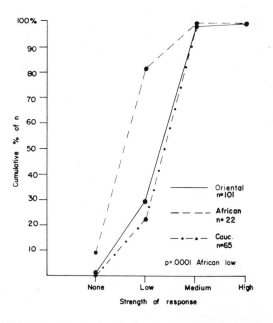

FIG. 5-18 The Babinski reflex, a splaying-out of the toes when the inside of the sole is lightly stroked. The African neonates tended to exhibit a low response.

hold up the head in the prone (Fig. 5-19), in their strong neck and shoulders, evidenced in the pull-to-sit (Fig. 5-20), and in the briskness of the automatic walk (Fig. 5-11). More generally, the African infants were simply precocious in exhibiting fully integrated musculature at so early an age. For example, one Nigerian (Hausa) infant of 45 minutes of age had full head control in the pull-to-sit, exhibited a straight back with no kyphosis, and was able to hold a sitting position and look around the chamber while held by his hands. Another, 24 hours old, exhibited the Wolfe-Landau response, a full extension of the head and feet while rocking on the belly, a response not usually seen in Caucasians before the second or third month. The Nigerian infants were the only group who consistently exhibited *lordosis*, a concavity of the back when pulled to sit — a herald of the subsequent excellent posture seen throughout sub-Saharan Africa (Fig. 5-21). In the same vein, kyphosis, a collapsed rounding of the back in the sitting position, was very low (Fig. 5-12). In areas other than motor behavior, no noteworthy differences were seen between the African and other babies.

As for follow-up data on this motor precocity, Geber and Dean (1957) and Ainsworth (1967) found that the African babies in Uganda continued to

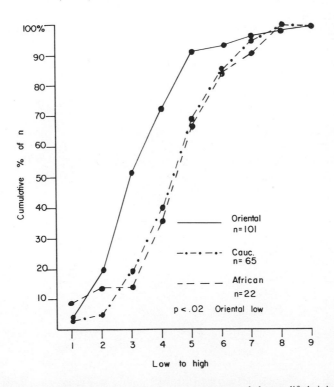

FIG. 5-19 Head-lift in prone. Oriental infants, as a group, tended not to lift their heads from the bedding; by contrast, African infants frequently lifted the head, neck, and shoulders.

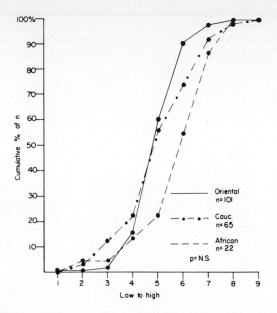

FIG. 5-20 Pull-to-sit. African neonates tended to have less head-lag when pulled by the hands to a sitting position from the supine. This difference, however, did not reach statistical significance.

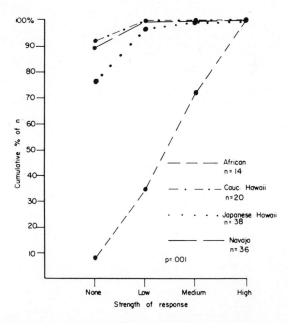

FIG. 5-21 Lordosis, the tendency to arch the back with the rump jutting out. African infants exhibited far and away the most lordosis. Variations in African *n* are due to the fact that these scales were introduced after the start of the African study.

be substantially advanced beyond European norms through approximately 3 years of age, even as Bayley (1965) and others (Curti et al., 1935; Knobloch & Pasamanick, 1958; Walters, 1967) had found on comparing black and white children in the United States. While this dichotomous performance was not maintained beyond 3 years in any of these studies, it is clear that none of the measures used tested whole-body motor coordination beyond that age. Obviously, beyond 3 years, children are very agile, and standardized test kits cannot begin to tap their true motor capabilities. A good motor test, for example, would reveal how well a youngster throws a ball, hits a target, climbs, catches, or runs, and no current test does so.

Ordinary observation, however, among black and white children in the United States would lead to the rather confident prediction that, were such tests available, black children would continue to out-perform white children beyond childhood. Further, while there are no controlled data on the subject, it would appear that Afro-Americans are far over-represented in all professional sports in which they have been given equal opportunity, as well as on the United States Olympic teams. Nor can one easily accept the explanation that Afro-Americans tend to be channeled into sports because little else is available to them. It is probable that American boys of all ethnic groups share the dream of becoming a sports hero, and there is no evidence that Afro-American preadolescents act on this ambition more than do other ethnic groups. It would appear instead that the subsequent rate of success among Afro-Americans is higher, and our interim conclusion is that the motor precocity among African and Afro-American infants heralds superior whole-body coordination in later life.

Before leaving this section, it should be acknowledged that the apparent genetically based motor precocity in African infants is a touchy issue to some and logical discussion has suffered as a result. Ainsworth (1967), for example, in an otherwise excellent study, first reported motor precocity at birth in her Ghanda (Uganda) sample and then explained the continued motor precocity with speculation about maternal permissiveness and "postural adjustments to being held and carried during the earliest months [p. 328]." At no time did she seriously consider genetic differences as a possibility, although logic would immediately suggest such an hypothesis, given its early onset.

Similarly, Geber, who had been among the first to report relative motor precocity at birth among the Ghanda, somehow omitted these data in explaining a later study of older Ghanda infants. There she emphasized the availability, nurturance, and physical closeness of the mother to the infant (Geber, 1958) as the basis for the perceived differences. Geber and Dean (1958) went on to say, but presented no data, that African infants of the Europeanized middle class were less precocious than those of the lower class, implying that the difference was due to differences in rearing. Leiderman et al. (1973) do present data, and to the opposite effect. They report that middle-class Kikuyu infants in Tigoni, Kenya, were more advanced in both the mental and motor scales of the Bayley Test than were lower-class infants. Such differences are understandable, given decisive differences in nutrition favoring the middle classes, and unlike Geber's claim, make considerable sense.

Warren (1972), in a most helpful review of infant testing in sub-Saharan Africa, found evidence for African motor precocity in 10 out of 12 studies which were adequately conducted. (Two other studies were deemed inadequate.) Despite this apparently decisive ratio, Warren chose to favor the results of the two studies which yielded no differences. We can only assume that these apparently illogical positions have been taken because of the taboo on genetic explanations of ethnic differences seen in recent decades and the related problems of racism. (This is important and will be discussed in the final section of this chapter.)

Apparently one of the difficulties in the above findings involves the ill-intentioned hypothesis that human groups which exhibit motor precocity are "less sapient" in that the hominid line has been characterized by progressive infantilization. It is therefore important to report a recent study by Freedman and Strieby (unpublished data, 1973) using the Cambridge Neonatal Scales with 31 newborns of Punjabi extraction. The Punjabis are a Caucasian group of Northern India who have been highly successful economically in New Delhi, where the study was done. Our data indicate that this group is the most motorically precocious of any group yet seen, including African and Australian aboriginal newborns. They had the strongest neck muscling of any group as indicated by the highest average *pull-to-sit* and the best ability to support body weight as indicated by the highest average *straightening-of-legs* response. Thus, within the one race of Caucasians, differences wide enough to encompass the other groups have been found, and it would appear that motor precocity is related to localized adaptations rather than to broad phyletic trends. We hope these findings will help lay to rest unwarranted and mischievous speculation regarding the relative phyletic position of one or another group of mankind.

AUSTRALIAN ABORIGINAL GROUP

The Australian aborigines, who were a hunting and gathering people before European contact, are frequently classified as a separate "Australoid" race (cf. Coon, 1962). It is now generally assumed that they first entered over land bridges from Indonesia and New Guinea some 50,000 years ago, and that they eventually became land-locked, with little opportunity for genetic exchange. There is in fact a good deal of homogeneity among the aborigines, and all languages on the Australian continent are thought to be related (Elkin, 1954). Also, all groups share similar blood-type patterns, for example, the near absence of "B" (Weiner, 1971). There are, nevertheless, many differences among aboriginal groups, and the present sample can only be considered an initial foray.

The sample consisted of 17 babies born in Darwin Hospital to aboriginal parents in February of 1972. The parents were from various subgroups in Northern Australia, most of whom live on or near Christian missions spotted throughout the northern territories; it is, in fact, largely the mission influence which determines which parents will have a baby in the hospital. There is an air service, run by the government, to transport expectant mothers to Darwin. As in other groups, mothers were not included who were under-nourished or in any way abnormal.

Perhaps the most dramatic difference in this population of newborns was the fact that almost all babies were wide awake as soon as they were removed for examination, thus achieving the highest ranking of all on *initial state*. On this rating, which runs from deep sleep (one) through maximal alertness (six), aboriginal infants averaged 3.791 to a Caucasian (United States) average of 2.926 ($p<.05$). Despite their wide-eyed appearance, however, the average aboriginal baby would not or could not follow moving objects, and consequently the aborigines achieved low scores on *following an object* compared to United States Caucasians ($p<.01$), and similarly, *turning to sounds* was low ($p<.001$). It is fascinating that these results form a pattern not heretofore seen in any other group. All other groups demonstrated a distinct positive correlation between initial state and subsequent scores of alertness; among the aborigines, however, a wide-eyed look was not an indication of readiness to turn toward stimuli, and only a few did so. Speculation on the meaning of this pattern would seem fruitless at this time, and further studies are now being planned.

There were a number of other differences from United States Caucasians. On the group of items assumed to be indicators of temperament, the aborigines differed from the Caucasian group in approximately the same way as did the Oriental groups. Thus, the aborigines were less excitable, less irritable, less labile in mood, less quick to cry, more consolable, and more likely to quiet themselves when left alone than United States Caucasians.

On motor items, on the other hand, the aboriginal group resembled the Nigerian sample. They were also extremely wiry (average weight 3016 grams compared to 3516 grams among United States Caucasians) and were stronger than the Caucasian sample in the neck, back, and legs. While differences in pull-to-sit were not quite significant, aboriginal newborns were clearly better able to hold up body weight when supported in a standing position ($p<.001$). Finally, they showed the most outstanding defense reaction to a cloth-on-the-face of any group.

Thus, the aboriginal sample provides a unique grouping of traits not heretofore seen. It is superficially tempting to relate this to the fact that in blood groupings, too, Australoids exhibit a unique pattern vis-à-vis the other groups studied (cf. Weiner, 1971). That fact is usually attributed to the lack of gene-flow to and from the Australian subcontinent, whereas gene-flow was clearly possible among all the other groups studied.

In any event, and before serious hypotheses may be formed regarding the meaning of these unique patterns in newborn behavior, further work is needed to substantiate whether or not they are truly characteristic of the wider aboriginal population.

SOME POSSIBLE SELECTIVE FORCES

Given such differences among various newborn populations, and assuming they reflect gene-pool differences, what have been the forces which have led to them? The most obvious potential factor is the already mentioned "founder principle," the notion that the founding stock of a population has given it a persisting genetic and phenotype character. In addition, selective forces have undoubtedly played a part as well.

Although any discussion of selective forces is perforce speculative, a particularly good example appears to be the possible selection for differential motor precocity at birth attendant upon traditional modes of food acquisition. This hypothesis stems from the Australian aboriginal data, a people whom we know with some certainty were continuously hunters and gatherers throughout prehistory. That is, they have been isolated on the Australian continent at least 12,000 years, and there is no evidence that they were ever agricultural or pastoral.

It will be recalled that in the aboriginal sample the neck, back, and legs were strikingly strong at birth, especially as compared with the Oriental or Caucasian populations. It would therefore appear significant that the aborigines are highly nomadic and have never developed special modes of transport for infants, such as cradleboards or slings. At best, the infant was carried against the chest or under the arm on a bark food-carrier, or over the back in a skin pouch (Basedow, 1929). Also, there is no lying-in period for the newborn during which strength might be achieved through maturation, for in this hunting and gathering people, living at a primitive subsistence level, a month's pause at one place was hardly possible. New babies were (and are) usually carried on the hip or in the arms. Given the high degree of nomadism and the lack of transport devices, it would seem imperative that the baby be well-muscled and that the head not roll about as if it were not quite attached (as was common among the Oriental and Caucasian samples).

Among the three Oriental groups and in European tradition, by contrast, newborns are usually not transported nor taken out-of-doors for several weeks. In Chinese and Japanese tradition, for example, newborns are kept indoors until the 1-month celebration. Certainly none, including the Navajo — who were also a nomadic people until recently — move about with their babies as quickly after birth as do the aborigines; when the traditional Navajo did transport the baby, it was always on a cradleboard.

Among the Hausa, too, where necks and backs of newborns were almost as fully developed as among the aborigines, it is customary for mothers or mothers' helpers to transport babies within a few days after birth in a cloth sling across the back. If the average Caucasian or Oriental neonate were jostled in this way, there would be considerable concern for the rolling head. While it is not clear whether or not the Hausa were nomadic through recent prehistory, African agriculture is relatively underdeveloped and very likely did not start till "historical" times. Thus we can assume that, as with the Australian aborigines, most of Hausa history involved hunting and gathering, with the present settled pattern but hundreds of years old. In any event, and whether or not these reconstructions are found to be true, it appears that mode of infant transport within a culture is closely related to the average physical states of infants, and this in turn seems another example of the complementariness of cultural practice and biological readiness.

Another instance of feedback between cultural practice and physiological status may be the differential twinning rates seen in Africa. Most black African groups and Afro-Americans exhibit higher rates of fraternal twinning than do Europeans and European-Americans (see Fig. 5-22). Note that it is the fraternal twinning rate which differs significantly, and we may

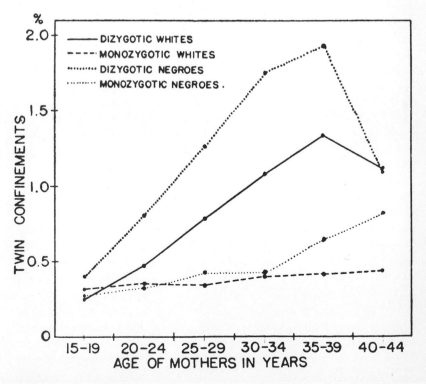

FIG. 5-22 Frequency of twin confinements in relation to age of mothers in the United States, 1938. From Stern (1960).

assume that this involves higher proportions of women with a genetic disposition toward multiple ovulation. Of greater interest, however, are Nylander's (1971) statistics from the university teaching hospital in Ibadan, Nigeria, which indicate that tribes that exalt the birth of twins tend to have exceedingly high twinning rates (e.g., the Yoruba with about 45 sets per 1000 births), whereas the few tribes in which the arrival of twins is a disappointment have substantially lower rates (e.g., the Eastern Ijaw of the Niger-Delta with 30 per 1000). The reasons for the differential rates of twinning would appear to lie at the level of selection; it appears most probable that infanticide has played a role in the achievement of the lower rates (cf. Leis, 1965) and, more speculatively, extra care has played a role in the higher rates, each serving to lower or raise, respectively, the proportion of multiple ovulators in the population.

An apparent contradiction are the Ibos, whose twinning rate is high and who are also reputed to kill twins. However, in a personal communication, LeVine has noted that it is possible that the Ibo reputation is undeserved; his Nigerian informant insists that twins are only killed by the Eastern Ijaw and not by other Nigerian groups, reputations notwithstanding. Clearly, accurate information in such areas is difficult to obtain, and the speculative nature of this discussion must be stressed.

As for ethnic differences found in behavior such as temperament and sensory alertness, the easiest explanation is via the "founder principle." It is, however, also possible that different ecological adaptations have fostered differences in temperament and alertness via natural selection. Although this would involve sheer speculation, there is a model for how such selection might occur.

Ginsburg and Laughlin (1967) have demonstrated that only seven generations of selection were necessary to produce excellent seeing-eye dogs from a group of German shepherd dogs not previously exhibiting this phenotype. No external blood line of "good" seeing dogs was introduced, but by selecting the best of each generation, sufficient "repackaging" of genes occurred in but seven successive matings to produce radically new gene frequencies. Their results involved striking changes in temperament, physical conformation, and sensory alertness, and there is ample evidence that any number of other factors may be similarly selected for (Fuller & Thompson, 1960). While it is unlikely we will ever be able to reconstruct the histories of comparable cultural selective pressures, the animal work seems a reasonable paradigm for what has probably often occurred at the human level over much longer time spans and via complex biosocial interactions.

THE PROBLEMS OF RACISM

It is unrealistic to leave off discussion of gene-pool differences and behavior without considering the issue of racism. Recently, Jensen (1969) published a monograph in which IQ differences between racial groups were related to gene-pool differences. The monograph consisted largely of data long available and well known, but the publication came at a time when the Afro-American struggle for equal rights was at its height. Jensen made the mistake of ignoring this fact and naively expected both black and white Americans to thank him for his considerable efforts. Instead, he was personally villified and his monograph became a sort of devil's manual. Jensen's recent retort to his critics (1973), while thorough and logically tight, nevertheless has had the net effect of continuing a seemingly endless controversy based (when all is told) not on fact and logic, but on heated feelings involving a people's sense of worth. In our view, it is important to consider such feelings in a chapter such as this, for they can be the most important part of the story.

On the basis of how they are used, the terms racism, nationalism, and tribalism are to a great extent interchangeable. Each depends on the contrast of an "in-group" and an "out-group," with one's own group appearing largely "good" and the other's group largely "bad." The universality of this type of thinking has been often documented, most notably by Sumner (1906).

Whereas tribalism or group rivalries appear to go back to man's pre-hominid past (Dart, 1955), nationalism and especially racism appear to be relatively new versions of the old story. It is, in fact, helpful to realize the rather arbitrary nature of "in-group" affiliations, for one then sees the process as a need in search of a context.

Similar behavior can be found among other primates, and most terrestrial monkeys (e.g., the macaques) owe primary allegiance to one troop and treat conspecifics in neighboring troops as rivals (cf. Koford, 1963). Even those individual monkeys who were formerly members of ego's troop and have switched to another, are considered "enemies." There are numerous comparable examples among humans. To mention one, among the warlike Dani of New Guinea, even sisters and brothers may become one another's enemy as they move to different villages because of exogamous mating patterns (Heider, 1970).

The point is that where at one time there was intertribal enmity there is now nationalism and racism, and it seems to be the nature of man to form in-groups and out-groups on some basis or other. The urge to do so is apparently deep-seated; that is to say, it is a product of our evolutionary past, but the particular grouping is entirely dependent upon historical context.

One of the consequences of this behavioral trend is the down-grading of the out-group and simultaneous up-grading of the in-group. This is where *interpretation* of data plays such a large role. Jensen's data have thus been interpreted as a denigration of Afro-Americans, as well they might, for publication came at a time when American blacks were seeking to resurrect group pride destroyed by their enslavement over a century ago.

The present author, then, is fully aware that any "facts" about ethnic differences may be used in the service of raising and lowering a group's standing. Unfortunately, there is little one can do to eliminate this possibility. For example, were the out-group to have higher average IQ's than the majority in-group, the latter could nevertheless manage to use that as negative evidence, as witnessed by the treatment of Jewish intellectuals in Nazi Germany. Even silence is of no help since people generate their own pseudo-data about one another.

The author's hope, then, is that a chapter such as this will help bring the issue of ethnic differences from under the wraps of folk knowledge, where maximal distortion usually occurs, into the area of science where disproof is at least possible. The contention is an old one — that which festers in the dark may clear up in the light of day.

In closing, we can only stress again that men everywhere are much more alike than they are different. Lewontin's (1971) analysis of 17 widely sampled blood factors (gene loci) showed that each major racial group within itself can account for 93.7% of all human genetic variation. There is, however, no point in ignoring the differences should one want to study them, provided that the questions asked are potentially constructive ones. The anticipation that racist-minded men will distort such data cannot discourage us, for they will do their worst in any event.

We will give the final word to the sociologist, Marvin Bressler (1968), who has commented on this topic as follows:

> Since every identifiable group is the product of a unique history which may have included exposure to differential selection processes, it would not be surprising if genetic rather than environmental influences sometimes explained a higher proportion of the variance in observed behavior . . . . An ideology that tacitly appeals to biological equality as a condition for human emancipation corrupts the idea of freedom. Moreover, it encourages decent men to tremble at the prospect of "inconvenient" findings that may emerge in future scientific research. This unseemly anti-intellectualism is doubly degrading because it is probably unnecessary [p. 197].

APPENDIX
SMILING IN BLIND INFANTS AND
THE ISSUE OF INNATE VS. ACQUIRED
(1964)

INTRODUCTION

Darwin (1872) wrote that many of the expressions of the congenitally blind, since they could not be learned by visual imitation, must be innate. He quoted the case of congenitally deaf-blind Laura Bridgeman, reported in 1851 by Lieber, to illustrate his point, and among the expressions he listed as innate were smiling and laughing. Darwin also noted that his own children first smiled at about forty-five days of age, and he reasoned that since this was too early for imitation to have played a role it was also evidence that smiling in man is innate. As further evidence, he noted its universal presence in man.

As for the survival value of the baby's smile, Darwin presented what would today be an obvious hypothesis concerning the joy it creates within the adult caretaker. (See Goldstein, 1957, for citations and discussion of function; see also Ambrose, 1960.) This paper, then, is primarily concerned with the "innateness" of the baby's smile, and with the clarification of this problem provided by studies of blind infants.

NORMATIVE DATA, IMITATION, AND FEAR OF STRANGERS

In the sections which follow, observations and studies will be reported in which the age of the infant appears to play an important role in the development of smiling. Aside from hereditary causes for individual differences (Freedman, 1965), a major difficulty of focusing on age is the fact that different environments can slow or speed development of smiling, usually depending on the amount of social stimulation (Kaila, 1932; Spitz and Wolf,

1946; Ahrens, 1954; Brackbill, 1958; Ambrose, 1961; Gewirtz, 1963; Wolff, 1963). Also, the reported first age of smiling may often be an artifact dependent on the amount of time the observer spends with the infant; the more time he spends, the greater are his chances for observing a smile. The stress throughout the paper will therefore be on sequence, rather than age, in developmental events.

With regard to imitation, observers agree that deferred imitation, i.e. imitation removed in time from the act imitated, does not normally occur until after the first year (Valentine, 1930; Piaget, 1951; Freedman and Keller, 1963). Thus smiling to a non-smiling stimulus in the first months of life cannot reasonably be called imitative, even in seeing children.

Another general point is that smiles are increasingly reserved for familiar persons, beginning at about five months of age in family-reared infants (Freedman 1961; Freedman, 1963), and at about eight months of age in institution-reared infants (Spitz, 1950; Malliardi *et al.,* 1961; Ambrose, 1961). Soon afterwards infants begin to react with overt fear when confronted with a stranger (Schaffer, 1963; Tennes and Lampl, 1966), and this rising fear of strangers is a major factor in the waning of smiling in many of the investigations to be reported.

EARLY NON-ELICITED SMILING

In the first weeks of life in full-term infants, and over a longer period in prematures, one often sees smiling after a feed as the infant is falling off to sleep. All modern observers agree that these smiles are not due to escaping gas, as the old-wives' tale would have it, and no eliciting stimulus has been discovered (Kaila, 1932; Spitz and Wolf, 1946; Koehler, 1954; Wolff, 1963; Freedman, 1963). Non-elicited smiling thus falls into the general category which Lorenz (1937) calls "vacuum activities," i.e. behaviour which appears in the absence of normal eliciting stimuli, usually in an early stage of development. Wolff (1963) has a similar interpretation:

> Particularly in prematures, but also in full-term infants, the smile may often be preceded by a twitching myclonus at the corners of the mouth which has at least a superficial resemblance to an electrophysiological event and gives some further support to the notion that smiling in the early days after birth may be a spontaneous discharge. A final piece of indirect evidence for this supposition was the observation that, like erections and spontaneous startles, smiling tends to occur with a high frequency during drowsiness when the eyes close.

SMILING TO TOUCH AND TO SOUND

Non-elicited smiles tend no longer to appear by the end of the first month, but instead, touching various parts of the face, especially the lips (Smets, 1962), and a variety of auditory stimuli, may bring about smiling. Hetzer and Tudor-Hart (reported in Bühler, 1933) tested 126 infants, ranging from one day to five months of age, with various acoustical stimuli including the human voice. While general reactions to the voice were only moderate, the reaction of smiling was almost exclusively to voice. Various modifications of the human voice at two months all resulted in smiling. There was no difference in smiling to mother's or other people's voices, or to nuances of vocal expression, within the first five months.

Wolff (1963) found that smiling to acoustical stimuli occurred in the third week of life in a detailed study of eight precocious and highly stimulated infants. Such smiling occurred after non-elicited smiling had dropped out, and before smiling to visual stimuli (see below) had developed. While smiling might be elicited by a bell, whistle or rattle at this stage, a high-pitched human voice was easily the most effective stimulus used. Wolf, in the course of her work with Spitz (1946), also made the observation that a high-pitched voice more readily elicited smiling than a low-pitched voice (personal communication).

L'Allier (1961) studied 120 institutionalized infants ranging in age from one to thirty-three weeks; fifteen infants were tested in each of eight consecutive four-week periods. A series of sixteen stimuli was presented to each infant and the frequency of smiling noted. Maximal smiling to all stimuli occurred between three and four months, and when all ages were considered together, various musical instruments were the poorest elicitors of smiles. The best elicitors were as follows:

	Frequency		Frequency
Voice (*E* unseen)	19	Voice and face (moving)	80
Voice and caress (*E* unseen)	31	Face	75
Voice and picked-up (*E*'s face in profile)	35	Voice and face and caress	65
Voice and caress and picked-up	39	Voice and face and caress and picked-up	46
Picked-up and caressed	25		

In a study of 88 family-reared infants, Laroche and Tcheng (1963) also found "voice and face" to be the best elicitor of smiling, over the first half year. In this study "voice" alone was superior to a "static face" but a "moving face" or "smiling face" elicited about as many smiles as did "voice" alone. In this population, maximum smiling to all stimuli occurred between four and six months.

Clearly, voice is a highly efficient stimulus to smiling. In L'Allier's study, however, the visualized moving face was the most efficient stimulus, and this is in accord with the bulk of current data.

SMILING TO VISUAL STIMULI

By far the greatest interest and greatest amount of work has been in this area. Starting with the highly original work of Kaila (1932), there have been several studies of infant smiling to various forms of visual stimulation (Spitz and Wolf, 1946; Ahrens, 1954; Wilson, 1960). Beginning at the end of the first month and into the second and third months, infants begin to stare into the observer's eyes, and for the first time eye-to-eye contact is obtained. Soon afterwards smiling occurs as the infant stares in this way, and such smiling is usually subjectively felt by the observer as the first true social smile probably because of the eye-to-eye contact (Wolff, 1963).

Kaila (1932), working in Charlotte Bühler's nursery in Vienna, became interested in the infant's "fascinated" staring into the adult face just preceding the smile, and set out to find what elements of the face the infant actually fixed upon. He made his observations on 70 infants over varying periods of time, in an essentially "naturalistic" study. Kaila used several two-dimensional cardboard models which were held above the infant's crib. These included one resembling a human face; one with the bottom half, below the bridge of the nose, blanked out; one containing just two large light eyes; and a mask containing two distinct dark eyes. He also presented his own face at various angles, ranging from full face to profile.

Kaila came to the conclusion that the infant was initially attracted to a Gestalt configuration consisting of the eyes in *en face* position ("der menschlichen Augenpartie"), and he held that "der menschlichen Augenpartie" is the first differentiated object in the life-space of the infant. In accord with Gestalt thinking, he theorized that the central nervous system was so constructed that "resonance" occurred to this particular configuration, which gave the figure psychological "pregnanz."

Spitz and Wolf (1946) tested 251 infants of various races and environments and corroborated Kaila's observations. They also added a third element to Kaila's Gestalt of the *en face* eyes: movement. They found the nodding head or nodding model elicited smiles more readily than one held still (corroborated by Laroche and Tcheng, 1963, see above). Also, a grimacing mouth was found to be as effective as a smiling one, so that movement of the mouth rather than specific shape was deemed most important. This finding, of course, threw doubt on such observations as Washburn's (1929) that the smiling face of an adult is the best elicitor of infant smiles. In both Kaila's and Spitz's studies, as in the study of Laroche and Tcheng (1963), maximal smiling to the presented stimulus occurred between three and six months of age, and thereafter the experimenter's face, and models of a face, ceased to be effective. It should be added that the work of Spitz and Wolf also served the important function of bringing these findings to the attention of English-reading workers.

Ahrens (1954), continuing the same approach and using a greater variety of two-dimensional models, came to some rather attractive conclusions. However, it should be noted that, as in Kaila's studies, there is much informality in reporting, and because of the complicated nature of the undertaking every procedure could not be done with every child. It is not clear how many different infants were observed in all, but there are a number of charts with specified procedures, subjects and results. All of Ahrens' observations were made in an institution for infants.

In the second month the most adequate stimulus Ahrens found was a face-sized card with eye-like dots, and a six-dotted model proved more effective than similar cards with one or two dots. At older ages greater and greater detail of a face was demanded before the infant would smile, beginning with the top half of a face, and including the mouth by the fifth month. By seven months these infants required a model with a broad mouth, and by eight months only an actual human face would do.

There was an attempt to refine Spitz's finding regarding movement by varying the speed with which the model was moved, but the results were complex and unsatisfactory. Movement of the models, however, had its clearest positive effect between two and four months.

By the time of this study, ethology had appeared as an exceedingly virile movement in animal behaviour, and Ahrens made the irresistible comparison, since made by many, between the smile of the baby and the gaping or begging responses of thrush and herring-gull chicks (Tinbergen, 1951). Adult herring gulls have a red spot on the underside of their yellow beaks, and naive chicks will gape (i.e. gaping is "released") when a model of the adult beak is presented at a proper angle (sign-stimulus). In varying the visual pattern by means of a variety of models, one was found which elicited a greater rate of gaping than did the natural stimulus: a small white stick with several dark red rings on it. Such a stimulus is called a "super-normal sign-stimulus" (Lorenz, 1952).

Similarly, in Ahrens' study, smiles in the first month were most readily elicited by what can be considered an exaggeration of the eye-part of the face. The six-dotted model elicited more smiling than a face and, in ethological terms, this model could also be considered a "supernormal sign-stimulus." Ethological conceptions of smiling have since appeared in a number of reports (e.g. Koehler, 1954; Gray, 1958; Ambrose, 1960).

SMILING IN CONGENITALLY BLIND INFANTS

Kaila and Ahrens were strictly visual in their theoretical thinking. Neither dealt with the problem posed by smiling in the blind, nor the related problems concerning smiling to sound or other stimuli. What then is known about smiling in the congenitally blind, and what does this information tell us about the mechanisms which bring about smiling?

Before reviewing the literature, a few remarks about blindness are in order. By current standards a child is considered blind if the corrected vision on his best eye is measured at less than 20/200. Considerably less vision is necessary, however, to move about and explore new objects and places (Parmelee *et al.* , 1959). A regard for bright light is often present when the source of blindness is a defective lens, as in cataracts or in retrolental fibroplasia, but the infant is still considered blind. So-called searching nystagmus, a ceaseless jerky motion of the eye, is usually present after the first month. Its exact nature is not known, but it has been described somewhat romantically as physiological searching for a foveal image.

Until recently, there have been only scattered case reports on behavior in congenitally blind infants, and in none of these reports was the degree of blindness detailed, nor are we usually told the etiology of the blindness.

Thompson (1941) quantified various aspects of facial movement, via motion picture film, in laughing, smiling, and crying, of twenty-six blind children, eleven of whom were blind at birth. There was a control group of twenty-nine seeing children of the same age range (seven weeks to thirteen years, six months). The only marked difference was a decrease in the amount of facial movements, after six years of age, in the smiles of those who were blind at birth. Thompson felt that this drop occurred because imitation was necessary to sustain the full smiling response. She also found heightened individual differences in smiling among the younger blind children, and she attributed this finding, as well, to the lack of opportunity for imitation. Imitation, she hypothesized, tended also to stylize expression and limit random muscular movement.

Thompson filmed only one child in its first year, at seven weeks and again at eleven and twelve months. It was noted that at seven weeks there was a barely perceptible retraction of the corners of the mouth in smiling; by eleven months there was a round-mouthed smile, and at twelve months the mouth had the more mature elliptical shape. Thompson compared this finding with that of Washburn (1929), who observed the same sequence of development at about the same ages in fifteen seeing infants, and she concluded that smiling appears on a "maturational" basis in the blind.

Gesell *et al.* (1949) reported on a congenitally blind child who smiled on hearing her sister's voice at an examination when sixteen weeks old. Koehler (1954) briefly reported on two cases in which smiling occurred at "the normal time" in one, and in the third month, "just after eating," in the other.

In recent years, soon after the discovery that supra-oxygenation of the incubator causes retrolental fibroplasia (RLF), a degeneration of the lens, a major longitudinal study of sixty-six RLF's was launched at the University of Chicago.

The report on this study by Norris *et al.* (1957) gave no specific data on smiling, but the statement is made that at four months these infants responded to human beings and demanded personal attention, as do seeing children at the same age. Elonen, the psychologist on this project, has told me privately that all the infants she saw "smiled normally."

Parmelee (1955) reported on questionnaires sent to parents of RLF children in California. He used only those responses reported from written records in baby books ($N = 28$) and found that the first smiling, with one exception, occurred between two and five months. Since these infants were on the average ten weeks premature, the first smiles could be said to have appeared on schedule. Dunn (1962) gathered data in lengthy interviews with parents of twelve congenitally blind children. These included eight with RLF, and one each with retinoblastoma, glaucoma, cataracts, and a cortical syndrome (a retardate). He found that with the exception of the retarded infant, all smiled in response to social stimulation between ten weeks and six months, and when corrections for prematurity were made, all smiled at about the same time as their sighted siblings, that is, between one and a half and four months. All, including the mentally retarded infant, smiled spontaneously and "without any instruction by the parents."

As for negative evidence, there are no reports available of blind infants who do not smile. It is safe to conclude, then, that vision is not a prerequisite for social smiling.

CURRENT INVESTIGATION

We have been able to directly observe the first elicited smiles, within two weeks of onset, in four congenitally blind infants. Each observational and testing period averaged about one and one half hours, and a good deal of cinema film has been taken and studied. Our four cases included one of congenital glaucoma and auridia, observed and tested at 4 months; one with primary vitreous hyperplasia as well as cranial synostosis, observed and tested at 3½ months; one with Rubella-induced cataracts observed and tested four times, between 2½ and 6 months; one with Rubella induced cataracts observed and tested on a weekly basis, between 2 and 4 months, and again at 6 months. In each case the ophthalmological report was bilateral blindness (i.e. vision less than 20/200 in each eye). In addition we noted that while all four infants tended to stare in the direction of bright light there was no visual pursuit of any objects, including a moving pen-light and a dangling red ring (each moved horizontally, vertically, and in a circle and repeated several times).

The Nancy Bayley Infant Mental and Motor Scales (Bayley, 1960) were administered each session and mental and motor performance, aside from visual items, was within normal limits in each case. Developmental tests, however, are a crude estimate of overall development in blind infants since in the first four months all scales are composed primarily of visual items.

The procedures for eliciting smiling were as follows (Bayley, 1960):

> When child is first placed in the crib, stand at his side, lean over with your face
> about twelve inches above the child's, (a) unsmiling for about 5 sec to 10 sec; (b)
> unsmiling but speaking softly ("hello baby," or speak child's name); (c) then smile,
> nod; (d) make a clicking sound while smiling and nodding; (e) then speak to him
> softly while smiling and touch his body lightly. Note whether the child responds with
> a smile to situations (a), (b), (c), (d), or (e), or whether he laughs, and whether he
> vocalizes. If the smile does not occur on the first presentation, repeat the test at a later
> time, when the infant is in a contented mood.

In each instance the ostensible eliciting stimuli for smiling were touch, voice, or the two combined, and we were struck that in each of the four subjects these first elicited smiles were extremely fleeting, i.e. they quickly formed and disappeared as in normal eyes-closed smiling in the first weeks of life (see above). Normal non-elicited smiling was also reported in two of the blind infants, and occurred at the usual time, in the first month. Following these observations, we asked parents of older blind children whether the first elicited smiles were of a similar fleeting nature, and we have since accumulated six cases of congenital blindness where such smiling is definitely recalled by the parents.

In the two cases we observed through six months of age, these fleeting smiles gradually changed to normal prolonged smiling, and the six retrospective cases, too, were reported as smiling normally by six months. This has led to two interim hypotheses. (1) The initial elicited smiles were reflexive in nature, since there was the typical sharp onset and almost immediate waning. (2) In these early months prolonged social smiling seems to require visual regard as a maintaining stimulus.

SMILING IN INFANTS WITH OTHER ANOMALIES

No careful studies of smiling in deaf infants have been reported but we have obtained retrospective data on two deaf infants whose course of smiling was described as completely normal.

The deaf-blind reported in the literature smile. Darwin's (1872) reference to Laura Bridgeman has already been mentioned, and Goodenough (1932) reported on a one-year-old girl, blind and deaf from birth, in whom smiling and laughing were appropriately expressed. Thompson (1941) reported that four deaf-blind cases were not markedly different from her blind subjects (see above) in laughing, smiling, and crying.

Infants with Down's syndrome (trisomy of the 21st chromosome) may smile normally and with full eye-to-eye contact, albeit several months later than normal (personal observations; see also Benda, 1960), and Dameron's (1963) remarks to the contrary seem to be in error. Although no studies are in print, I have questioned workers in the field and the general opinion was that smiling is present in all but the most severely impaired defectives. If there is any generalization to draw from this, it is that smiling tends to remain intact despite substantial biological impairment.

INNATE VERSUS LEARNED

The notion of "innateness" has never sat well in American psychology and the early work of Dennis (1935) was the first attempt to contest such an interpretation of smiling. Dennis and his wife observed a pair of infants over their first year under conditions of minimal stimulation. He found, as did many of the above authors, that the human face was the best eliciting stimulus for smiling, but it should be noted that since by design he avoided vocalizing to the babies, he gathered little data on responsiveness to voice.

Dennis concluded that the smile appeared as a response to reduction in tension, although he admitted his data did not necessarily suggest such a position. He wondered why, for example, the baby did not smile at its milk bottle and to other objects associated with reduction in tension, but achieved no clear answer to these questions.

In dealing with the position that smiling is an innate response to a human face, Dennis referred to his own review of the literature on congenitally blinded children who had had cataracts removed. He wrote, "In accounts of their early visual reactions (after the operation), there is nothing to suggest that they instinctively smiled at the human face, or even that they instinctively chose the human face for fixation." There was apparently nothing to suggest the opposite either, and Dennis himself agreed that facile counter-arguments are available, such as the waning of instinct.

In the section concerned with normative data on smiling, we have seen that time of onset and amount of smiling is affected by environmental events. For example, Brackbill (1958) has shown that smiling can be increased and decreased by schedules of social reinforcement, while Gewirtz (1963) and Ambrose (1961) have shown that time of onset and amount of smiling can vary with the amount of social stimulation. However, these studies were not concerned with the origin of smiling or the neurophysiological mechanisms involved. Recently, however, Schneirla (1959) addressed himself to this problem on a theoretical level.

Schneirla, in taking an anti-instinctivist pro-learning position, postulated that the smile is derived from a rudimentary "grimace" (early non-elicited smiling in our terminology). The "grimace," he hypothesized, is induced by low-level stimulation of the facial nerve and it thereafter becomes associated with social stimuli. Schneirla termed even the developed smile of three months a "grimace," apparently because it served the argument that smiling is gradually differentiated from early diffuse responses.

Since no data were offered to support the case that stimulation of the facial nerve elicits early eyes-closed smiling, we can assume Schneirla considered some form of external stimulation logically necessary, and his discussions on other topics in the same article and elsewhere (1960) bear this out. However, the work of Weiss and others (Weiss, 1954) shows that external stimulation is not necessary for all CNS activity, so that data and not logic is needed in this case.

In our own work (Freedman, 1965), we have found that many infants never showed non-elicited "grimace" smiling, yet they developed normal social smiling at the usual time. Also, when non-elicited smiling was present, the gradual and continuous development from diffuse to well-formed smiling, postulated by Schneirla, was not observed. Instead, there was a distinct noncontinuity between early non-elicited smiles and later social smiles which entail eye-to-eye contact. Other observers agree that before smiling to the face develops, there is a non-smiling period in which eye-to-eye contact first takes place (Spitz and Wolf, 1946; Ahrens, 1954; Wolff, 1963), and by this time non-elicited smiling appears only rarely (Wolff, 1963).

In addition there is great variation in onset of social smiling and some infants are extremely precocious under routine hospital care (see Gewirtz, 1963; Laroche and Tcheng, 1963, for literature on age of onset). We have closely observed one infant whose first social smiles, i.e. smiling with his eyes on the caretaker's face, occurred at 3 days of age. This infant smiled consistently thereafter, exhibiting both "non-elicited" and elicited smiling throughout the first month. The infant was under routine care so that it is less pertinent to speak of learning and more pertinent to speak of a precocious capacity for smiling.

Finally, a learning view, such as Schneirla's or Dennis', should account for the fact that certain stimuli are better elicitors of smiling than others. As discussed above, the best eliciting stimuli are normally the human voice and the human face, whereas various non-living objects, more directly associated with the reduction of tension, are not smiled at. Schneirla has dealt with this point by suggesting that if the feeding bottle could be visualized during feeding instead of "just felt," the bottle would henceforth elicit smiling. However, Wilson (1960) has performed such an experiment and shown this is not the case: various stimuli visually associated with feeding were quite ineffective in eliciting smiles.

We may conclude that learning or Pavlovian explanations can tell us something about the relative strength and frequency of smiling responses under different environmental conditions, but they tell us little regarding the origin of smiling or the mechanisms involved.

What then, do the "nativists" tell us? In our own work, we have found that identical twins exhibit greater concordance than fraternal pairs in time of onset and in amount of social smiling (Freedman, 1965). Such studies, of course, say only that heredity is playing some role but nothing about the nature of this role. Ethological thinking, on the other hand, has led to the postulation of a specific neurophysiological mechanism (see section on visual elicitation of smiling), but unfortunately the evidence indicates that this hypothesis is also inadequate.

It is based on the assumption that a specific visual stimulus, a moving face-like pattern, acts as a "releaser" by disinhibiting the "innate releasing pattern," which results in smiling; but as we have seen smiling occurs regularly in the absence of vision. The moving face-like pattern must therefore be considered a facilitator of smiling rather than a primary elicitor.

Lehrman's (1954) sweeping critique of ethology contains several parallel cases, from animal behavior, in which identification of a specific "releaser" turned out to be misleading. One famous example, "short neckedness" in birds (as in hawks), had been identified as a "releaser" of escape responses in gallinacious chicks (Tinbergen, 1948); subsequent work has shown the relationship to be a good deal more complex (Curio, 1963), and in one study, gallinacious chicks which showed this escape response had apparently learned which birds not to fear (Schleidt, 1961).

In general, the fight between nativistic and learning positions has helped very little in clarifying the mechanisms behind smiling in human babies. The representatives of both positions have so far drawn too narrow a picture, and we are reminded of other similar arguments. For example, anti-instinctivists often cite Kuo's (1932) work which makes the point that pecking in chicks is not an innate response but is dependent on the physical juxtaposition of head and heart in the egg (Lehrman, 1954; Schneirla, 1960). An instinctivist, however, can answer this argument easily by pointing out that the positions of the fetal head and heart, etc., have been channelled by evolutionary changes which must ultimately be reflected in changes at the genetic level.

On the other hand, as Lehrman has pointed out, when ethologists have spoken of organized patterns of behavior as "innate," the door to further investigation of this behavior has often been shut. For to hypothesize that a behavior is innate can only mean that the behavior appears to be evolutionally meaningful and/or that it appears to be a reflection of the organism's genotype. Beyond this, only careful investigation of the behavioral pattern will help us understand it. Beach (1955) makes the same point.

CONCLUSIONS

It is probable that cybernetic models will eventually provide an adequate theoretical basis for dealing with tangled problems like the present one. For the present, however, the evidence that the infant's smile is "innate," given the above use of the term, can be found in much of the data cited. The lack of ability for deferred imitation, i.e. imitation removed in time from the act imitated, eliminates imitation as an explanation of the young infant's smiling to non-smiling stimuli; social smiling in blind infants precludes some sort of (hypothetical) primitive imitation; the reflexive nature of early social smiling observed in blind infants suggests an electrophysiological discharge; the twitching-myoclonic pattern of early non-elicited smiling, present in the seeing and in the blind, is similarly suggestive; the greater concordance in smiling patterns within identical-twin pairs compared to fraternal-twin pairs implies hereditary control; the inability, despite repeated attempts, to demonstrate either tension reduction or conditioning as the cause of early smiling implies a non-learned aspect; in the nonblind, over the first months, the facilitation of smiling with specific "supernormal" visual stimuli suggests an ethological-type "releasing" (read facilitating) mechanism; facilitation of the earlier smiles by a high-pitched voice can be similarly interpreted.

Some less direct evidence for innateness is: the universal presence of smiling in the great variety of cultures; the continued appearance of smiling in the congenitally blind although facial movement, in general, is greatly reduced after six years of age; the fact that smiling is intact, even if slow in developing, in defective children. Finally, there are the strong but tautological arguments regarding evolutionary function, such as, the joy the baby's smile creates in the caretaker and its continued importance as a signal of mutual positive feeling throughout life.

In conclusion, we who investigate behavior can benefit from the embryologist, N. K. Brooks (quoted by Openheimer, 1954): "When we say the development of the egg is inherent must we not also say what are the relations with reference to which it is inherent? When we say it is induced, must we not also say what are the relations with reference to which it is induced? Is there any way to find this out except scientific discovery?"

SUMMARY

The literature on smiling in infancy was briefly summarized and data were cited which appear to support the thesis that smiling in infancy is an "innate" expression. Particular emphasis was placed on observations of blind infants since ethologically oriented theories hold that smiling comes about as an "innate" response to certain visual "sign stimuli". It was found that blind, deaf, and blind-deaf infants smile, which indicates that no single sensory channel is the exclusive releaser of smiling. On the other hand, it was found that vision definitely facilitated smiling since blind infants did not exhibit normal prolonged smiling until 5 or 6 months of age; instead, they exhibited fleeting, reflex-like smiling. Finally, examination of theoretical positions in current innate vs. acquired controversies pointed-up weaknesses in each position.

BIBLIOGRAPHY

Ahrens, R. Beitrag zur Entwicklung des Physiognomie und Mimikerkennens, tiel I, II. *Zeitschrift fuer Experimentelle und Angewandte Psychologie*. 1954, **2**,412-454, 599-633.

Ainsworth, M.D. *The effects of maternal deprivation: A review of findings and controversy in the context of research strategy*. Public Health Papers (Geneva: World Health Organization), 1962, **14**.

Ainsworth, M. D. *Infancy in Uganda*. Baltimore: Johns Hopkins Press, 1967.

Allport, G. *Personality: A psychological interpretation*. New York: Holt, 1937.

Ambrose, J.A. The smiling and related responses in early human infancy: An experimental and theoretical study of their course and significance. Unpublished doctoral dissertation, University of London, 1960.

Ambrose, J.A. The development of the smiling response in early infancy. In B. M. Foss (Ed.), *Determinants of infant behaviour I*. London: Methuen, 1961, 179 – 201.

Ambrose, J.A. (Ed.) *Stimulation in early infancy*. New York: Academic Press, 1969.

Anderson, J.E. The limitations of infant and preschool tests in the measurement of intelligence. *Journal of Psychology*, 1939, **8**, 351-379.

Apgar, V., & Hames, L.S. Further observations on the newborn scoring system. *American Journal of Diseases of Children*, 1962, **104**, 419-428.

Appell, G., & Aubry, J. *Maternal deprivation in young children*. Film: 16 mm; 22 minutes; sound. New York University Film Library; Tavistock Child Development Research Unit, London; United Nations, Geneva, 1951.

Baerends, G.P., & Baerends-Van Roon, J.M. An introduction to the ethology of cichlid fishes. *Behaviour, Supplement*, 1950, **1**, 1-243.

Balint, M. Individual differences of behavior in early infancy and an objective way of recording them. *Journal of Genetic Psychology*, 1948, **73**, 57-117.

Bandura, A., Ross, V., & Ross, S. *Journal of Abnormal and Social Psychology*, 1963, **66**, 3-11.

Basedow, H. *The Australian Aboriginal*. Adelaide: F.W. Peerce, 1929.

Bateman, A.J. Intra-sexual selection in *Drosophila*. *Heredity*, 1948, **2**, 349-368.

Bateson, G. *Steps to an ecology of mind*. San Francisco: Chandler, 1972.

Bateson, G., & Mead, M. *Karba's first years*. Film: 16 mm; sound. New York University Film Library, 1942.

Bayley, N. *Manual of directions for an infant scale of mental development*. Laboratory of Psychology, National Institute of Mental Health, 1960. (mimeographed).

Bayley, N. Comparison of mental and motor test scores for ages 1–15 months by sex, birth order, race, geographical location and age of parents. *Child Development*, 1965, **36**, 379-411.

Bayley, N. *Bayley scales of infant development*. New York: Psychological Corp., 1970.

Beach, F.A. The descent of instinct. *Psychological Review*, 1955, **62**, 401-410.

Beekman, S. The relation of gazing and smiling behavior to status and sex in interacting pairs of children. Unpublished master's thesis, Committee on Human Development, University of Chicago, 1970.

Bell, R.Q., & Costello, N.S. Three tests for sex differences in tactile sensitivity in the newborn. *Biologia Neonatorum*, 1964, **7**, 335-347.

Benda, C.E. *The child with Mongolism*. New York: Grune & Stratton, 1960.

Benjamin, J.D. Prediction and psychopathologic theory. In L. Jessner & E. Pavenstadt (Eds.), *Dynamic psychopathology in childhood*. New York: Grune & Stratton, 1959, 6-77.

Birren, J.E. (Ed.) *Handbook of aging of the individual*. Chicago: University of Chicago Press, 1959.

Blanck, S. Dimorphism in seated postures. Unpublished manuscript, Committee on Human Development, University of Chicago, 1971.

Bower, T.G.R. The visual world of infants. *Scientific American*, 1966, **215**, 80-92. (a)

Bower, T.G.R. Slant perception and shape constancy in infants. *Science*, 1966, **151**, 832-834. (b)

Bower, T.G.R. Phenomenal identity and form perception in an infant. *Perception & Psychophysics*, 1967, **2**, 74-76. (a)

Bower, T.G.R. The development of object permanence: some studies of existence constancy. *Perception & Psychophysics*, 1967, **2**, 411-413. (b)

Bower, T.G.R. Object permanence. Unpublished lecture, University of Chicago, 1968.

Bower, T.G.R. Object perception in infants. *Perception*, 1972, **1**, 15-30.

Bower, T. G. R., & Patterson, J. B. The separation of place, movement, and object in the world of the infant. *Journal of Experimental Child Psychology,* 1973, **15**, 161– 168.

Bowlby, J. Maternal care and mental health. *Monograph Series* (Geneva: World Health Organization), 1952, **2**.

Bowlby, J. *Attachment*. New York: Basic Books, 1969.

Brackbill, Y. Extinction of the smiling response in infants as a function of reinforcement schedule. *Child Development*, 1958, **29**, 115-124.

Brazelton, T.B., & Freedman, D.G. The Cambridge neonatal scales. In J.J. van der Werff ten Bosch (Ed.), *Normal and abnormal development of brain and behavior*. Leiden: Leiden University Press, 1971.

Brazelton, T.B., Robey, J.S. & Collier, G.A. Infant development in the Zinacanteco Indians of Southern Mexico. *Pediatrics*, 1969, **44**, 274-290.

Bressler, M. Sociology, biology and ideology. In D.C. Glass (Ed.), *Genetics*. New York: Rockefeller University Press, 1968.

Brooks, J., & Lewis, M. *Attachment behavior in thirteen-month-old opposite-sex twins*. Princeton, N.J.: Educational Testing Service, 1973.

Brown, R. *Words and things*. Glencoe, Ill.: Free Press, 1958.

Bühler, C. The social behavior of children. In C. Murchison (Ed.), *A handbook of child psychology*. Worcester, Mass.: Clark Univ. Press, 1933, 374– 416.

Burlingham, D. *Twins; A study of three identical pairs*. New York: International Universities Press, 1952.

Burns, R.K. Role of hormones in the differentiation of sex. In W.C. Young (Ed.), *Sex and internal secretions*. Baltimore: Williams & Wilkins, 1961, 76– 158.

Cameron, J., Livson, N., & Bayley, N. Infant vocalizations and their relationship to mature intelligence. *Science*, 1967, **157**, 331-333.

Campbell, B. *Human evolution*. Chicago: Aldine, 1966.

Carr-Saunders, A. *The population problem*. London and New York: Oxford University Press, (Clarendon) 1922.

Casler, L. Maternal deprivation: a critical review of the literature. *Monographs of the Society for Research in Child Development,* 1961, **26** (Whole No. 2).

Cassirer, E. *An essay on man*. New Haven: Yale University Press, 1944.

Caudill, W., & Weinstein, H. Maternal care and infant behavior in Japan and America. *Psychiatry*, 1969, **32**, 12-43.

Chance, M.R.A. Attention structure as the basis of primate rank orders. *Man*, 1967, **2**, 503-518.

Chiang, I. *The Chinese eye; an interpretation of Chinese painting*. London: Methuen, 1960.

Chomsky, N.A. *Aspects of the theory of syntax*. Cambridge, Mass.: M.I.T. Press, 1965.

Condon, W.S. & Sander, L.W. Neonate movement is synchronized with adult speech: Interactional participation and language acquisition. *Science*, 1974, **183**, 99-101.

Coon, C.C. *The origin of races*. New York: Knopf, 1962.

Critchlow, V., & Bar-Sela, M.E. Control of the onset of puberty. *Neuroendocrinology*, 1967, **2**, 101-162.

Crow, J.F. Mutation in man. In A.G. Steinberg (Ed.), *Progress in medical genetics*. New York: Gruen-Stratton, 1961, 1–26.

Crow, J.F. Inbreeding and heterosis. In I.H. Herskowitz (Ed.), *Study guide and workbook for genetics*. New York: McGraw-Hill, 1960.

Curio, E. Probleme des Feinderkennens bei Fögeln. *Proceedings of the 13th International Ornithology Congress*, 1963, 206-239.

Curti, M., Marshall, F.B., Steggerda, M., & Henderson, E.M. The Gesell schedules applied to one-, two-, and three-year old Negro children of Jamaica, B.W.I. *Journal of Comparative and Physiological Psychology*, 1935, **20**, 125-156.

Dameron, L.E. Development of intelligence of infants with Mongolism. *Child Development*, 1963, **34**, 733-738.

Darlington, C.D. *The evolution of genetic systems*. New York: Basic Books, 1958.

Dart, R. The cultural status of the South African man-apes. *Smithsonian Report* for 1955. Washington, D.C.: Smithsonian Institution, 1956, 317–338.

Darwin, C. *The voyage of the Beagle*. 1839. (Reprinted: New York: Doubleday, 1962.)

Darwin, C. *The origin of species*. 1859. (Reprinted: New York: Collier, 1962.)

Darwin, C. *The expression of the emotions in man and animals*. London: Murray, 1872. (Reprinted: Philosophical Library, New York, 1955.)

Dawson, J.L.M. Effects of sex hormones on cognitive style of rats and men. *Behavioral Genetics*, 1972, **21**, 21-42.

Dayton, G.O., Jr., Jones, M.H., Ain, P., Rawson, R.A., Steele, B., & Rose, M. Developmental study of coordinated eye movements in the human infant. I. Visual acuity in the newborn human: A study based on optokinetic nystagmus recorded by electrooculography. *Archives of Ophthamology,* 1964, **71**, 865–870.

Dennis, W. An experimental test of two theories of social smiling in infants. *Journal of Social Psychology*, 1935, **6**, 214-223.

Dennis, W. *The Hopi child*. New York: Appleton-Century, 1940.

DeVore, I. (Ed.) *Primate behavior; Field studies of monkeys and apes*. New York: Holt, Rinehart and Winston, 1965.

Diamond, M. A critical evaluation of the ontogeny of human sexual behavior. *Quarterly Review of Biology*, 1965, **40**, 147-175.

Diamond, M., Diamond, L.A., & Mast, M. Visual sensitivity and sexual arousal levels during the menstrual cycle. *Journal of Nervous and Mental Disease,* 1972, **155**, 170–176.

Drillien, C.M. *The growth and development of the prematurely born infant*. Baltimore: Williams & Wilkins, 1964.

Dunn, M.R. Interpersonal relations in blind infants. Unpublished manuscript, Univ. of California School of Medicine, San Francisco, 1962.

Edelman, M. Peer group formation in young children; I. Perception. Unpublished doctoral dissertation, Committee on Human Development, University of Chicago, 1973.

Eibl-Eibesfeldt, I., & Hass, H. Film studies in human ethology. *Current Anthropology*, 1967, **8**, 477-479.

Eimas, P.D., Siqueland, E.R., Jusczyk, P., & Vigorito, J. Speech perception in infants. *Science*, 1971, **171**, 303-306.

Eisenberg, R.B., Griffin, E.J., Coursin, D.B., & Hunter, M.S. Auditory behavior in the human neonate: A preliminary report. *Journal of Speech and Hearing Research*, 1964, **7**, 245-269.

Elkin, A.P. *The Australian aborigines*. Sydney: Argus and Robertson, 1954.

Erikson, E.H. *Childhood and society*. New York: Norton, 1950.

Erlenmeyer-Kimling, L., & Jarvik, L.F. Genetics and intelligence: A review. *Science*, 1963, **142**, 1477-1479.

Escalona, S., & Heider, G.M. *Prediction and outcome*. New York: Basic Books, 1959.

Etkin, W. (Ed.) *Social behavior from fish to man*. Chicago: University of Chicago Press, 1967.

Ewer, R.F. *Ethology of mammals*. London: Logos Press, 1968.

Fantz, R.L. The origin of form perception. *Scientific American*, 1961, **204**, 459-463.

Fenichel, O. *The psychoanalytic theory of neuroses*. New York: Norton, 1945.

Fischer, K. Genetic contributions to individual differences in language acquisition. Paper presented at the biennial meeting of the Society for Research on Child Development, April, 1973.

Fiske, A. Human kinship genetics. Unpublished manuscript, Committee on Human Development, University of Chicago, 1973.

Flory, C.D. Sex differences in skeletal development. *Child Development*, 1935, **6**, 205-212.

Fourcher, L. The balloon test. Unpublished manuscript, Committee on Human Development, University of Chicago, 1968.

Freedman, D.G. The effects of indulgent and disciplinary rearing in four breeds of dogs. Unpublished doctoral dissertation, Brandeis University, Waltham, Mass., 1957.

Freedman, D.G. Constitutional and environmental interactions in rearing of four breeds of dogs. *Science*, 1958, **127**, 585-586.

Freedman, D.G. The infant's fear of strangers and the flight response. *Journal of Child Psychology and Psychiatry*, 1961, **4**, 242-248.

Freedman, D.G. Development of the smile and fear of strangers; with an inquiry into inheritance of behavior. Film: 16 mm, sound. University of Pennsylvania, 1963. Psychological Cinema Register, PCR-2140.

Freedman, D.G. Smiling in blind infants and the issue of innate vs. acquired. *Journal of Psychology and Psychiatry*, 1964, **5**, 171-184.

Freedman, D.G. Hereditary control of early social behavior. In B.M. Foss (Ed.), *Determinants of infant behaviour* III. London: Methuen, 1965, 149-159.

Freedman, D.G. A biological view of man's social behavior. In W. Etkin (Ed.), *Social behavior from fish to man*. Chicago: University of Chicago Press, 1967, 152-188.

Freedman, D.G. The origin of social behavior. *Science Journal, (London)*. Nov. 1967, 69-73.

Freedman, D.G. An evolutionary framework for behavioral research. In S.G. Vandenberg (Ed.), *Progress in human behavior genetics*. Baltimore: The Johns Hopkins Press, 1968, 1-6.

Freedman, D.G. An evolutionary approach to research on the life cycle. *Human Development*, 1971, **14**, 87-99. (a)

Freedman, D.G. The impact of behavior genetics and ethology. In H.E. Rie (Ed.), *Perspectives in child psychopathology*. Chicago: Aldine, 1971, 219-266. (b)

Freedman, D.G. The development of social hierarchies. In L. Levi (Ed.), *Society, stress and disease: Childhood and adolescence*. London: Methuen, 1973.

Freedman, D.G., Boverman, H., & Freedman, N.A. Effects of kinesthetic stimulation on smiling in premature infants. Paper presented at the meeting of the American Orthopsychiatric Association, San Francisco, April, 1966.

Freedman, D.G., & Freedman, N.A. Differences in behavior between Chinese-American and European-American newborns. *Nature* (London), 1969, **224**, 1227.

Freedman, D.G., & Keller, B. Inheritance of behavior in infants. *Science*, 1963, **140**, 196-198.

Fries, M., & Woolf, D. Some hypotheses on the role of the congenital activity type in development. *Psychoanalytic Study of the Child*, 1953, **8**, 48.

Fuller, J.L., & Thompson, W.R. *Behavior genetics*. New York: Wiley, 1960.

Garai, J.E., & Scheinfeld, A. Sex differences in mental and behavioral traits. *Genetic Psychology Monographs*, 1968, **77**, 169-299.

Geber, M. The psychomotor development of African children in the first year and the influence of maternal behavior. *Journal of Social Psychology*, 1958, **47**, 185-195.

Geber, M., & Dean, R.F.A. Gesell tests on African children. *Pediatrics*, 1957, **20**, 1055-1065.

Geber, M., & Dean, R.F.A. Psychomotor development in African children: The effect of social class and the need for improved tests. *Bulletin of the World Health Organization*, **18**, 1958, 471-476.

Geber, M., & Dean, R.F.A. Precocious development in newborn African infants. In Y. Brackbill & G. Thompson (Eds.), *Readings in infancy and childhood*. New York: Free Press, 1966, 120-126.

Gesell, A., Ilg, F., & Bullis, C.E. *Vision, its development in infant and child*. New York: Hoeber, 1949.

Gewirtz, J.L. Changes in the course of human smiling through the first eighteen months of life. Unpublished manuscript, National Institute of Mental Health, 1963.

Gibson, E.R., & Walk, R.D. The visual cliff. *Scientific American*, 1960, 202.

Ginsburg, B.E. Genetic parameters in behavior research. In J. Hirsch (Ed.), *Genetics and behavior*. New York: McGraw-Hill, 1968, 1-24.

Ginsburg, B.E., & Laughlin, W.S. Genetic potential and social structure. Paper presented at the Columbia University Forum, Fall, 1967.

Goldberg, S., & Lewis, M. Play behavior in the year-old infant: Early sex differences. *Child Development*, 1969, **40**, 22-31.

Goldfarb, W. Emotional and intellectual consequences of psychologic deprivation in infancy: a re-evaluation. In P. Hoch & J. Zubin (Eds.), *Psychotherapy of childhood*. New York: Grune & Stratton, 1955, 105-119.

Goldstein, K. The smiling of the infant and problem of understanding the "other." *Journal of Psychology*, 1957, **44**, 175-191.

Goldstein, K. *The organism*. Boston: Beacon Press, 1963. (a)

Goldstein, K. *Human nature in the light of psychopathology*. New York: Schocken Books, 1963. (b)

Goldstein, K., & Sheerer, M. Abstract and concrete behavior. *Psychological Monographs*, 1941, **53**, (No. 2, Whole No. 239).

Goodenough, E. W. Interest in persons as an aspect of sex difference in the early years. *Genetic Psychology Monographs*, 1957, **55**, 301-316.

Goodenough, F.L. Expression of the emotions in a blind-deaf child. *Journal of Abnormal and Social Psychology*, 1932, **27**, 328-333.

Gorman, C.N. Navajo vision of earth and man. *The Indian Historian*, 1973, **6**, 19-22.

Gorman, J.J., Cogan, D.G., & Bellis, S.S. A device for testing visual acuity in infants. *Sight Saving Review*, 1959, **29**, 80-84.

Gray, P.H. Theory and evidence of imprinting in human infants. *Journal of Psychology*, 1958, **46**, 155-166.

Green, N. An exploratory study of aggression and spacing behavior in two preschool nurseries: Chinese-American and European-American. Unpublished master's thesis, Committee on Human Development, University of Chicago, 1969.

Hafez, E.S.E., & Scott, J.P. The behavior of sheep and goats. In E.S.E. Hafez (Ed.), *The behavior of domestic animals*. Baltimore: Williams & Wilkins, 1962, 297-333.

Hall, K. R. L. & DeVore, I. Baboon social behavior. In I. DeVore (Ed.), *Primate behavior: Field studies of monkeys and apes*. New York: Holt, Rinehart and Winston, 1965, 53-110.

Hamilton, W.D. The genetical evolution of social behavior. *Journal of Theoretical Biology*, 1964, **7**, 1-52.

Hampson, J.L., and Hampson, J.G. The ontogenesis of sexual behavior in man. In W.C. Young (Ed.), *Sex and internal secretions*. Baltimore: Williams & Wilkins, 1961, 1401-1432.

Hardin, G. *Nature and man's fate*. New York: Mentor, 1961.

Haring, D.G. Comment on Japanese personal character: Pre-war. In D.G. Haring (Ed.), *Personal character and cultural milieu*. New York: Syracuse University Press, 1956, 405-411.

Harlow, H.F., & Harlow, M. Learning to love. *American Scientist*, 1966, **54**, 244-272.

Harlow, H.F., & Zimmerman, R.R. Affectional responses in the infant monkey. *Science*, 1959, **130**, 421-432.

Harris, G. W. The Upjohn lecture of the endocrine society: Sex hormones, brain development and brain function. *Endocrinology*, 1964, **75**, 627-648.

Harrison, G.A. Human genetics. In G.A. Harrison, J.S. Weiner, J.M. Tanner, & N.A. Bernicot (Eds.), *Human biology—An introduction to human evolution, variation and growth*. London and New York: Oxford University Press, 1964, 101–184.

Haynes, H.M., White, B.L. & Held, R. Visual accommodation in human infants. *Science*, 1965, **148**, 528-530.

Hebb, D.O. Heredity and environment in mammalian behavior. *British Journal of Animal Behaviour*, 1953, **1**, 43-47.

Hediger, H. Environmental factors influencing the reproduction of zoo animals. In F.A. Beach (Ed.), *Sex and behavior*. New York: Wiley, 1965, 319–354.

Heider, K.G. *The Dugum Dani: A Papuan culture in the highlands of West New Guinea*. Chicago: Aldine, 1970.

Hess, E.H. Imprinting. *Science*, 1959, **130**, 133-144.

Hinde, R.A. Interaction of internal and external factors in integration of canary reproduction. In F. A. Beach (Ed.), *Sex and behavior*. New York: Wiley, 1965, 381–415.

Hochberg, J.E. Nativism and empiricism in perception. In L.J. Postman (Ed.), *Psychology in the making*. New York: Knopf, 1966, 255–330.

Honzik, M.P. Developmental studies of parent-child resemblance in intelligence. *Child Development*, 1957, **28**, 215-228.

Honzik, M.P. Personality consistency and change: Some comments on papers by Bayley, Macfarlane, Moss, Kagan and Murphy. *Vita Humana*, 1964, **7**, 67-72.

Hull, E. Sex differences in infant test performances. Unpublished manuscript, Committee on Human Development, University of Chicago, 1967.

Hutt, S.J., Hutt, C., Lenard, H.G., Bernuth, H.V., & Muntjewerff, W.J. Auditory responsivity in the human neonate. *Nature (London)*, 1966, **218**, 888-890.

Jay, P. (Ed.) *Primates*. New York: Holt, Rinehart and Winston, 1968.

Jensen, A.R. How much can we boost I.Q. and scholastic achievement. *Harvard Educational Review*, 1969, **39**, 1-123.

Jensen, A.R. *Genetics and education*. New York: Harper and Row, 1973.

Jensen, G. Sex differences in developmental trends of mother-infant monkey behavior *(M. nemestrina)*. *Primates*, 1966, **7**, 3, 403.

Jinks, J.L. *Extrachromosomal inheritance*. Englewood, N.J.: Prentice-Hall, 1964.

Jirari, C. Form perception, innate form preferences and visually-mediated head-turning in human neonates. Unpublished doctoral dissertation, Committee on Human Development, University of Chicago, 1970.

Jumonville, J. Influence of genotype-treatment interaction in studies of emotionality in mice. Unpublished doctoral dissertation, Department of Psychology, University of Chicago, 1968.

Kagan, J. *Change and continuity in infancy*. New York: Wiley, 1971.

Kagan, J., & Moss, H.A. *Birth to maturity*. New York: Wiley, 1962.

Kaila, E. Die Reaktion des Saugling auf das menschliche Gesicht. *Annales Universitatis fennicae Aboensis, Series B,* 1932, **17**, 1-114.

Kessler, J.W. *Psychopathology of children*. Englewood Cliffs, N.J.: Prentice-Hall, 1966.

Kimura, G. Functional asymmetry of the brain in dichotic listening. *Cortex*, 1967, **3**, 163-178.

Kinsey, A.C. *Sexual behavior in the human female*. Philadelphia: Saunders, 1953.

Kinsey, A.C., Pomeroy, W.B., & Martin, C.E. *Sexual behavior in the human male*. Philadelphia: Saunders, 1948.

Klinghammer, E. Factors influencing choice of mate in altricial birds. In H.W. Stevenson, E.H. Hess, & H.L. Rheingold (Eds.), *Early behavior: Comparative and developmental approaches*. New York: Wiley, 1967, 5–42.

Kluckhohn, C., & Leighton, D. *The Navajo*. Cambridge, Mass.: Harvard University Press, 1946.

Knobloch, H., & Pasamanick, B. The relationship of race and socioeconomic status to the development of motor behavior patterns in infancy. *Psychiatric Research Reports*, 1958, **10**, 123-133.

Koehler, O. Das Lacheln als angeborene Ausdrucksbewegung. *Menschliche Vererbung und Konstitutionslehre*, 1954, **32**, 390-398.

Koford, C.B. The Rhesus of Cayo Santiago Island. Film, Atlanta: National Institute of Neurological Diseases and Blindness, 1963.

Korner, A.F. Neonatal startles, smiles, erections and reflex sucks as related to state, sex and individuality. *Child Development*, 1969, **40**, 1039-1053.

Korner, A.F. Sex differences in newborns with special reference to differences in the organization of oral behavior. *Journal of Child Psychology and Psychiatry,* 1973, **14**, 19–29.

Korner, A.F., & Grobstein, R. Individual differences at birth: Implications for mother-infant relationship and later development. *Journal of the American Academy for Child Psychiatry*, 1967, **6**, 676-690.

Kovach, J. K., & Hess, E. H. Imprinting: Effects of painful stimulation upon the following response. *Journal of Comparative and Physiological Psychology*, 1963, **56**, 461-464.

Kuchner, J. Untitled, unpublished doctoral dissertation, University of Chicago, 1973.

Kuo, Z. Y. Ontogeny of embryonic behavior in Aves. IV. The influence of prenatal behavior upon postnatal life. *Journal of Comparative Psychology*, 1932, **14**, 109-121.

Lack, D. *Darwin's finches*. London and New York: Cambridge University Press, 1947.

Lack, D. Preface. *Darwin's finches*. New York: Harper, 1961.

L'Allier, L. Smiling as a result of aural stimuli. Unpublished doctoral dissertation, University of Montreal, 1961.

Laroche, J.L., & Tcheng, F. *Le sourire du nourisson*. Louvain: Publication Universitaire, 1963.

Laser, J. Infant reactions to adult and child strangers. Unpublished manuscript, Committee on Human Development, University of Chicago, 1966.

Lee R.B., & DeVore, I. (Eds.) *Man the hunter*. Chicago: Aldine, 1968.

Lehrman, D.S. A critique of Konrad Lorenz's theory of instinctive behavior. *Quarterly Review of Biology*, 1954, **28**, 337-363.

Leiderman, P.H., Babu, B. Kagia, J., Kraemer, C., & Leiderman, G.F. African infant precocity and some social influences in the first year. *Nature* (London), 1973, **242**, 247-249.

Leis, P.E. The nonfunctional attributes of twin infanticide in the Niger Delta. *Anthropology Quarterly*, 1965, **38**, 97-111.

Lenneberg, E. *Biological foundations of language*. New York: Wiley, 1967.

Leonard, M.R. Problems in identification and ego development in twins. *Psychoanalytical Study of Children*, 1961, **16**, 300-318.

LeVine, R.A. Outsiders' judgments: An ethnographic approach to group differences in personality. *Southwestern Journal of Anthropology*, 1966, **22**, 101-116.

LeVine, R.A. Cross-cultural study in child psychology. In P.H. Mussen (Ed.), *Carmichael's manual of child psychology*. (3rd ed.) New York: Wiley, 1970, 559–612.

Levine, S., & Mullins, R.F. Hormonal influences on brain organization in infant rats. *Science*, 1966, **152**, 1585-1592.

Lewis, M. *Infant speech*. London: Routledge and Kagan Paul, 1951.

Lewis, M. Infants' responses to facial stimuli during the first year of life. *Developmental Psychology*, 1969, **2**, 75-86.

Lewis, M., Bartels, B., Campbell, H., & Goldberg, S. Individual differences in attention. *American Journal of Diseases of Children*, 1967, **113**, 461-465.

Lewis, M., Kagan, J., & Kalafat, J. Patterns of fixation in the young infant. *Child Development*, 1966, **37**, 331-341.

Lewontin, R.C. The adaptation of populations to varying environments. *Cold Spring Harbor Symposia on Quantitative Biology*, 1951, **22**, 395-408.

Lewontin, R.C. The apportionment of human diversity. *Evolutionary Biology*, 1971, **6**, 381-398.

Lipsitt, L.P., & Levy, N. Electroactual threshold in the human neonate. *Child Development*, 1959, **30**, 547-554.

Lipton, E.L., & Steinschneider, A. Studies in the psychophysiology of infancy. *Merrill-Palmer Quarterly*, 1964, **10**, 102-117.

Lorenz, K. Companionship in bird life. In C.H. Schiller (Ed.), *Instinctive Behavior*. New York: International Universities Press, 1957, 83-128. Translation of Der Kumpan in der Umwelt des Vogels. *Journal Ornithologie*, 1935, **83**, 137–213, 289–413.

Lorenz, K. The nature of instinct. In C.H. Schiller (Ed.), *Instinctive Behavior*. New York: International Universities Press, 1957, 129-175. Translation of Über die Bildung des Instinctbegriffes. *Die Naturwissenschaften*, 1937, **25**, 289–300, 307–318, 324–331.

Lorenz, K. The past twelve years in the comparative studies of behavior. In C.H. Schiller (Ed.), *Instinctive Behavior*. New York: International Universities Press, 1957, 288-310. Translation of Die Entwicklung der vergleichenden Verhaltensforschung in den letzten 12 Jahren. *Verhandlungen der Deutschen Zoologischen Gesellschaft in Freiburg*, 1952, 36-58.

Lorenz, K. *On aggression*. New York: Harcourt, Brace & World, 1966.

Maccoby, E.E. (Ed.) *The development of sex differences*. Stanford: Stanford University Press, 1966.

Maccoby, E.E., & Jacklin, C.N. Stress, activity and proximity seeking: Sex differences in the year-old child. *Child Development*, 1973, **44**, 34-42.

MacFarlane, J.W. Perspectives on personality consistency and change from the guidance study. *Vita Humana*, 1964, **7**, 115-125.

MacKinnon, D.W. The structure of personality. In J. McV. Hunt (Ed.), *Personality and behavior disorders*. New York: Ronald Press, 1944, 3-48.

MacKinnon, D.W. (Ed.) *Selection of personnel for the office of strategic services: Assessment of men*. New York: Rinehart, 1948.

Mallardi, A., Mallardi, A.C., & Freedman, D.G. Studio su primo manifestarso dell paura dell'estraneo nel bambino: Osservazioni comparative tra sogetti allevati in famiglia e soggetti allevati in comunita chiusa. *Atti de VI Congresso Nazionale della S.I.A.M.E., Bari*, 1961, 254-256.

Mason, W.A. The effects of social restriction on the behavior of Rhesus monkeys: I. Free social behavior. In R.E. McGill (Ed.), *Readings in animal behavior*. New York: Holt, Rinehart and Winston, 1965.

Mason, W.A., Green, P.C., & Posepanko, C.J. Sex differences in affective-social responses of Rhesus monkeys. *Psychonomic Science*, **15**, 1959, 74-83.

Masters, W.H., & Johnson, V.E. The sexual response cycles of the human male and female: Comparative anatomy and physiology. In F.A. Beach (Ed.), *Sex and behavior*. New York: Wiley, 1965, 512-534.

Mayr, E. Behavior and systematics. In A. Roe & G.G. Simpson (Eds.), *Behavior and evolution*. New York: Holt, Rinehart and Winston, 1958.

Mayr, E. *Animal species and evolution*. Cambridge, Mass.: The Belknap Press of Harvard University Press, 1963, 341-360.

McKusick, V.A. *Human genetics*. Englewood, N.J.: Prentice-Hall, 1964.

McLean, J. D. Sex-correlated differences in human smiling behavior: A preliminary investigation. Unpublished manuscript, Committee on Human Development, University of Chicago, 1970.

McNeill, D. Developmental psycholinguistics. In S. Smith & G.A. Miller (Eds.), *Genesis of language*. Cambridge, Mass.: MIT Press, 1966, 1-92.

McNeill, D. *The acquisition of language*. New York: Harper and Row, 1970.

McNeill, D. Sentence structure in chimpanzee communication. Unpublished manuscript, Committee on Cognitive Processes, University of Chicago, 1972.

Mead, M. *Sex and temperament in three primitive societies*. New York: Morrow, 1935.

Mead, M. *Male and female*. New York: Morrow, 1949.

Meili, R. *Anfange der Charakterentwicklung*. Bern: Hans Huber, 1957.

Messer, S.B., & Lewis, M. Social class and sex differences in the attachment and play behavior of the one-year-old infant. *Merrill-Palmer Quarterly*, 1972, **18**, 295-306.

Meyers, W.J., & Cantor, G.N. Observing and cardiac responses of human infants to visual stimuli. *Journal of Experimental Child Psychology*, 1967, **5**, 16-25.

Mitchell, G., & Brandt, E.M. Behavioral differences related to experience of mother and sex of infant in the rhesus monkey. *Developmental Psychology*, 1970, **3**, 149.

Money, J. Determinants of human sexual behavior. Unpublished manuscript, 1970.

Montagu, M.A. (Ed.) *Marriage: Past and present*. Boston: Sargent, 1956.

Moss, H.A. Sex, age and state as determinants of mother-infant interaction. *Merrill-Palmer Quarterly*, 1967, **13**, 19-35.

Moss, H.A., & Robson, K. The role of protest behavior in the development of mother-infant attachment. Paper presented to meetings of American Psychological Association, San Francisco, Sept. 1968.

Murdock, G.P. World ethnographic sample. *American Anthropology*, 1957, **59**, 664-687.

Murphy, L.P. Factors in continuity and change in the development of adaptational style in children. *Vita Humana*, 1964, **7**, 96-114.

Nakamura, H. *Ways of thinking of Eastern peoples: India, China, Tibet, Japan*. Honolulu: East-West Center Press, 1964.

Neilon, P. Shirley's babies after fifteen years. *Journal of Genetic Psychology*, 1948, **73**, 175-186.

Nichols, R. C. The resemblance of twins in personality and interests. *Research Reports* (National Merit Scholarship Corp.), 1966, **2**, 1-23.

Nisbett, R.E., & Gurwitz, S.B. Weight, sex and the eating behavior of newborns. *Journal of Comparative Physiology and Psychology*, 1970, **73**, 245-253.

Norris, M., Spaulding, P.J., & Brodie, F. *Blindness in children*. Chicago: University of Chicago Press, 1957.

Nylander, P.O.S. Ethnic differences in twinning rates in Nigeria. *Journal of Biosocial Science*, 1971, **3**, 151-158.

Oetzel, R.M. Annotated bibliography. In E. Maccoby (Ed.), *The development of sex differences*. Stanford: Stanford University Press, 1966, 223-331.

Omark, D. Adult human responses to infant sounds. Unpublished master's thesis, Committee on Human Development, University of Chicago, 1967.

Omark, D. Peer group formation in young children: II. Action. Unpublished doctoral dissertation, Committee on Human Development, University of Chicago, 1973.

Openheimer, J. Section I. Problems, concepts, and their history. In B.H. Willier, O.H. Weiss, & V. Hamburger (Eds.), *Developmental analysis*. Philadelphia: Saunders, 1954, 1–24.

Papousek, H. Conditioning during early postnatal development. In Y. Brackbill and G.G. Thompson (Eds.), *Behavior in infancy and early childhood*. New York: Free Press, 1967, 259–274.

Parker, R., & Freedman, D.G. Sex differences in children at play. Film: 16 mm; sound. University of Pennsylvania, 1971. Psychological Cinema Register, PCR 2245.

Parmelee, A.H., Jr. The developmental evaluation of the blind premature infant. *AMA Journal of Diseases of Children*, 1955, **90**, 135-140.

Parmelee, A.H., Jr., Fiske, C.E., & Wright, R.H. The development of ten children with blindness as a result of retrolental fibroplasia. *AMA Journal of Diseases of Children*, 1959, **98**, 198-220.

Parsons, T., and Bales, R. *Family socialization and interaction process*. Glencoe, Ill.: Free Press, 1955.

Peiper, A. *Cerebral function in infancy and childhood*. (Transl. by B. Nagler & H. Nagler) New York: Consultants Bureau, 1963.

Petre-Quadens, O. Ontogenesis of paradoxical sleep in the human newborn. *Journal of Neurological Science*, 1967, **4**, 153-157.

Piaget, J. *Play, dreams and imitation in childhood*. New York: Norton, 1951.

Piaget, J. *The origins of intelligence in children*. New York: Norton, 1952.

Pinneau, S.R. The infantile disorders of hospitalism and anaclitic depression. *Psychological Bulletin*, 1955, **52**, 429.

Potter, C.E.L. *Fundamentals of human reproduction*. New York: McGraw-Hill, 1948.

Price, B. Primary biases in twin studies. *American Journal of Human Genetics*, 1950, **2**, 293-352.

Rensch, B. *Evolution above the species level*. New York: Columbia University Press, 1960.

Reppucci, C.M. Hereditary influences upon distribution of attention in infancy. Unpublished doctoral dissertation, Harvard University, 1968.

Rheingold, H.L., Gewirtz, J.L., & Ross, A.W. Social conditioning of vocalizations in the infant. *Journal of Comparative Physiology and Psychology*, 1959, **52**, 68-73.

Riesen, A.H. Stimulation as a requirement for growth and function in behavioral development. In D.W. Fiske and S.R. Maddi (Eds.), *Functions of varied experience*. Homewood, Ill.: Dorsey Press, 1961. 57-80.

Sade, D.S. Inhibition of son-mother mating among free-ranging Rhesus monkeys. *Scientific Pschoanalysis*, 1968, **12**, 18-38.

Schaefer, E.S., & Bayley, N. Maternal behavior, child behavior and their intercorrelations from infancy through adolescence. *Monographs of the Society for Research in Child Development*, 1963, **28**, (Whole No. 3), 1–127.

Schaffer, H.R. Some issues for research in the study of attachment behavior. In B.M. Foss (Ed.), *Determinants of infant behaviour II*. London: Methuen, 1963, 179–200.

Schaffer, H.R. The onset of fear of strangers and incongruity hypothesis. *Journal of Child Psychology and Psychiatry*, 1966, **7**, 95-106.

Schaffer, H.R., & Emerson, P.E. The development of social attachments in infancy. *Monographs of the Society for Research in Child Development*, 1964, **29**, (Whole No. 3), 1–77.

Schleidt, W.M. Reaktionen von Truthuhnern auf fliegende Raubvögel und Versuche zur Analyse ihrer AAM's. *Zeitschrift fuer Tierpsychologie*, 1961, **18**, 534-560.

Schneirla, T.C. An evolutionary and developmental theory of biphasic processes underlying approach and withdrawal. In M.R. Jones (Ed.), *Nebraska symposium on motivation*. Lincoln: University of Nebraska Press, 1959, 1–41.

Schneirla, T.C. Instinctive behavior, maturation-experience and development. In B. Kaplan & S. Wapner (Eds.), *Perspectives in psychological theory*. New York: International Universities Press, 1960, 1-33.

Schultz, A.H. Some factors influencing the social life of primates in general and of early man in particular. In S.L. Washburn (Ed.), *Social life of early man*. Chicago: Aldine, 1961, 58-90.

Schultz, A.H. The recent hominoid primates. In S. Washburn & P.C. Jay (Eds.), *Perspectives on human evolution*. Vol. I. New York: Holt, Rinehart and Winston, 1968, 122-195.

Scott, J.P., & Fuller, J. *Genetics and social behavior of the dog*. Chicago: University of Chicago Press, 1965.

Scrimshaw, N.S., & Behar, M. Protein malnutrition in young children. *Science*, 1961, **133**, 2039-2047.

Shafer, R. Athapaskan and Sino-Tibetan. *International Journal of American Linguistics*, 1952, **18**, 12-19.

Sheldon, W.H., & Stevens, S.S. *The varieties of temperament*. New York: Harper, 1942.

Shirley, M. M. The first two years: A study of twenty-five babies, Vol. III. Personality Manifestations. *Institute of Child Welfare Monograph Series*. Minneapolis: University of Minnesota Press, 1933.

Smets, A.M. Le sourire en reaction à une stimulation tactile simple. 1962. Reported in J.L. Laroche & F. Tcheng *Le sourire du nourisson*. Louvain: University in Louvain, 1963.

Southwick, C.H. (Ed.) *Primate social behavior*. New York: Van Nostrand, 1963.

Spitz, R.A. Hospitalism. *Psychoanalytic study of the child*. New York: International Universities Press, 1945, 53–74.

Spitz, R.A. Anxiety in infancy. *International Journal of Psychoanalysis*, 1950, **31**, 139-143.

Spitz, R.A. *A genetic field theory of ego formation*. New York: International Universities Press, 1959.

Spitz, R. A. *The first year of life*. New York: International Universities Press, 1965.

Spitz, R.A., & Wolf, K.M. The smiling response: A contribution to the ontogenesis of social relations. *Genetic Psychology Monographs*, 1946, **34**, 57-125.

Spock, B. *Baby and child care*. New York: Pocket Books, 1955.

Stern, K. *Principles of human genetics*. (2nd ed.) San Francisco: W.H. Freeman, 1960.

Stevens, C. An ethological investigation of social interaction among third graders. Unpublished master's thesis, Committee on Human Development, University of Chicago, 1972.

Stockard, C.R. *The physical basis of personality*. New York: Norton, 1931.

Sumner, W.G. *Folkways*. Boston: Ginn, 1906.

Tanner, J.M. *Education and physical growth*. London: University of London Press, 1961.

Taylor, D.C. Differential rates of cerebral maturation between sexes and between hemispheres: Evidence from epilepsy. *Lancet*, 1969, **2**, 140-142.

Tennes, K.H., & Lampl, E.E. Some aspects of mother-child relationship pertaining to infantile separation anxiety. *Journal of Nervous and Mental Disease*, 1966, **143**, 426-437.

Thoman, E., Leiderman, H., & Olson, J. Neonate-mother interaction during breast feeding. *Developmental Psychology*, 1972, **6**, 110.

Thompson, J. Development of facial expression of emotion in blind and seeing children. *Archives of Psychology*, 1941, no. 264.

Thorpe, W.H. *Learning and instinct in animals*. (2nd ed.) London: Methuen, 1963.

Tinbergen, N. Social releasers and the experimental method required for their study. *Wilson Bulletin*, 1948, **60**, 6-51.

Tinbergen, N. *The study of instinct*. Oxford: Oxford University Press, 1951. Out of Print.

Tinbergen, N. The shell menace. In T.E. McGill (Ed.), *Readings in animal behavior*. New York: Holt, Rinehart and Winston, 1965, 532-540.

Trivers, R.L. The evolution of reciprocal altruism. *Quarterly Review of Biology*, 1971, **46**, 35-57.

Trivers, R.L. Parental investment and sexual selection. In Campbell, B. (Ed.), *Sexual selection and the descent of man, 1871–1971*. Chicago: Aldine, 1972, 136-179.

Trivers, R.L. Parent-offspring conflict. *American Zoologist*, 1974, In Press.

U.S. Public Health Service. *Vital statistics*. Arizona: Window Rock, 1969.

Valentine, C.W. The psychology of imitation with special reference to early childhood. *British Journal of Psychology*, 1930, **21**, 105-132.

Vandenberg, S.G. Hereditary factors in normal personality traits (as measured by inventories). *Recent Advances in Biological Psychiatry*, 1967, **9**, 65-104.

van Lawick-Goodall, J. The behavior of free-living chimpanzees in the Gombe Stream Reserve. *Animal Behavior Monograph*, 1968, **1**, III, 161-311.

Vine, I. The significance of facial-visual signalling in human social development. In I. Vine & M. von Cranack (Eds.), *Expressive movement and nonverbal communication*. New York: Academic Press, 1971.

von Koenigswald, G. H. R. *The evolution of man*. Ann Arbor: University of Michigan Press, 1962.

Von Uexküll, J. (1938) A stroll through the world of animals and men. In C.H. Schiller (Ed.), *Instinctive behavior*. New York: International Universities Press, 1957, 5–82.

Waddington, C. H. Genetic assimilation of an acquired character. *Evolution,* 1954, **7**, 118-126.

Waddington, C.H. *New patterns in genetics and development*. New York: Columbia, 1962.

Waddington, C.H. *The nature of life*. New York: Harper Torchbook, 1966.

Walters, C.E. Comparative development of Negro and white infants. *Journal of Genetic Psychology*, 1967, **110**, 243-251.

Warren, N. African infant precocity. *Psychological Bulletin*, 1972, **78**, 353-367.

Washburn, R.W. A study of the smiling and laughing of infants in the first year of life. *Genetic Psychological Monographs*, 1929, **6**, 397-535.

Washburn, S.L., & DeVore, I. Social behavior of baboons and early man. In S.L. Washburn (Ed.), *Social Life of Early Man*. Chicago: Aldine, 1961, 91–105.

Watson, J.S. Operant conditioning of visual fixation in infants under visual and auditory reinforcements. *Developmental Psychology*, 1969, **1**, 508-516.

Weiner, J.S. *Man's natural history*. London: Weidenfeld and Nicolson, 1971.

Weir, R. Some questions on the child's learning of phonology. In R. Smith and G.A. Miller (Eds.), *Genesis of language*. Cambridge, Mass.: MIT Press, 1966, 153-168.

Weiss, P.A. Nervous system (neurogenesis). In B.H. Willier, P.A. Weiss, & V. Hamburger (Eds.), *Analysis of development*. Philadelphia: Saunders, 1954, 346–401.

White, S.H. Evidence for a hierarchical arrangement of learning processes. In L.P. Lipsitt & C. C. Spiker (Eds.), *Advances in child development and behavior*. Vol. 2. New York: Academic Press, 1965, 187–220.

Wickelgran, L. Convergence in the human newborn. *Journal of Experimental Child Psychology*, 1967, **5**, 74-85.

Wiener, N. *Cybernetics*. New York: Wiley, 1948.

Wilkins, L. *The diagnosis and treatment of endocrine disorders of childhood and adolescence*. (3rd ed.) Springfield, Ill.: Charles C. Thomas, 1965.

Williams, G.C. *Adaptation and natural selection*. Princeton: Princeton University Press, 1966.

Willier, B.H., Weiss, P.A., & Hamburger, V. (Eds.) *Analysis of development*. Philadelphia: Saunders, 1955.

Wilson, J.P. Nursing experience and the social smile. Unpublished doctoral dissertation, University of Chicago, 1960.

Witkin, H.A., Lewis, H.B., Hertzman, M., Machover, K., Bretnall Meissner, B., & Wapner, S. *Personality through perception*. New York: Harper, 1954.

Wolfe, C. Human smiling behavior. Unpublished manuscript, Committee on Human Development, University of Chicago, 1971.

Wolff, P.H. Observations on the early development of smiling. In B.M. Foss (Ed.), *Determinants of infant behaviour II*. London: Methuen, 1963, 113–133.

Wolff, P.H. The natural history of crying and other vocalizations in early infancy. In B.M. Foss (Ed.), *Determinants of infant behaviour IV*. New York: Barnes and Noble, 1969.

Wynne-Edwards, V.C. *Animal dispersion in relation to social behavior*. New York: Harper, 1962.

Young, W.C. The organization of sexual behavior by hormonal action during the prenatal and larval periods in the vertebrates. In F. Beach (Ed.), *Sex and behavior*. New York: Wiley, 1965.

Young, W.C., Goy, R.W., & Phoenix, C.H. Hormones and sexual behavior. In J. Money (Ed.), *Sex research; New developments*. New York: Holt, Rinehart and Winston, 1965.

Zelazo, P.R. Newborn walking: From reflexive to instrumental behavior. Unpublished manuscript, Department of Psychology and Social Relations, Harvard University, 1974.

AUTHOR INDEX

Numbers in *italics* refer to the pages on which the complete references are listed.

SUBJECT INDEX

A

Activity, 163, 164
Affiliative behavior, *see* Sex differences
African infants, 146, 147, 161, 164, 165–170, 171, 173–174
Afro-American infants, 146, 147, 164, 173
Aggression, 43, *see also* Secondary sex characteristics, Sex differences
Alertness, 171
  and natural selection, 174
Altricial development, 18–23
  in doves, 19
  in human infants, 21–23
  in predators, 19–20
  in primates, 21–22
Anger, 43
Auditory responsivity, 23, 24, 30, *see also* Sex differences, Smiling
Australian Aboriginal infants, 170–172, 173

B

Balinese infants, 145
Behavior, *see also* Critical periods, Imprinting, Reflexive behavior, Systems-theory
  adaptive, *see* Phylogeny, adaptive mechanisms
  evolved, 9–11
  innate vs. acquired, 6–8, 185–188
  "instinctive," *see* Systems-theory
  species-specific, 4, 28

Behavior genetics, 3–4, 82–85, 143–144, *see also* Heredity and environment, Personality, Phylogeny
  dogs, 85–91
  rodents, 92–94
  twins, 94–109, 112–140, 141–143
Biology, 5–6
  causal mechanisms in, 8–9
    DNA, 8
    embryological development, 8–9
    gene mutation, 8

C

Caretaker-infant interactions, 23, 28–29, 43–44, 45, 50, *see also* Crying, Dominance-submission hierarchies, Imprinting, Sex differences, Smiling, Systems-theory
  critical periods in development of attachments, 47–49
  differential parental treatment, 62
  mother-infant interactions, 3, 71, 156
    Caucasian, 156–157
    Chinese-American, 156–157
  parent-offspring conflict, 46
Caucasian infants, 146, 147, 148–159, 160, 161, 162, 163–165, 166, 167, 168, 171, 172, 173
Chinese-American infants, 148–157, 160, 172

208